Aircraft of the United States' Military Air Transport Service

1948 to 1966

Airman 2nd Class William Chapman guards a MATS C-97C of the 146th ATW, Van Nuys, California.
California ANG, courtesy of 1Lt M J Kasiuba

Dedication

The pilots and flight crew who flew the aircraft operated by the Military Air Transport Service deserve high praise for their professionalism and devotion to duty under often trying conditions. But this book is humbly dedicated to the tens of thousands of nameless mechanics, cooks, technicians, duty drivers, supply personnel, security officers, administrative staff, and watchstanders who dedicated themselves to a job well done behind the scenes. Without your untiring and largely unheralded efforts, the Military Air Transport Service would not have been so competent, so efficient, or so successful.

Aircraft of the United States' Military Air Transport Service 1948-1966

ISBN 1 85780 087 7

Published by Midland Publishing Limited
24 The Hollow, Earl Shilton
Leicester, LE9 7NA, England
Tel: 01455 847815 Fax: 01455 841805
E-mail: midlandbooks@compuserve.com

Midland Publishing Limited
is an imprint of Ian Allan Publishing Limited

Worldwide distribution (except N. America):
Midland Counties Publications (Aerophile) Ltd
Unit 3 Maizefield, Hinckley Fields
Hinckley, Leicestershire,
LE10 1YF, England
Tel: 01455 233747 Fax: 01455 233737
E-mail: midlandbooks@compuserve.com

United States trade distribution:
Specialty Press Publishers & Wholesalers Inc.
11605 Kost Dam Road, North Branch
MN 55056, USA
Tel: 612 583 3239 Fax: 612 583 2023
Toll free telephone: 800 895 4585

Printed in England by
Ian Allan Printing Limited
Riverdene Business Park
Hersham, Surrey, KT12 4RG

Aircraft of the United States' Military Air Transport Service 1948 to 1966

Nicholas M Williams

Midland Publishing
Limited

Introduction and Acknowledgements

The aircraft of today's Air Mobility Command seem almost ghost-like in their operations. Nondescript camouflaged transports arrive and depart airfields with little fanfare, cruising far overhead with only whispy contrails and a faint rumble marking their passage. It seems incredible that two generations have not heard the drone of a MATS transport, shimmering in bright yellow and blue aluminum, breaking the evening stillness.

In the 50 years since its formation, a nostalgic look back seems fitting to celebrate not only the varied roles MATS undertook, but also to look in amazement at the multitude of aircraft types which were flown. Many of the aircraft described in this book will be familiar to long-time MATS men and women who flew, crewed or maintained them. Other types may well surprise some readers who were unaware of the widely varied missions which were performed under the MATS umbrella. A few aircraft included in this book may provoke argument about whether they truly were MATS aircraft after all.

Surprisingly little has been published relating to the MATS' 'trash haulers' and its many subordinant services. Most available sources have dealt with personalities and subjective, behind-the-scenes personal narratives. In contrast, this is not a 'people book', but an objective, in-depth look at the missions and aircraft of MATS. Much of the information has been gleaned from previously published books, articles and histories, as well as thousands of pages of microfilm histories of units obtained from the Air Force Historical Research Center at Maxwell Air Force Base, the Naval Aviation History and Archives Unit, as well as the individual historical offices of the Air Weather Service, Air Force Communications Command etc, various Air Force bases, and the newsletters of the many alumni associations.

As a starting point, MATS' own published figures for aircraft types, dates and numbers of aircraft flown have been used. In many cases, the published figures have proven incorrect or contradictory, and have been revised.

The Author is indebted to the following individuals who 'went the extra mile' in sharing information and answering a seemingly endless stream of questions: Robert M Johnson, Chief, and Dick Gamma, Archie DiFante, and Essie Roberts of the Archives Branch, Air Force Historical Research Agency; Dan Hagedorn, Paul Wood, Norman Richards, and Peter Callejas of the Archives Reference Team, National Air and Space Museum; David W Menard of the Air Force Museum; James A Moyers, Historian, Air Force Communications Agency; aircraft photographers and historians Jack M Friell, Harry Gann, William T Larkins, Robert L Lawson, Douglas D Olson and Norm Taylor; fellow author and historian Wayne Mutza; Lillian E Nolan, Chief, History Office of the HQ Air Force Weather Agency; and Mrs Marcella Gerdes.

Also contributing important, and often priceless, information or photos were: Robert D Archer; Norman Avery; Gerald H Balzer; Ann K Hussey, Chief of the Office of History, and Shawn M Bohannon, Historian, Kelly AFB; Dana Bell; Carl H Bernhardt, Historian, Air Resupply and Communications Association; Roger F Besecker; Phil Butler, John W Christianson; Barry J Collman; Major E D Davis, 1708th Ferrying Wing Association; Larry Davis; John M Davis; Robert F Dorr; Robert Esposito; Jeffrey L Ethell; Steve Ginter; Jennifer M Gradidge; Dave Hansen; Thomas E Hatch; Tom Hildreth; Ken M Hiltz Jr; George M Horn and Dale C Kingsbury of the Air Force Photo Mapping Association; Walter House; Thor Johnson; Mike Kasiuba; R W Koch; Leo J Kohn; John Lameck; Alwyn T Lloyd; Terry M Love; Paul Madsen; Jim Meehan; Dewey S McClellan of the AACS Alumni Association; Claude McCullough; David R McLaren; Peter Mersky; Robert C Mikesh; Jay Miller; Lt Col Stephen H Miller; Kent Mitchell of the Hagerstown Aviation Heritage Museum; Robert Parmerter; Lionel N Paul; Fred Pernell, Still Picture Branch, National Archives; Brian Pickering of Military Aircraft Photographs; Howard Plunkett; Matt Rodina; Colin M Smith; Peter C Smith; Otha C Spencer, Historian, Air Weather Reconnaissance Association; Paul D Stevens; Bill Stratton, International Liaison Pilot and Aircraft Association; Baldur Sveinsson; Scott A Thompson; Robert S Wardner; CM Sgt Brian Wasko; Clyde Wilkes; and Tommy R Young, Historian, HQ Air Mobility Command.

Thanks also to the staff at Midland Publishing, for embracing the result of my labors and guiding it through to publication.

I would welcome any correspondence on the topic of MATS, – via my publishers' please, – the address details are on page 2.

Finally, to my ever-patient wife Linda and my children Lauren and Chris, my thanks for your understanding for all the time over the past few years when I was not there for you.

May 1999

Nicholas M Williams
Waverly, IA
USA

Opposite page: **C-135B, 61-2663, one of 45 Stratolifters flown by MATS prior to delivery of the C-141.** Clyde Gerdes Collection

This page, below: **A MATS International Date Line certificate awarded for a flight from Hickam to Wake.** P J Bloom, via author

MEASUREMENT

The very nature of this subject has resulted in measurements of length, area, volume and weight being quoted in the narrative in Imperial units. It is appreciated that some readers will be more familiar with the Metric system of measurement and the following list of equivalents is tendered to be helpful in that respect. Note: meter (US spelling); metre (in Europe).

Length: 1 inch (in) = 25.4 millimeters (mm); 1 foot (ft) = 30.48 centimeters (cm); 1 yard (yd) = 0.9144 meters (m); 1 mile = 1.609 kilometers (km).

Area: 1 square inch (in^2) = 6.45 square centimeters (cm^2); 1 square mile = 2.59 square kilometers (km^2); 1 acre = 4047 square meters (m^2); 2.471 acres = 1 hectare

Volume: 1 cubic inch (in^3) = 16.38 cubic centimeters (cm^3); 1 cubic foot (ft^3) = 28,316.846 cubic centimeters (cm^3); 1 pint (pt) = 0.568 litres (l or lit); 1 US gallon = 3.788 liters; 1 Imperial/UK gallon = 4.546 litres.

Weight: 1 ounce (oz) = 28.35 grams (gm); 1 pound (lb) = 0.4536 kilograms (kg); 1 ton (t) = 1.016 metric tonnes.

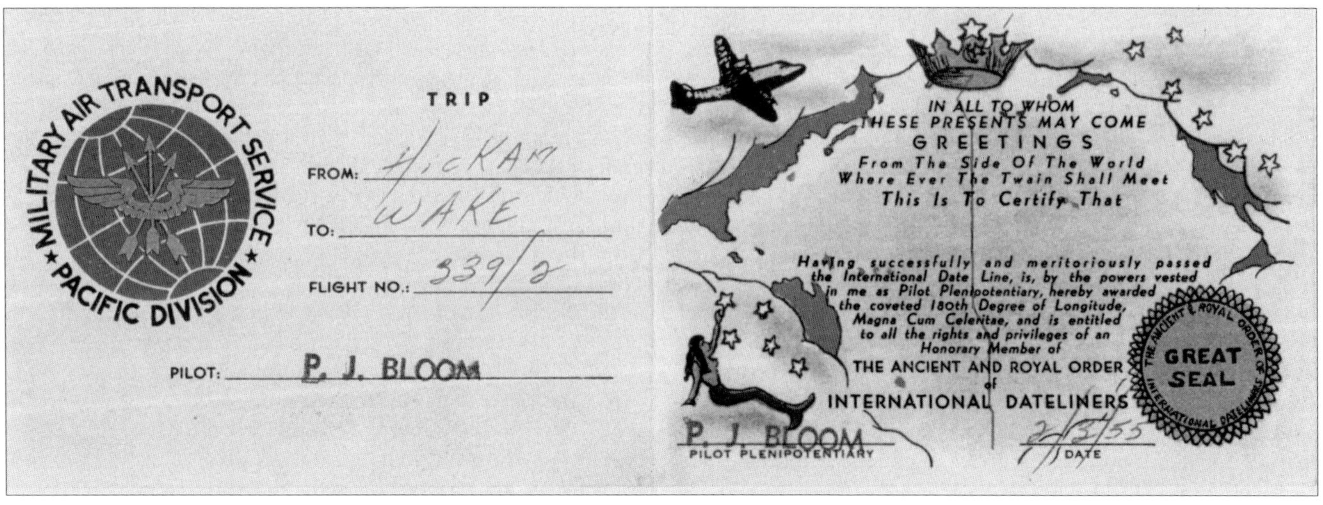

MILITARY AIR TRANSPORT SERVICE ★ PACIFIC DIVISION ★

TRIP

FROM: Hickam

TO: WAKE

FLIGHT NO.: 339/2

PILOT: P. J. BLOOM

IN ALL TO WHOM THESE PRESENTS MAY COME

GREETINGS

From The Side Of The World Where Ever The Twain Shall Meet

This Is To Certify That

Having successfully and meritoriously passed the International Date Line, is, by the powers vested in me as Pilot Plenipotentiary, hereby awarded the coveted 180th Degree of Longitude, Magna Cum Celeritae, and is entitled to all the rights and privileges of an Honorary Member of

THE ANCIENT AND ROYAL ORDER of INTERNATIONAL DATELINERS

GREAT SEAL

THE ANCIENT ROYAL ORDER OF INTERNATIONAL DATELINERS

P. J. BLOOM

PILOT PLENIPOTENTIARY

2/3/55

DATE

Contents

Below: **Convair T-29B, 51-5122, in April 1963 while being operated as a MATS transport.** MAP

Title page: **Douglas C-133B, 59-529, one of fifty MATS Cargomasters, above the San Francisco Bay with the Golden Gate Bridge in the background.** Douglas, courtesy of Harry Gann

Left: **MATS Pacific Division C-118A, 53-3249, flown by the 33rd ATS, 1705th ATG, McChord AFB, Washington, at Elmendorf AFB, Alaska, in October 1955.** Air Force, courtesy of Norm Taylor

Photograph overleaf on page 8: **C-121G, 54-4067 *City of Campbell*, of the Naval Air Transport Wing, Pacific, at Elmendorf AFB, Alaska, in January 1958, after the Constellations of Navy Squadrons VR-7 and VR-8 at NAS Moffett Field, California, had been transferred to the Air Force.** Norm Taylor

Photograph overleaf on page 9: **Mechanics make repairs to Air Evacuation Douglas C-54E belonging to the 1700th Air Transport Group, Kelly AFB, Texas.** US Air Force

Commanders of the Military Air Transport Service

Lt Gen Laurence Kuter
1st June 1948 to 28th October 1951

Lt Gen Joseph Smith
15th November 1951 to 30th June 1958

Lt Gen William Tunner
1st July 1958 to 31st May 1960

General Joe Kelly Jr
1st June 1960 to 18th July 1964

General Howell Estes Jr
19th July 1964 to 31st December 1965

Part I

HISTORY

Chapter 1

Air Corps Ferrying Command

Like his brethren in the US Army Air Corps pursuit and bombardment communities, the airman in a 1935-era transport unit could not foresee the rapid advancements in both equipment and organization that would be made by the Air Corps and US Army Air Forces over the next ten years. Before 1935, the Air Corps possessed only a few dozen cargo aircraft which were attached to individual airfields and air depots. Few of these aircraft were fitted with larger cargo doors, as trains were commonly used to transport bulky cargo and freight was flown only in emergencies. An even smaller number of personnel transports were assigned to the various headquarters. However, in an Air Corps reorganization beginning in March 1935, the first Army Air Corps transport squadron was established at Patterson Field, Ohio, and the foundation for a unified air transport structure was laid.

The types of true transport aircraft possessed by the Air Corps also began to stabilize at this time. Where previously the Air Corps practice had been to order small numbers of a wide variety of aircraft to be used for utility and transport operations, increasing numbers of military versions of the Douglas DC-2 and DC-3 were ordered beginning with a single XC-32 in 1935 and 18 C-33s, based on the DC-2, in 1936. These aircraft gradually replaced Ford C-3/C-4 Tri-Motors, twin-engined Curtiss C-30 Condors and Bellanca C-27 Airbus transports.

By 1939, thirty-five Douglas C-39s, also based on the DC-2 but with a DC-3 center wing section, equipped the following units of the newly-organized 10th Air Transport Group at Patterson Field, Ohio:

1st Transport Squadron	Patterson Field, Ohio
2nd Transport Squadron	Langley Field, Virginia
3rd Transport Squadron	Duncan Field, Texas
4th Transport Squadron	McClellan Field, California
5th Transport Squadron	Olmstead Field, Pennsylvania
6th Transport Squadron	Olmstead Field, Pennsylvania
7th Transport Squadron	McClellan Field, California

Anticipating its eventual participation in the expanding European war, in September 1940 the US Army Air Corps ordered an additional 545 C-47s, the first large order for the Skytrain predating wartime orders totalling thousands of aircraft. Initial orders for the long-range, four-engined Douglas C-54 Skymaster also were placed at this time.

The impetus for the Air Corps' initial organizational build-up came not only from transport needs, but also from a need to supply American allies with aircraft. By 1941, with war raging in Europe and England desperate for aircraft of all types, the Air Corps Ferrying Command was formed on 29th May 1941, supplementing ferrying operations already established by Canadian and British civil airlines. Commanded by Col Robert Olds, the Ferrying Command was given two missions: to assume the task of ferrying American-built British Lend-Lease aircraft from American factories to departure points in Canada and the eastern and southern US; and to maintain a special Air Ferry Service to meet War Department requirements, a task which was to develop into the transport component of the Air Transport Command's mission in less than a year.

An insignia was adopted by the Ferrying Command which was used, basically unchanged, over the following six years: a light blue or orange circle containing the top portion of a white globe, with a red and dark blue stylized bird – reminiscent of a sundial – superimposed over it. At the left margin of the circle, spelled out in International Morse Code, were the letters 'ACFC' standing for the Air Corps Ferrying Command. The same insignia was used later when the Air Transport Command was formed, with 'AFATC' spelled out in International Morse Code for Air Forces Air Transport Command, reflecting the name change, on 20th June 1941, to the US Army Air Forces. In this insignia, the separate letters' dots and dashes were painted in alternating red and dark blue to differentiate them.

On lst July 1941, a Consolidated B-24 Liberator was flown from Bolling Field, DC, to Prestwick, Scotland, via Montreal and Gander, the first North Atlantic shuttle flight made by the Army Air Forces Ferrying Command. Twenty-two subsequent shuttle flights were made between July and October while the weather was favorable, at a rate of six round trips per month. This service was dubbed the 'Arnold Line' after Commanding General of the Air Forces, General Henry H (Hap) Arnold.

Later in 1941, two Army Air Forces globe-circling missions reaffirmed the feasibility of long-range transport routes. The first, in September, used two B-24s to transport presidential envoy W Averell Harriman's contingent to Moscow to draft a Lend-Lease agreement. On their return flights, one B-24 flew westward via Cairo, Africa, South America, the Caribbean, and Florida. The other aircraft returned via the Middle East, India, Singapore, Darwin, Wake Island, and Hawaii. In November, a B-24 flown by Lt Col Caleb V Haynes and Major Curtis E LeMay (later to head the Strategic Air Command), returned from a 26,000 mile mission carrying Major General Brett, Chief of the Air Forces, to the Middle East.

Following the Japanese attack on Pearl Harbor on 7th December 1941, the Ferrying Command temporarily ceased all operations to the Allies. After having delivered over 1,300 aircraft to the British, it switched its emphasis to supplying aircraft and war materiel to overseas American units. The Ferrying Command was divided, on 29th December 1941, into two wings: the Domestic Wing with six sectors within the US, and a Foreign Wing split into the North Atlantic Sector, headquartered at Presque Isle, Maine; the Transatlantic Sector, with headquarters at Bolling Field, DC; the South Atlantic Sector at Morrison Field, West Palm Beach, Florida; and the Pacific Sector at Hamilton Field, California. As the war expanded, new wings soon were added: the Caribbean Wing at Morrison Field and the Africa-Middle East Wing headquartered at Cairo, Egypt.

Ferrying Command's first foreign ferrying operation began only three days after Pearl Harbor, when four B-24s were delivered to the Middle East. Not generally appreciated is the fact that the success of these early world-wide ferry and transport routes flown by Ferrying Command and Air Transport Command personnel were the result of commercial airline pioneering efforts. Not only did the military benefit from the routes flown by Pan American Airways, BOAC, and their joint subsidiary Atlantic Airways Ltd, but once war broke out the influx of many highly-trained airline personnel into Ferrying Command and Air Transport Command structure, in administrative as well as flight and maintenance positions, aided the rapid expansion of the ATC throughout the war.

On 14th April 1942, the president of American Airlines, C R Smith, was made the Executive Officer of Ferrying Command with the rank of Colonel. Smith then began assigning responsibilities to the various airlines to assist in the war effort. Even with this valuable help from airline-trained personnel, Ferrying Command was not able to immediately meet all of the War Department's strategic transport demands, and so contracts were signed with the airlines to fill this gap. As early as July 1941, Pan American Airways created two subsidiaries to provide facilities and regular transport services to Cairo and Khartoum. In December, Pan American Airways itself agreed to a contract with the government to transport men and supplies to Teheran over its African route, and by April 1942 airlines were contracted to fly routes over the Atlantic and to Alaska. Consolidated Aircraft Corporation entered the fray in April 1942, operating its own LB-30s and C-87s, transport versions of their B-24 bomber, from the San Diego factory westward across the Pacific under the name of Consairways.

Opposite page top: **Lockheed Y1C-36, one of only three purchased by the Army Air Corps in 1937.**
Peter M Bowers, courtesy of Clyde Gerdes Collection

Right: **The Douglas C-39, shown here in pre-1942 markings, was the military version of the DC-2.**
Peter M Bowers, courtesy of Clyde Gerdes Collection

Chapter 2

Air Transport Command

In recognition of the new shift in emphasis in the Ferrying Command's mission, on 20th June 1942 the organization was re-designated as the Air Transport Command (ATC). The ATC was given exclusive responsibility for the War Department's strategic airlift missions, and it absorbed all Army Air Forces transport units from other commands except the Troop Carrier Command. Over the following year, this restructuring, providing centralized control of all strategic air transport without interference from theater commanders (except during emergencies), caused some backlash from the theater commands until this relationship between the ATC and theater commands could be clarified.

With the creation of the Air Transport Command, two divisions were formed: the Ferrying Division and the Air Transport Division. Five wings also were established: the North Atlantic, South Atlantic, Pacific, Caribbean, and Africa-Middle East. By the end of 1942, the Africa-Middle East Wing had been split into the North African and the Central African Wings, and two new wings, the Alaskan and the India-China Wings, had been formed. Also established at this time was a Special Air Missions squadron operating out of Bolling Field, DC, charged with the responsibility for transporting government and military VIPs throughout the world.

During the war, the ATC expanded its sphere of operations as new territories were liberated. In November 1942, six Consolidated C-87s were used by the ATC to establish a regular trans-Sahara route between Accra and Oran, while in January 1943 regular services were flown between Prestwick and Marrakesh using Douglas C-54s. A new European Wing also was established in January, and in July regular routes to Australia were begun. In February 1944, direct ATC flights between New York and Calcutta were started, with London-Paris, Marseilles-Casablanca and New York-Paris flights beginning in October. While a detailed accounting of the ATC's exploits during the Second World War is outside the scope of this book, one accomplishment stands out and deserves mention: 'The Hump'. The ATC had activated its India-China Wing in December 1942 to provide airlift support to the Chinese Government and America and its allies fighting in China. Operating from bases in India and flying routes over the tallest and most rugged mountains in the world, the Himalayas, nicknamed 'The Hump', ATC Curtiss C-46, Douglas C-47 and contracted C-87 fuel transports flew the largest sustained air supply campaign up to that time.

When the India-China Wing was activated on 1st December 1942, at Assam in India, its goal was to deliver 2,500 tons of materiel to China by February 1943, and 5,000 tons per month thereafter. This was to be accomplished by flying from bases in Assam to Kunming, China, using either of two main routes. The southern route was a direct, 520 mile trip which crossed a 'low' Himalayan ridge at 16,000ft. However, this route exposed the transports to Japanese-held territory for 45 minutes. A northerly route avoided this hazard, but was 200 miles longer and still required crossing the Himalayas at 16,000ft.

These were not the only hazards that were faced by 'Hump' crews. Bases at Assam and Kunming were subject to occasional Japanese raids. Navigation aids were non-existent, and poor weather at Kunming often resulted in aircraft 'stacked' above the airfield waiting their turn to land. Monsoon weather from April through October helped produce 200 inches of rain during the year, and even during the 'dry' season from October to January or February, violent storms often swept through the entire region.

In November 1942, before the India-China Wing's activation, the 10th Air Force had delivered 819 tons of supplies to China. At first meeting its goal, the ATC delivered 2,871 tons in February 1943, but bad weather in April lowered the delivered tonnage considerably. In mid-May, the ATC was directed to not only meet the previously-mentioned 5,000 ton goal for July, but to deliver 7,500 tons in August and 10,000 tons during September 1943. Known as 'Project 7' or the '10,000 Ton Objective', the Wing found that to meet this new goal it would need an additional 93 C-46s, 25 C-47s, and 24 C-87s, 10,000 tons of extra equipment, and the construction of eight new airfields.

Poor weather during the summer of 1943, and the loss of at least two dozen aircraft to Japanese fighters during the fall and early winter, hindered the wing from reaching this goal until December, when 12,594 tons of supplies were delivered. By August 1944, the 'Hump' crews were transporting over 23,000 tons per month and at war's end 'Hump' aircraft were delivering an astounding 71,000 tons per month, most of this by aircraft of the India-China Wing of the Air Transport Command. In recognition of the ATC's feat, President Roosevelt presented the wing with a Presidential Unit Citation, supposedly the first instance of a 'non-combat' unit having received this honor.

Opposite page top: **ATC Douglas C-53 41-20092 operated under contract by Pan American Airways, being loaded with cargo at Miami for a flight to South America.** US Air Force, via NASM

Upper right: **ATC insignia, 20th June 1942 to 1st June 1948**

Below: **A Consolidated LB-30B, carrying British serial number AM927, one of 20 Liberator transports ordered by the UK. After 'special duties' (tests?) in the US, this particular airplane is believed to have been damaged and not delivered. After the Second World War it was flown as a VIP transport with US civil registration marks and was eventually acquired by the Confederate Air Force.** Clyde Gerdes Collection

After the war, Air Transport Command's mission shifted into reverse. Victory in Europe in May 1945 saw the ATC returning 84,000 veterans and thousands of aircraft to the US, although many aircraft were held in storage depots in Germany, Italy, and Egypt for sale by the Army-Navy Liquidation Commission.

By V-J Day on 2nd September 1945, Air Transport Command consisted of more than 300,000 military and civilian personnel and over 3,700 aircraft, including nearly 1,200 C-47s, 770 C-46s, 700 C-54s, and 200 C-87s. ATC aircraft flew to every continent through its one domestic and eight foreign divisions.

However, within a year of V-J Day, demobilization had reduced the ATC's strength to less than 60,000 personnel and 1,500 aircraft, and its route structure had been consolidated into just three global divisions: the Atlantic Division, Pacific Division, and European Division. By mid-1947, the ATC's main transport fleet had been reduced to roughly 600 aircraft: 302 C-54s, 289 C-47s, six C-46s, and a handful of newer transports such as the Lockheed C-69 and Douglas C-74. By March 1948, further budget cutbacks had reduced the Air Transport Command to 130 C-47s, 130 C-54s, ten C-74s, three Boeing C-97s, and one Douglas C-118 used by the Special Missions Squadron to transport President Truman. To maintain its worldwide services, with this reduced capability, ATC soon was forced to contract out airlift and maintenance services with civil air carriers.

On a brighter note, in a move to improve efficiency the Army Air Forces assigned a number of services to Air Transport Command in March 1946: the Army Airways Communications System, the AAF's Weather Service, Flight Service, Aeronautical Chart Service, and the Office of Flying Safety. On 13th March 1946, the AAF Air Rescue Service was established and was assigned to the ATC on 1st April. ATC also was given command responsibility for a number of widely-scattered transport bases, including Kindley, Bermuda; Dhahran, Saudi Arabia; Lajes, Azores, and Wheelus, Tripoli, Libya.

272374
2374

Photographs on the opposite page:

Top: **ATC Douglas C-54B 42-72374 the *Flying Cross*, near Kunming, China, in June 1945.** US Air Force, via Dana Bell

Bottom: **ATC Curtiss C-46A 42-96569 flying 'The Hump' with snow-capped Himalayas in the background.** US Air Force, via NASM

Photographs on this page:

Top: **Douglas C-47B 43-16255 one of nearly 1,200 Skytrains flown by the Air Transport Command during the Second World War.** US Air Force, via the Clyde Gerdes Collection

Bottom: **C-54E 44-9122 displays the flamboyant markings of the Pacific Division of Air Transport Command, 1947.** Leo J Kohn

Above: **Boeing YC-97 45-59590 seen here above San Francisco Bay,was one of six early Stratofreighters flown by the ATC on a regularly-scheduled freight run between California and Hawaii.** US Air Force, via David Menard

Left: **The familiar MATS tail band was first seen on Air Transport Command aircraft. C-54D 42-72550 carries an early 'buzz number' on its aft fuselage.** APN

Bottom: **This Air Evacuation C-54D, 42-72742, belonging to Air Transport Command's Continental Division, could accommodate up to 30 patients in the domestic medevac role. The nose inscription was in red with black borders.** US Air Force, courtesy of Dana Bell

Opposite page, left and right: **Naval Air Transport Service insignia: for 20th October 1943 to 19th April 1945 and for 19th April 1945 to 1st June 1948.**

Chapter 3

Naval Air Transport Service

Although smaller in size than the Army Air Forces Air Transport Command, the Naval Air Transport Service's early history mirrors that of the ATC. Prior to Pearl Harbor, the Navy's air transport aircraft and their crews were assigned to various utility squadrons and commands with no formal coordinating organization developed. The aircraft themselves mostly were small utility and converted patrol types, with neither reinforced floors nor cargo doors to handle bulky loads. The appearance of the Douglas DC-2 in 1935 enabled the Navy to re-equip its utility squadrons with this modern transport, designated as the R2D-1, replacing a handful of Ford Tri-Motor transports. Eventually, early models of the DC-3 were procured in increasing numbers, beginning with the R4D-1 in February 1942.

Five days after Pearl Harbor, on 12th December 1941, the Naval Air Transport Service (NATS) was created during a meeting between Secretary of the Navy Frank Knox and Captain C H 'Dutch' Schildhauer, who outlined his plan to create a global air transport network 'between naval establishments and areas of naval operations'. To aid in developing this the Navy was forced to sign contracts with Pan American Airways and American Export Airlines. Eventually, both airlines' Pacific and Atlantic Division routes, aircraft, and personnel were brought into the NATS system. In actuality, until NATS began to receive the long-range Douglas R5D (C-54) Skymaster in 1943, Pan American Airways Boeing 314 'Clippers' served as the mainstay of NATS' Pacific operations. After the Japanese defeat in the South Pacific in 1943, Pan American/NATS aircraft were reassigned to the mainland-Honolulu route exclusively. By January 1944, Pan American still shouldered approximately half of the Navy's requirements, and it was not until January 1945 that the contract carrier's contribution had dwindled to just 20 per cent.

The first NATS squadron, VR-1, was established on 9th March 1942, at NAS Norfolk, Virginia, to serve the Atlantic area. Beginning operations with four R4D-1s, 27 officers and 150 enlisted men, VR-1's first missions went south to supply naval forces fighting the German submarine threat along the Atlantic Coast and the Caribbean Sea. VR-2 was established the following month at NAS Alameda, California, with one R4D-1. In May, a VR-2 Sikorsky VS-44 flying boat made the inaugural transpacific NATS flight to Honolulu. VR-3 was established in July 1942 at NAS Olathe, Kansas, with its mission to connect the various continental naval stations, training centers, and supply bases. The squadron made its first transcontinental flight on 6th September.

The unavailability of true long-range transport aircraft and the scarcity of airline trained personnel caused the build-up of NATS to progress slowly. The first NATS wing, the Pacific Wing at NAS Honolulu, was not established until October 1942. The Atlantic and West Coast Wings were formed in March 1943, and in November 1943 the Naval Air Ferry Command was established with three squadrons based in California, Ohio, and New York. By the end of 1943, the Naval Air Transport Service had grown to include four wings made up of ten transport and three ferry squadrons flying 173 aircraft. Its 8,000 personnel operated flights throughout the Pacific area, to Alaska, Rio de Janeiro, and eastward to Europe and Africa on four transatlantic routes.

Not to be outdone by its Army Air Forces counterparts, the Naval Air Transport Service continually strove to acquire the best equipment for its trans-oceanic routes. Navy planners originally had conceived a NATS fleet made up exclusively of flying boats, and had converted a number of four-engined Consolidated PB2Y Coronado and twin-engined Martin PBM Mariner patrol boats to personnel and cargo transports and VIP carriers.

The first R5D-1 appeared in April 1943. Comparable to the Army Air Forces C-54, the Navy eventually acquired over 200 of the long-range Skymasters. But the Navy's crown jewel during the war undoubtedly was the 148,000 lb Martin Mars. Although only the prototype XPB2M-1R contributed to any extent during the war after being modified to a transport, it did so in record-breaking style.

The Mars went into service with VR-8 at NAS Patuxent River, Maryland, in November 1943, and almost immediately demonstrated its capabilities. On 30th November, the Mars, with a crew of sixteen, made a 28-hour non-stop flight of 4,375 miles from Patuxent River to Natal, Brazil, delivering 13,500 lbs of cargo. Assigned to VR-2 at NAS Alameda, California, in January 1944, the XPB2M-1R made 78 round trips between San Francisco and Honolulu until its retirement in March 1945, delivering over three million pounds of cargo and personnel.

The six production JRMs which were built served the Navy well while flying with the NATS, starting in 1945, and later with the Fleet Logistic Support Wing, until being retired in 1956.

By January 1945, the NATS fleet consisted of over 100 R5D Skymasters, a few twin-engined R4D Skytrains, 32 Convair PB2Y-3R Coronados, four Boeing 314s, and the single Martin Mars, the Martin PBM Mariner flying boats having been retired the previous October.

At the end of the war, the Naval Air Transport Service could boast of a fleet of 429 aircraft and a personnel strength of over 26,000. However, rapid post-war demobilization lowered this number considerably. By 1946, NATS had been reduced to just over 200 aircraft, and by 1947 NATS' total transport inventory averaged just 116 aircraft made up mostly of R5D, R4D and the handful of production JRM Mars flying boats.

Left: **The Consolidated PB2Y-3R was one of NATS' main cargo and personnel transports during the Second World War.** Peter M Bowers Collection

Below: **Consolidated PB2Y-3R, Bu7090, operated for the Naval Air Transport Service during the Second World War by Pan American Airways on its complex launch and retrieval lift.** Pan American via Thor Johnson

Top: **Naval Air Transport Service R5D-3, 50845, approaches one of the Hawaiian Islands during a shuttle flight from California in December 1944.** Navy by Lt Cdr Horace Bristol

Bottom: **Cadets from Leonard Hall School wait to board *King Kong*, NATS R5D-1 39161 of VR-1, at NAS Patuxent River, Maryland in 1947.** Navy, via Steve Ginter

Above: **Consolidated PB2Y-3R, 7083, carrying the neutrality flag and the Pan American Airways emblem as Pan American operated the Coronado under contract.** Pan American Airlines, courtesy of Thor Johnson

Below left: **Passengers walk ashore for lunch from a NATS PBM Mariner transport while it is being refueled at Kingston, Jamaica, in August 1943.** Navy, by Lt J G Wayne Miller

Below right: **The prototype Martin XPB2M-1R Mars heads west from San Francisco in October 1944.** Navy, courtesy of Clyde Gerdes Collection

Above: **Consolidated PB2Y-3R, 7241, flies over the NATS terminal on Oahu, Hawaii, in 1946.** Navy

Below: **Douglas R5D-3, 56528, of the Naval Air Transport Service over the Pacific coastline in August 1947.** Navy

Chapter 4

Military Air Transport Service 1948 to 1950

'We have learned and must not forget that from now on air transport is an essential of air power, in fact, of all national power.'

General Henry H Arnold
Commanding General, US Army Air Forces
February 1945

General 'Hap' Arnold had long been considering what role the post-war Air Transport Command would play. By November 1945, Arnold saw the continuing need for an organization serving as a link between installations around the world and capable of deploying troops quickly during emergencies, such as airlifting an entire Army corps to either Alaska or Iceland with the assistance of the civil airlines reserve fleet.

Economy and efficiency were foremost on the minds of Congress in the late 1940s. Passage of the National Security Act of 1947 created the Department of Defense, and former Secretary of the Navy James F Forrestal was appointed as the first Secretary of Defense. The Act also established the United States Air Force as an independent department on 18th September 1947, equal to the Army and Navy Departments. Both the Congressional Committee on National Aviation Policy and the President's Air Policy Commission recommended that, to avoid duplication of effort, the Air Force's Air Transport Command and the Navy's Naval Air Transport Service be merged into one agency for the strategic transport of personnel and cargo.

On 15th January 1948, Defense Secretary Forrestal issued a memorandum proposing the creation of the Military Air Transport Service (MATS). Forrestal followed this on 1st March with a formal order to combine the ATC and NATS into the MATS. MATS would be operated by the Air Force for the Department of Defense, with the Navy furnishing personnel and aircraft proportionate to its own transportation needs. MATS was established as a major Air Force command, under the jurisdiction of the Chief of Staff, USAF, but it also served as a global air transport agent for the Department of Defense and other authorized government agencies. Significantly, both the Air Force and Navy retained smaller tactical and non-scheduled transport units as part of their overseas commands, such as USAF-Europe's European Air Transport Service, and the Troop Carrier Command, Tactical Air Command and the support squadrons of the Strategic Air Command for the Air Force, and the Fleet Logistic Support Wings/Fleet Logistic Air Wing for the Navy.

The spirit of Air Force/Navy unification within MATS was evident from the top down. Commanding the new organization was Major General Laurence S Kuter, who had previously commanded the ATC's Atlantic Division, with the Navy's Rear Admiral John P Whitney, former head of the Naval Air Transport Service, serving as Vice Commander. MATS Headquarters was established at Gravelly Point, Virginia, but was moved to Andrews AFB, Maryland, in November 1948.

4.1 Transport Operations

On 1st June 1948, the Military Air Transport Service began operations with a total inventory of 824 aircraft (766 Air Force and 58 Navy) and 54,164 Air Force, Navy and civilian personnel. The main airlift force was made up of 239 C-47s and 234 C-54s, although the ten MATS C-74s and four MATS C-97s made up an important component of its growing airlift capability in 1948. As a 'stand alone' combined organization, 'MATS' had replaced 'USAF' and 'NAVY' on the wings of most of its aircraft, and the now-familiar MATS globe with three winged arrows, representing the three services, was painted on their fuselages in dark blue and yellow. The Military Air Transport Service was split into three divisions: Atlantic, Continental and Pacific. The routes flown by these divisions were in a constant state of flux as new routes were opened, old ones closed, and priorities and aircraft types changed over the years, and the following account will have to serve as only a general description of the first few years of MATS' existence.

The Atlantic Division of MATS, with its roots as the Ferrying Command's 22nd Ferrying Wing, which was established on 12th June 1942, was headquartered at Westover AFB, Massachusetts. From Westover AFB, Atlantic Division's routes spread eastward:

- to Frankfurt, Germany, via Newfoundland, the Azores, England and France;
- to Dhahran, Saudi Arabia, via Newfoundland, the Azores, French Morocco, and Tripoli;
- to Bermuda and the Azores;
- to Newfoundland, Labrador and Iceland; and
- to Winnipeg and Churchill, Canada.

The Atlantic Division also maintained a network of routes in Europe, the Mediterranean, and the Near East. The division operated a scheduled medical air evacuation service between Westover AFB, Fairfield-Suisun AFB, California, and Kelly AFB, Texas. Finally, the Atlantic Division had jurisdiction over Kindley AFB, Bermuda; Lajes Field, Azores; Wheelus Field, Libya, and Dhahran, Saudi Arabia.

The Continental Division of MATS, which began as the Domestic Division of the Air Corps Ferrying Command on 28th December 1941, had its headquarters at Kelly AFB, Texas. The division maintained the following air routes:

- to Kodiak, Alaska, using aircraft of Navy MATS squadron VR-3, from NAS Moffett Field, Calif., via McChord AFB, Washington, and on to Adak and Shemya in the Aleutians;
- to Fairbanks, Alaska, from Great Falls AFB, Montana, via Edmonton, Fort Nelson and Whitehorse, Canada;
- to Anchorage from Great Falls AFB via McChord AFB;
- to Tokyo from McChord AFB via Anchorage and Shemya;
- to Tokyo from Kelly AFB and Brookley AFB, Alabama, via Hickam AFB, Hawaii, and Midway Island;
- to Hickam AFB from Brookley AFB;
- to Rio de Janeiro from Brookley AFB via West Palm Beach, Florida, Ramey AFB, Puerto Rico, Waller AFB, Trinidad, and Belem, Brazil; and
- from Brookley AFB to Balboa, Canal Zone.

The Continental Division also operated a domestic air evacuation service throughout the United States, connecting Travis AFB, Westover AFB, Washington, DC, Brookley AFB, Biggs AFB, Texas, and Hill AFB, Utah. Finally, the 1254th ATS Special Missions squadron, organized in October 1948 and headquartered at Washington National Airport, was tasked with the responsibility for transporting governmental and Washington, DC-based military VIPs, and was controlled by the Continental Division of MATS.

The Pacific Division, which essentially was an expanded version of the old Naval Air Transport Service network of routes, had its headquarters at Hickam AFB, Hawaii, and operated a shuttle service between Hickam AFB and Travis AFB, California, linking up with Continental Division flights. The Pacific Division's routes westward were:

- from Hickam AFB to Tokyo via Midway Island;
- from Hickam AFB to Tokyo via Wake Island and Iwo Jima;
- from Hickam AFB to Manila, Philippines, via Johnston Is, Kwajalein, and Guam;
- from Guam to Tokyo;
- from Guam to Iwo Jima and Kwajalein;
- from Manila to Okinawa and Tokyo;
- from Manila to Dhahran via Bangkok, Calcutta, New Delhi and Karachi.

At Dhahran, the western terminus of the Pacific Division met the eastern terminus of the Atlantic Division, thus completing the MATS world-wide route system.

As previously mentioned, in March 1946 the Air Transport Command had absorbed a number of Army Air Forces services, as well as the newly-created Air Rescue Service. With the formation of MATS, these services continued to function under the MATS umbrella.

Opposite page, top: **Douglas C-54E, 44-9042, is being painted in new MATS markings at Fairfield-Suisun AAF in September 1948.** William T Larkins

Below: **A Continental Division C-47B, 45-885, departs from NAS San Diego in December 1950.** Navy by AF3 Vallejo, courtesy of Robert L Lawson

4.2 Airways & Air Communications Service

The Airways and Air Communications Service (AACS), headquartered at Andrews AFB, provided communications and navigational services to nearly 200 locations worldwide, including control towers, direction finders, radio ranges, Ground Control Approach (GCA), Instrument Landing System (ILS), air-to-ground and point-to-point radio, radar beacons, message centers and cryptocenters. The AACS also maintained trained and fully equipped mobile units for immediate tactical deployment wherever needed. After post-war demobilization, in June 1946 the AACS was reduced to just 8,635 Army Air Forces personnel, but by June 1948 this number had grown to over 17,000 including civilians. The AACS operated a growing fleet of aircraft of its own, mostly administrative but also a small number used as electronic check aircraft.

4.3 Air Weather Service

The Air Weather Service (AWS), with headquarters at Andrews AFB, operated, as it does today, a number of weather stations, mobile units, and aerial reconnaissance squadrons on a worldwide basis. The organization was charged with the responsibility for providing the Air Force and other governmental agencies with operational and planning forecasts for any air route, terminal, or geographic location. Weather information collected by the AWS was transmitted around the world by the AACS.

In 1948, the Air Weather Service possessed 67 RB-29s and ten RB-17s distributed among its widespread weather reconnaissance squadrons:

8th Weather Squadron	Ft McAndrews AB, Newfoundland
9th Weather Squadron	March AFB, California
10th Weather Squadron	McClellan AFB, California
11th Weather Squadron	Elmendorf AFB, Alaska
12th Weather Squadron	Mitchel AFB, New York
15th Weather Squadron	Kadena, Okinawa
16th Weather Squadron	Scott AFB, Illinois
18th Weather Squadron	Wiesbaden, Germany
19th Weather Squadron	Smoky Hill AFB, Kansas
20th Weather Squadron	Yokota AB, Japan
24th Weather Squadron	Kelly AFB, Texas
25th Weather Squadron	Robins AFB, Georgia
26th Weather Squadron	Brookley AFB, Alabama
30th Weather Squadron	North Guam AFB, Guam

4.4 Air Rescue Service

The organization that was to evolve into the Air Rescue Service underwent a bewildering series of designations, redesignations and headquarters movements under the ATC beginning in January 1946. The Air Rescue Service (ARS) was officially designated in May 1946, and was concerned only with the various air rescue units located within the continental US. When the Military Air Transport Service was formed and assumed control over the Air Rescue Service, the ARS was assigned the additional responsibility for all rescue units located in Europe, North Africa and the Middle East, with those units located in the Far East being absorbed in May 1949.

In 1948, during the first year of MATS control of the Air Rescue Service, 2,082 aviation-related alerts were answered. Typically, after receiving an alert, the ARS made an extended radio check of all airports along the missing airplane's route, alerted other co-operating agencies (Coast Guard, Flight Service, Civil Air Patrol, etc), and finally alerted its own crews for a possible mission. Preliminary search plans would then be formulated, including all known information regarding the airplane, its pilot and passengers, and the *en route* weather. If this communications check proved negative, the aircraft was listed as missing and the search officially was begun. Specially trained para-rescue teams were maintained at selected bases, each made up of a para-doctor, two medical technicians, and two survival specialists. Of the more than 2,000 aircraft alert responses made by the ARS in 1948, only 193 actual missions were completed, the remaining alerts proving false due to overdue aircraft, unclosed flight plans, overdue position reports, or for other reasons.

Air Weather Service C-47D, 45-933, at Little Rock, Arkansas, with 'MATS' under its left wing. Leo J Kohn

All-yellow R-5D, 43-46640, photographed in April 1947 at Hayward, California, a year after the Air Rescue Service had been assigned to the Air Transport Command.
William T Larkins, courtesy of Dana Bell

By December 1948, the ARS possessed a fleet of 127 aircraft:

1 C-45	15 C/SC-47	1 C-64	19 H-5
1 L-4	23 L-5	14 L-13	19 OA-10A
25 SB-17	3 SB-29	6 SC-82	

ARS structure after reorganization in September 1949:

1st Rescue Squadron (Headquarters, MacDill AFB, Florida)
Flight A MacDill AFB, Florida
Flight B Albrook AFB, Canal Zone
Flight C Ramey AFB, Puerto Rico
Flight D Kindley AFB, Bermuda

2nd Rescue Squadron (Headquarters, Kadena Field, Okinawa)
Flight A Kadena Field, Okinawa
Flight B Kadena Field, Okinawa
Flight C Clark AFB, Philippines
Flight D North AFB, Guam

3rd Rescue Squadron (Headquarters, Yokota AB, Japan)
Flight A Yokota AB, Japan
Flight B Yokota AB, Japan
Flight C Misawa AB, Japan
Flight D Ashiya AB, Japan

4th Rescue Squadron (Headquarters, Hamilton AFB, California
Flight A Hamilton AFB, California
Flight B March AFB, California
Flight C McChord AFB, Washington
Flight D Hickam AFB, Hawaiian Islands

5th Rescue Squadron (HQ at Lowry AFB, Colorado)
Flight A Lowry AFB, Colorado
Flight B Biggs AFB, Texas
Flight C Maxwell AFB, Alabama
Flight D Selfridge AFB, Michigan

6th Rescue Squadron (HQ at Westover AFB, Massachusetts)
Flight A Westover AFB, Massachusetts
Flight B Harmon AB, Newfoundland
Flight C Goose AB, Labrador
Flight D Bluie West 1, Greenland

7th Rescue Squadron (HQ at Wiesbaden AB, Germany)
Flight A Wiesbaden AB, Germany
Flight B Lajes Field, Azores
Flight C Wheelus Field, Libya
Flight D Dhahran Field, Saudi Arabia

By the end of 1949, the ARS fleet had grown to 219 aircraft of all types, including 66 SB-17s, 38 L-13s, 40 H-5s, two SC-46s, four SA-16As and two H-6s.

4.5 Flight Service

The Flight Service, the only MATS service to operate entirely within the continental United States, had its headquarters located in Washington, DC. The Flight Service used a web of eight Flight Service Centers to: monitor all military flights; act as a clearing authority for all military flights departing locations where other clearing authority was not available; notify Air Defense Control Centers of movements of military aircraft within specified areas; notify the Air Rescue Service of lost or overdue aircraft; maintain up-to-date information on landing fields, navigational facilities, availability of fuel and other conditions that might affect flight safety; and process all reports of reckless flying. The Flight Service also maintained a hurricane evacuation plan, designating refuge bases for all aircraft located in areas affected by hurricane conditions.

The eight Flight Service Centers were located at Orlando AFB, Florida; Hamilton AFB, California; Lowry AFB, Colorado; March AFB, California; Maxwell AFB, Alabama; McChord AFB, Washington; Olmsted AFB, Pennsylvania; and Wright-Patterson AFB, Ohio. The Flight Service possessed a small fleet of administrative C-45, C-47 and C-54 aircraft.

4.6 Berlin Airlift

Almost as if on cue, the Russians issued a Cold War challenge to MATS only 24 days after its formation. After the Second World War, the city of Berlin had been partitioned into four sectors by the Allied armies of America, England, France and Russia.

Unfortunately, this division made Berlin an island surrounded by Russian occupied and controlled territory. The western allies had a written agreement with the Russians for the use of three air corridors into the western sectors of the city, but no guarantees existed for roads, railways, or inland waterways into Berlin.

Air Rescue Service C-47D, 43-16256, at Hayward, California, in April 1947 before the formation of the US Air Force and MATS. William T Larkins

SB-17G, 44-83700, wearing the colors of the Air Rescue Service at Hamilton Field, California, in 1948. Note the airplane's 'buzz number' on the tail. William T Larkins

Berlin Airlift C-47s line the ramp at Tempelhof AB in 1948. The C-47s soon were replaced by C-54s on the airlift. Air Force, courtesy of Clyde Gerdes Collection

This situation became painfully clear at 6am on Friday 25th June 1948, when the Russians blockaded all land and water routes into the western sectors of Berlin, citing 'technical difficulties' in the repair of these facilities. For several days previously, the Russians had been harassing US military freight trains travelling to Berlin, demanding to be allowed to inspect each car, all in a thinly-disguised attempt to force the allies out of the city. General Lucius D Clay, the US Commander in Germany, urged that an armed convoy be sent to open a road to Berlin. But as the Joint Chiefs of Staff refused to allow force to be used in the operation, Clay withdrew the option and instead recommended that an airlift be implemented to supply the city with necessities. After receiving quick approval for the airlift, Clay ordered Lt Gen Curtis E LeMay, Commander of USAF (Europe), to devise and implement a plan to airlift supplies into Berlin using the three air corridors into the western sectors of the city. The American airlift began on 26th June when 32 C-47s from the European Air Transport Service and the 60th Troop Carrier Group carried 80 tons of supplies into Berlin.

Despite the best efforts of the Americans, and aircraft and crews supplied by the Royal Air Force Transport Command, it became obvious during the first month of the airlift that a massive and sustained effort would be required. Fewer than 100 C-47s were in USAF (Europe), and while new aircraft and crews were brought in from other Air Force and RAF units as well as from American and British civil airlines, still more aircraft would be needed to supply not only foodstuffs, but coal to be burned during the coming winter. The tonnage thought necessary to supply the city kept increasing nearly every week of the airlift.

On 23rd July 1948, the Military Air Transport Service was directed to establish an Airlift Task Force Headquarters in Germany, operating under General LeMay. MATS chose Maj Gen William H Tunner, Deputy Commander for Air Transport, to head the task force. Tunner brought a large portion of his MATS headquarters staff with him to Germany, and his team began outlining a plan to make the most efficient use of the airlift fleet. Supporting the airlift were the Airways and Air Communications Service, which screened its hundreds of installations worldwide for trained personnel and specialized equipment for the airlift, and the Air Weather Service, which moved three additional weather reconnaissance squadrons to Europe and extra personnel to the airlift bases being used.

While the Berlin Airlift, or 'Operation Vittles' as it was known to the Americans, became a MATS administered operation, it is important to note that a number of other military and civil entities made significant contributions to the overall effort. The American and British aircraft were organized into the Combined Airlift Task Force, headquartered in Wiesbaden, which included RAF Dakotas (C-47s), Avro Yorks and Handley Page Hastings, as well as RAF Short Sunderland and Aquila Airways Short Hythe flying boats which carried supplies into Havel Lake, and BEA Vickers Vikings, Flight Refuelling Ltd Avro Lancasters, Scottish Airlines Convair Liberator transports, and other British civil operators flying a variety of aircraft types. As the airlift expanded, the USAF (Europe) and troop carrier group units which initially had been committed were supplemented by C-54 squadrons from continental US, Alaskan and Caribbean commands.

When MATS had received its airlift call-to-arms in July 1948, the organization responded by sending nine squadrons of C-54s, totalling 81 aircraft, with 3 three-man crews per airplane. By the end of the year, 457 three-man flight crews from MATS would be assigned to the Airlift Task Force. MATS also established a Replacement Training Unit for 'Operation Vittles' crews at Great Falls AFB, Montana, flying 19 C-54s. At the airlift's peak, this unit was training thirty replacement crews a week. On 4th October, MATS C-74s began making three round trips per week between Brookley AFB, Alabama, and Frankfurt, Germany, carrying C-54 engines and parts for airlift Skymasters. Also, early in 1949 seven new MATS C-121s were based at Westover AFB to fly passengers to Germany via the North Atlantic route.

By the fall of 1948, MATS had supplied an additional 73 C-54s, including Pacific Division R5Ds from VR-6 and VR-8. These two 12-plane Navy MATS transport squadrons responded to the battle-cry, 'Ten Tons to Tempelhof', by becoming the most efficient squadrons of the entire airlift. VR-6 held the aircraft availability record of 81 percent, while VR-8 held the overall efficiency record, ending its tour at the conclusion of the airlift with the title of Most Efficient Squadron. Both squadrons held the record for heaviest average load for C-54/R5D aircraft carried between Rhein-Main and Berlin with 10.3 tons, and VR-6 set the record for daily utilization by averaging 18.6 hours per airplane during one 24-hour period. Another Navy MATS squadron, VR-3, supported the airlift by shifting its aircraft from domestic routes to the Westover AFB to Frankfurt, Germany, run.

In time, the tight scheduling of airlift traffic within the three corridors, and the greater capabilities of the C-54/R5Ds, resulted in the withdrawal of the C-47s and the near exclusive use of the Skymasters on the airlift. There were several significant exceptions to this policy, starting in mid-August 1948, when a single MATS C-74 from the 521st ATG, Mobile, Alabama, arrived at Rhein-Main Airfield to begin Vittles flights. C-74, 42-65414, landed at Gatow Airfield on the 17th carrying 20 tons of flour, and for the next six weeks the Globemaster flew 24 missions into the city, delivering 1,234,000 pounds of supplies.

Several airlift records were set by this C-74, as it averaged over 38,000 pounds of cargo per flight. On 18th September, Air Force Day, the C-74 flew six round trips into Berlin hauling a total of 250,000 pounds of coal and setting a new Airlift Task Force utilization record by flying 20 hours during the 24-hour effort. Also participating in the airlift, starting in September 1948, were five troop carrier C-82A Packets which were used to carry bulky loads, while a single Strategic Air Command YC-97A, 45-59595, joined the airlift in May 1949, carrying just over one million pounds of supplies into Berlin in 27 flights.

Following months of negotiations with the Soviets, an agreement was reached on 4th May 1949, and the blockade of Berlin was lifted on 12th May. However, General Clay requested, and received approval for, the airlift to continue so that a stockpile of supplies could be built-up that would last through the coming winter. The Airlift Task Force finally was disbanded on 1st September, and the last airlift C-54 landed at Tempelhof on 1st October. In 462 days of operations, the combined airlift had delivered 2.3 million tons of supplies in over 277,000 flights. It had been estimated that 4,500 tons per day would be required to supply the western sectors of Berlin, but the airlift actually had delivered an average of over 5,500 tons per day. For the United States forces, it was estimated that Air Force, Navy and Army participation had cost the country over $190 million, including $7.5 million in damaged and destroyed aircraft, and 31 Americans who lost their lives in 12 aircraft crashes.

The Berlin Airlift was considered a technical achievement and a diplomatic success, but to General Tunner and MATS planners the lessons learned were clear: that the future of air transport would rely on the design and procurement of larger aircraft. Just as the tonnage delivered had increased dramatically when the C-47s had been replaced on the airlift by C-54s, the successful use during 'Operation Vittles' of the five C-82As and the single C-97 and C-74 – however small their relative contributions were – demonstrated the all-around economies of larger aircraft in everything from the amount of fuel used to the number of flight crews needed. The subsequent success of aircraft such as the C-124, C-133, C-141 and C-5 has validated those lessons learned during the Berlin Airlift.

While 'Operation Vittles' became MATS' main focus of attention from mid-1948 to the fall of 1949, the organization continued to operate its worldwide network of transport routes, despite budget restrictions. The Air Rescue Service, Air Weather Service, and other MATS subordinate services slowly gained new aircraft as they struggled to overcome similar constraints. MATS also provided humanitarian support when needed, such as its 'Operation Snowbound' in January 1949. A severe blizzard had paralyzed parts of the central and western United States, and Air Rescue Service SC-47s and MATS C-54s were brought in to assist snowbound residents. These aircraft dropped 525 cases of 'C' rations, another 20,000 pounds of food, and 10,000 pounds of coal to those stranded by the storm, and 25,000 pounds of feed to isolated cattle.

In February, 'Operation Haylift' ended after 24 days of operations, using MATS C-47s and C-54s to drop nearly 1,900 tons of feed to blizzard-threatened cattle and sheep in Nevada and Utah. On the other side of the world, in September 1949 an Air Weather Service RB-29 collected air samples containing nuclear fission products, enabling the US to confirm that Russia had detonated its first atomic bomb.

Above: **During 'Operation Vittles', Douglas C-74s flew three round trips per week hauling C-54 engines and parts between Brookley AFB and Frankfurt, Germany.** Air Force

Below: **R5D-3, 50873, (formerly USAF serial 42-72450) of Navy MATS squadron VR-3 with NAS Moffett Field in the background.** Navy by AF1 Henry Weyandt, courtesy of Robert L Lawson

Chapter 5

Military Air Transport Service 1950 to 1960

5.1 Korean War

A second Cold War challenge was thrust upon the Military Air Transport Service only nine months after the end of the Berlin Airlift. On the morning of 25th June 1950, the Communist North Korean People's Army launched a full-scale invasion of South Korea. The North Korean Air Force entered combat in the afternoon by attacking the South Korean airfields at Seoul and Kimpo. The first American aircraft destroyed in the war was an already-damaged MATS Pacific Division C-54G, 45-518, which was strafed on the ground and destroyed by North Korean Yak fighters at Kimpo Airfield. The Military Air Transport Service's widespread involvement during the following 37 month duration of the war, through its transport operations as well as by the Air Rescue Service, Air Weather Service, Airways and Air Communications Service, and Air Resupply and Communications Service, is best described by treating each organization separately.

5.1.1 Transport Operations

MATS transport operations supporting the Korean War began in earnest in July 1950 when the Pacific Airlift was begun, primarily using MATS C-54s, C-74s, C-97s, and C-124s, contracted commercial air carrier aircraft, six Canadair North Stars (C-54s) from the Royal Canadian Air Force and three Belgian Sabena Air Lines DC-4s, some 250 aircraft in all. The Pacific Airlift delivered men and supplies as far west as Japan, returning eastward with war casualties and personnel on R&R. Once in Japan, this war materiel was re-loaded aboard Combat Cargo Command C-54s and C-119s for delivery into the Korean War Zone. The Combat Cargo Command, led by Maj Gen William H Tunner, adopted the lessons learned from the Berlin Airlift in creating a tight schedule of takeoffs and landings to supply Korea from bases in Japan. This arrangement of transferring personnel and supplies in Japan to smaller Combat Cargo Command aircraft was devised partly due to the fluid battle situation that existed early in the war, where airfield security was questionable, and due to the fact that many South Korean runways and taxiways were thought either too short or not sturdy enough to accommodate the larger MATS transports.

By the end of July, the Pacific Airlift was in full swing. On 24th August, the West Coast Airlift Task Force (Provisional) was organized, with its headquarters at Travis AFB. The Task Force had responsibility for integrating the civil airlines and United Nations aircraft into the airlift, and for controlling air traffic from the United States to Japan.

Three routes were used during the Pacific Airlift: the mid-Pacific route, from Travis AFB to Japan via Hickam AFB, Hawaii, and either Wake or Midway Islands, was the most-used cargo route during the Korean War, with a flying time for the 6,770 mile route of about 34 to 38 hours; the Northern Pacific or Great Circle route, from McChord AFB, Washington, via Elmendorf AFB, Alaska, and the Aleutians, was the most direct with a flying time of about 30 to 33 hours over 5,680 miles, and was the favored route for passenger traffic; the Southern Pacific route, from Travis AFB to Hickam AFB, Johnston Island and Kwajalein,

Top: **C-54E, 44-9031, resplendent in the full MATS markings at the Santa Monica Airport in the early 1950s.**
Douglas, courtesy of Norman Taylor

was the longest at 40 flying hours over 8,080 miles, and least-used route, employed only when poor weather precluded travelling the more northerly routes.

As the Pacific Division had fewer than sixty C-54s in its inventory, Lt Gen Laurence S Kuter, MATS Commander, directed other MATS divisions to supplement the Pacific Division on the airlift. In July, Atlantic and Continental Divisions furnished an additional forty C-54s, and the Tactical Air Command added two troop carrier groups to the force. At least one of these groups, the 62nd TCG at Kelly AFB, was reassigned to MATS in July 1950 and its C-54s were moved to McChord AFB, Washington, and placed under the operational control of the North Pacific Air Transport Wing (Provisional).

To keep up with the war's demands for more supplies, some 66 four-engine transports were chartered from 17 scheduled and non-scheduled commercial airlines. Despite this invaluable assistance, MATS averaged 186 round trips to Japan per month over the northern route alone. And, while the pre-war airlift requirements to Japan had been about 70 tons per month, by the end of September 1950 over 100 tons per day were being airlifted. On their return flights, MATS transports provided aeromedical evacuation from Japan to the United States for about 350 patients per month.

By November 1950, the Pacific Airlift had stabilized and the West Coast Airlift Task Force (Provisional) was disbanded and its responsibilities were assumed by the Continental Division of MATS. By March 1952, the Pacific Airlift was utilizing approximately 60 MATS, 60 commercial, and 15 United Nations transports. At war's end in July 1953, MATS had airlifted over 80,000 tons of cargo and 214,000 personnel over its Pacific Airlift routes. Its transports had returned eastward carrying over 43,000 casualties to the United States for further treatment.

5.1.2 Air Weather Service

When the Korean War broke out, weather services in the Pacific Theater of operations were provided by the 2143rd Air Weather Wing, Air Weather Service, MATS, with headquarters in Tokyo. The 2143rd AWW was made up of three ground weather squadrons: the 20th Weather Squadron in Japan; the 15th Weather Squadron in the Philippines; and the 31st Weather Squadron in Hawaii and the Marshall Islands. Each of these ground-based weather squadrons had many small, scattered weather-spotting detachments. In response to the Korean War, by November 1950 the 20th WS had placed 32 detachments around Japan and the Korean peninsula. The 2143rd AWW also had two weather reconnaissance squadrons, the 512th WRS, Yokota AB, Japan, and the 514th WRS on Guam, each with a complement of RB-29s, redesignated as WB-29s in August 1950.

The 512th WRS normally flew its 'Buzzard' weather reconnaissance flights over the South China Sea on a daily basis, but within 24 hours of hostilities a squadron RB-29 began flying a 'Buzzard Special' weather recon mission over Korea, not only reporting meteorological readings, but flying a zig-zag course over the country and reporting on tactical observations. By the end of September, the 512th WRS was flying two daily missions over Korea: 'Buzzard King' over North Korea and the Yellow Sea, and either 'Buzzard Dog' or 'Buzzard Easy' over adjacent areas.

On 13th July, an Air Weather Service RB-29 led the first B-29 strike against North Korea from Japan. However, despite the fact that the Air Weather Service's mission was amended on 29th August to exclude weather reconnaissance 'over areas where active enemy aerial resistance may be encountered', 512th WRS RB/WB-29 crews regularly flew weather recon 'combat missions' over South and North Korea. In February 1952, the first 512th WRS aircrews to have flown 50 of these missions were rotated stateside. In fact, until 9th June 1952, the squadron had the distinction of being the only Air Force unit to have had an aircraft over enemy-held territory every day since the war's beginning, accumulating some 750 combat missions during this period. The 514th WRS on Guam also had its share of war-related accomplishments. On 8th September 1950, Captain Charles R Cloniger received the Distinguished Flying Cross for continuing and completing a typhoon reconnaissance mission with one of his WB-29's engines feathered. The information his crew provided on this flight was invaluable to US forces preparing for the Inchon invasion.

In February 1951, the 512th WRS and 514th WRS were redesignated as the 56th and 54th Strategic Reconnaissance Squadrons, Medium, Weather, respectively. In May 1952, the 57th SRS at Hickam AFB, Hawaii, was assigned to the 2143rd AWW. By war's end in July 1953, the Air Weather Service had lost six men killed in action, and its units had earned 18 campaign streamers, three Republic of Korea Presidential Unit Citations, two Air Force Outstanding Unit Awards, and four service streamers.

5.1.3 Airways and Air Communications Service

The start of the Korean War saw the United States ill-prepared to counter the Communist onslaught. This was especially true in the area of air traffic control and navigation aids, which were the domain of MATS' Airways and Air Communications Service. Before the Northern Pacific route from the US to Japan could be used by Pacific Airlift transports, a number of the former Second World War bases in the Aleutian Islands had to be reactivated. The 1804th AACS Group in Alaska accomplished this task by mid-July 1950. The 1808th AACS Wing, headquartered in Tokyo, was responsible for air traffic control, navigation aids and air communications for the entire Far East and Pacific areas. The 1808th AACS Wing was composed of the 1809th AACS Group at Nagoya, Japan, the 1810th AACS Group at Hickam AFB, Hawaii, and the 1811th AACS Group at Kadena Air Base, Okinawa. Each group was subdivided into squadrons and detachments which operated airfield control towers, direction finder stations, and several Military Air Traffic Control (MATCon) centers. However, the only AACS controlled facility in Korea at the time was a low-power homing beacon at Kimpo Airfield, which quickly fell into enemy hands at the war's beginning.

On 26th June 1950, representatives of the 1808th AACS Wing and Headquarters, Far East Air Forces, met to determine what was needed to support air traffic control in the war zone. The first priority was the installation of a homing beacon at the port of Pusan, which was to be the main logistical base for United Nations forces. Secondly, three hundred AACS officers and men, skilled in the installation and operation of mobile communications equipment, were brought in from the United States to set up ten advance airfields throughout Korea. AACS detachments soon were established at Pusan, Taegu, and Pohang, and although the Pohang detachment had to abandon its position due to a North Korean assault, through the remainder of the year additional detachments were formed above the 38th parallel as the United Nations forces moved northward.

Top: **Douglas C-124A 50-1259 in early MATS markings as the Globemaster II flew the Pacific Airlift into the Korean War zone.** Bob Pickett, courtesy of Norm Taylor

Right: **Air Weather Service WC-54D, 42-72618, in 1959. This airplane most probably was used as an administrative transport.** MAP

Bottom: **The Airways and Air Communications Service used the Douglas Skymaster, such as this C-54D, 42-72503, for flight checking facilities as well as for administrative transport.** MAP

Above: **This radar screen was part of the survival equipment carried by this Grumman SA-16 Albatross of the 9th Rescue Squadron, Flight D, at Wiesbaden AFB, Germany, in May 1952.** Air Force, courtesy of NASM

A third priority was the establishment of IFR airways between Japan and Korea. The combination of mountainous terrain and often poor flying weather over both Korea and Japan made air traffic control difficult, if not dangerous, and so permanent altitude blocks were assigned to Combat Cargo Command and Tactical Air Wing aircraft.

These plans made for the control of air traffic above Korea and Japan solved most problems, but the sheer number of aircraft of all types around a few airfields – at times exceeding the volume of air traffic at Tempelhof Airdrome during the Berlin Airlift – demanded further steps. Subsequently, a new procedure was adopted by the AACS for air traffic within Korean airspace: all traffic below 12,000 feet would be controlled by the MATCons, while air traffic above 12,000 feet (with the exception of two wings of B-26s) would be monitored by the Tactical Air Control Center.

While the world of air traffic control may appear commonplace, even in a war situation, the men and women of the AACS distinguished themselves in Korea. During the retreat from North Korea by United Nations forces in November 1950, personnel of the 1973rd AACS Squadron remained at their stations directing takeoffs and landings of United Nations cargo aircraft as they evacuated UN personnel, earning the squadron a Distinguished Unit Citation for 'extraordinary heroism and fidelity'. In May 1952, the control tower operators and air traffic control personnel at Brady, Ashiya and Pusan East airfields were commended for their expert handling of Combat Cargo Command aircraft during the emergency airlift of the 187th Regimental Combat Team into Korea. At Pusan East Airfield alone, control tower personnel handled a takeoff or landing every three minutes in poor weather. And, on 21st June 1953, the Itazuke, Japan, GCA unit landed 26 C-46s at three minute intervals during minimum weather conditions, all with no advance warning.

5.1.4 Air Rescue Service

Of all the varied missions to come under the auspices of the Military Air Transport Service during the Korean War, the search and rescue (SAR) mission performed by the Air Rescue Service was by far the most spectacular. And, with the exception of Sikorsky H-5s and H-19s and Grumman SA-16As, this mission was accomplished with older Second World War vintage aircraft converted to the SAR role: the Consolidated-Vultee L-5, Douglas SC-47, Curtiss SC-46, and Boeing SB-17 and SB-29.

In June 1950, the Air Rescue Service had two squadrons based within the Korean war zone: the 2nd Rescue Squadron, with headquarters and Flights A and B based at Kadena Field, Okinawa, Flight C at Clark AFB, Philippines, and Flight D at North AFB, Guam; and the 3rd Rescue Squadron, with its headquarters and Flight A at Johnson AB, Japan, Flight B at Yokota AB, Japan, Flight C at Misawa AB, Japan, and Flight D at Ashiya AB, Japan. While the squadrons were administratively a part of the Air Rescue Service and MATS, their operations were controlled by the Far East Air Force and, for the 3rd Rescue Squadron in particular, the Fifth Air Force.

At the start of the war, the 2nd Rescue Squadron furnished local SAR and long-range SB-29s to accompany SAC B-29s as they crossed the Yellow Sea from their base in Okinawa into North Korea. The 3rd Rescue Squadron, being in closer proximity to the Korean peninsula, bore the brunt of search and rescue responsibilities during the war. The squadron possessed a mixed bag of SB-17, SB-29, SC-46, SC-47, and L-5 aircraft, as well as nine H-5s. As with the 2nd RS SB-29s, the 3rd RS SB-29 'Super Dumbos' accompanied SAC B-29s from their base at Yokota AB, Japan, across the Yellow Sea to North Korea, while the SB-17s, SC-46 and SC-47s performed shorter-range missions, often orbiting off the Japanese or Korean coasts.

On 7th July, twelve days after the start of hostilities, the 3rd RS sent two L-5s into Korea, but the lack of suitable landing sites hampered their effectiveness. A detachment of H-5s was sent from Flight D at Ashiya AB to Taegu on 22nd July to assist in the evacuation of wounded soldiers. The H-5s were so effective that the 3rd RS rushed additional H-5s into Korea early in August and, on 21st August, the squadron received an additional allocation of 14 H-5s. On 30th August, the 3rd RS organized Detachment F, whose L-5s and H-5s were used specifically to evacuate the wounded from forward positions.

For the remainder of the war, Detachment F (redesignated as Detachment 1, 3rd Air Rescue Squadron on 22nd June 1951) hopscotched up and down the Korean peninsula as the battle lines changed from day to day, evacuating thousands of wounded American and United Nations troops.

In March 1951, two new Sikorsky YH-19 helicopters were brought into Korea by an Air Proving Ground team. The aircraft were put to the test almost immediately, working alongside Detachment F H-5s as wounded and injured paratroopers were evacuated from a drop zone at Munsan-ni. The H-19 could carry eight litter patients or ten passengers and a pilot and medical technician, compared to the H-5's cabin accommodations for a pilot and medical technician only, with two patients carried in external litter capsules. But as a majority of Detachment F's front-line rescue missions involved only single pilot pick-ups, the detachment personnel looked upon the newer helicopter as a complement to the H-5, rather than as a replacement for it. After the detachment had begun to receive its allotment of H-19s in February 1952, it was felt that the aircraft's 120 mile range better suited it to perform overwater rescue missions using the built-in hydraulic-powered hoist line. Two H-19As subsequently were based on Cho-do Island and one at Paengnyong-do, which were designated bail-out sites for war damaged or mechanically disabled aircraft. A small number of 3rd ARS H-19s also participated in clandestine operations. The all-black Sikorskys picked up agents after completion of their intelligence-gathering or sabotage missions along North Korea's northwest coast.

Below: **SB-29, 44-87644, carries full defensive armament of turret-mounted machine guns as well as the 3,000 lb A-3 lifeboat.** Haney Collection, courtesy of Lionel N Paul

Left: **During the Korean War, the 3rd Air Rescue Squadron operated the Sikorsky H-5, which carried a paramedic as well as stretchers for evacuating the wounded.** Air Force, courtesy of NASM

Below: **SA-16A, 51-5294, in March 1956. The Albatross replaced the OA-10A Catalina as the Air Rescue Service's standard amphibian in 1950.** Air Force, courtesy of Clyde Gerdes Collection

In November 1952, all Air Rescue Service units were reorganized, with the 2nd Air Rescue Squadron becoming the 2nd Air Rescue Group and the 3rd ARS being redesignated as the 3rd ARG. Detachment 1, 3rd ARG became the 2157th Air Rescue Squadron, while the various flights became numbered squadrons.

As mentioned, the 2nd ARS/ARG on Okinawa initially was equipped with relatively short-ranged OA-10 and SB-17 aircraft. By March 1952, the squadron had received its fourth SB-29 'Super Dumbo' and it was able to provide escort services for SAC B-29s. Beginning on 8th May 1952, a squadron SB-29 would depart and orbit at sea as the SAC bombers took off and assembled. The SB-29 would accompany the Superfortresses until they crossed the Korean coast, then would orbit outside the coastline until the bombers had completed their mission, reversing the process on the return flight. A similar scenario was true for 3rd ARS/ARG SB-29s flying from Japan. While Flight D (39th ARS) aircrews orbited off the Korean coast with their SA-16As, Flight B (37th ARS) used their SB-17s and eventually SB-29s for route patrol and offshore orbit. When the SAC B-29s based in Japan began night operations late in 1952, a 3rd ARS SB-29 would trail the bomber stream and then orbit offshore until the attacking force returned. As North Korean fighters were always a threat to attack the SB-17s and SB-29s, these SAR aircraft were refitted with functional top and bottom turrets and tail guns.

The 3rd ARS received its first Grumman SA-16As a month after hostilities had broken out, and the amphibians were assigned to patrol the Tsushima Straits. The Albatrosses made their first water rescue a week after arrival and, despite being limited in their open sea landings to waves of less than five feet, the SA-16A's large cabin could carry a number of people, including a welcomed paramedic.

In the fall of 1950, the 3rd ARS assigned its SA-16As to strip alert at Wonsan and Seoul, re-positioning the aircraft at Taegu Airfield after the United Nations retreat in November. One of these strip alert Albatrosses participated in an amazing night-time rescue of a downed F-51 pilot from the Taedong River. While flights of Mustangs supressed gunfire from both banks of the river, the Albatross pilot, Lt John Najarian, landed his SA-16A in the shallow, debris-filled river. After picking up the pilot of the Mustang, Najarian successfully took off as the covering F-51s illuminated low-hanging high-tension power lines with their landing lights.

As the Korean War progressed, the US Army assumed an increasing role for front-line medevac, and the Air Rescue Service was able to concentrate its efforts on the search and rescue mission. As it was, the Air Rescue Service carried 9,680 military personnel to safety, with medevac cases from front-line units accounting for nearly 8,600 of these. In the 37 months of the war, the Air Rescue Service retrieved 170 Air Force crewmen from behind enemy lines: 102 by helicopter, 66 by SA-16s, and 2 by L-5 liaison aircraft. An additional 11 US Navy, 35 Marine Corps, 5 Army, and 33 airmen from allied forces were rescued from behind enemy lines, totalling nearly 1,000 men when all personnel are included. And, from within friendly territory, the ARS rescued a further 86 airmen. It should not be surprising, then, that the 3rd Air Rescue Squadron received the first Presidential Unit Citation of the war, or that its members were awarded over 1,000 personal citations and commendations.

5.1.5 Air Resupply and Communications Service

Also participating in the Korean War effort were elements of a newly-formed sub-command of MATS, the Air Resupply and Communications Service (ARCS). The ARCS was attached to MATS for less than three years, but its organization and subsequent Korean operations are noteworthy.

During the early stages of the Korean War, a scheme was hatched in the Pentagon to combine several overt and covert intelligence and propaganda missions into one organization that would counter the Communist threat on a worldwide basis both in hot and cold war scenarios. The Air Resupply and Communications Service was activated on 23rd February 1951, with its headquarters assigned to MATS Headquarters at Andrews AFB, although the ARCS headquarters were moved to Washington, DC, on 14th May

From the outset, the mission of the ARCS was not clearly defined, especially its peacetime function. Planning for the organization was complicated by the fact that Tables of Organization for wing headquarters and subordinate units were drawn up in early February 1951, before Tables of Equipment had been produced. In other words, planners were attempting to procure personnel before it had been decided what types of equipment they would be required to use. As no Air Force regulation had yet been issued, MATS proposed a draft, in April 1951, for a vague Air Force Regulation defining the ARCS' mission to 'Provide worldwide air resupply and communications service for all Air Force and other US military activities requesting such service.' Eventually, the missions of the ARCS were clarified as:

- the psychological warfare function, which called for the capability of preparing psychological warfare material in printed form, propaganda, and jamming enemy frequencies;
- aerial resupply, which called for the capability of introducing and evacuating ranger-type personnel behind enemy lines and supplying them and guerrilla units.

Pentagon planners envisioned seven ARCS wings, to be activated at three-month intervals and deployed overseas after six months of training. While MATS acted as the parent command of the ARCS, its wing operations actually would be directed by Headquarters US Air Force from the Psychological Warfare Division, Directorate of Plans. And, once established overseas, ARCS squadrons would function as tenant organizations, and would be under the operational control of the theater commander.

The first ARCS wing, the 580th Air Resupply and Communications Wing, MATS, was activated at Mountain Home AFB, Idaho, on 16th April 1951. It was planned that the 580th ARCW would be composed of five squadrons:

- an Aerial Resupply Squadron, which would transport and evacuate personnel and supplies behind enemy lines;
- an Airborne Materials Assembly Squadron, which would 'provide storage, maintenance, and aerial-type packaging of operational supplies, and the packaging of overt propaganda leaflets as a service to the US Air Force units engaged in leaflet attacks from the base area concerned';
- a Holding and Briefing Squadron, which provided for the

Top left: **The Air Resupply and Communications Service operated a number of aircraft, including this C-47D, 43-15732.** H Applegate, courtesy of David Menard

Left: **The red tail and outer wing panels on this MATS C-47A, 42-24303, indicate that it was operated in a cold weather climate.** Air Force, courtesy of Clyde Gerdes Collection

Below: **Flightline of the 580th Air Resupply Squadron, Wheelus AB, Libya, in 1953 with four B-29s, two C-119s and one SA-16.** Air Force, courtesy of Carl H Bernhardt Jr.

administration, briefing and supply of personnel assigned by other agencies for introduction behind enemy lines;
- a Communications Squadron, to provide a base area agent communications circuit, operating an around-the-clock broadcasting service over four frequencies simultaneously;
- a Reproduction Squadron, having the capability of reproducing covert propaganda material and up to four million overt propaganda leaflets a day.

The second ARCS wing to activate, on 23rd July 1951, was the 581st ARCW. The two ARCS wings trained with a number of aircraft, including the B-29, C-119, SA-16, C-47 and C-54, but were expected to receive additional types once deployed overseas.

In March 1952, an additional responsibility was given to the Air Resupply and Communications Service when all formal escape and evasion training in MATS was transferred to it from the Air Rescue Service. However, Headquarters MATS was becoming increasingly frustrated with the fact that there was 'no firm policy of any kind in USAF on the future of ARCS, subsequent to completing (the) training cycle of ARCS wings', and MATS Headquarters made it clear that they wanted to be relieved of responsibility for the program.

As this debate festered between Air Staff planners and Headquarters MATS, in July 1952 the 581st ARCW became the first wing to deploy overseas when it moved to Clark AFB, Philippines (later Kadena AFB, Okinawa), attached to the Thirteenth Air Force. The 580th ARCW moved its operations in October 1952 to Wheelus AFB, Libya, becoming attached to United States Air Forces in Europe.

The 581st ARCW soon became involved in the Korean War, using its B-29s to drop propaganda leaflets, leaflets warning North Korean civilians of impending raids, and to insert agents behind enemy lines. Early in October 1952, a small detachment of six pilots and 13 enlisted men was sent to Korea to operate four new H-19As under the Fifth Air Force for the insertion and retrieval of agents along the coastal mud flats north of the DMZ. Flying off Cho-do Island, these 581st ARCW H-19As often supplemented 3rd ARS aircraft and its own SA-16As in the rescue of downed American and allied airmen, plus agents from within North Korea. The full story of the 581st ARCW's exploits during the Korean War has yet to be told, but it is interesting to note that the last American prisoners of war to be released by the Chinese Communists, in August 1955, were the pilot and surviving crewmen of an ARCS B-29 that had been shot down during a leaflet-dropping mission near the Yalu River in January 1953.

As the Korean War was drawing to a close, ARCS planners realized that with no peacetime mission developed, the command would be expendable in the upcoming post-war budget tightening process.

Brigadier General Monro MacCloskey, Commander of the ARCS since September 1952, made a valiant attempt to inspire his personnel to come up with new peacetime tasks for the ARCS to perform, but to little avail. The 582nd ARCW, the third ARCS wing, activated on 24th September 1952, was suddenly inactivated on 14th August 1953, before its training had been completed (its successor, the 582nd ARG, was reorganized and deployed to RAF Station Molesworth, England, in 1954). On 1st January 1954, the Air Resupply and Communications Service was detached from MATS, although the organization continued to provide services to the Department of Defense on a much reduced scale.

5.2 Transport Operations

The decade from 1950 to 1960 saw erratic growth of the Military Air Transport Service, both in personnel and in its aircraft inventory. For MATS personnel strength, the decade began with just under 60,000 total personnel (officer, enlisted and civilian employees) in June 1950, just before the Korean War broke out, but by June 1952 this total had climbed to 105,000. The all-time peak personnel strength for MATS was reached in 1958 with nearly 128,000, but budget constraints and a restructuring of MATS transport operations resulted in a gradual decline in personnel through the early 1960s. And, while the Atlantic and Pacific Divisions of MATS continued to focus mainly on transport operations, the Continental Division formalized three of its missions in the early 1950s.

The first of these, aeromedical evacuation, became a high priority due to the outbreak of the Korean War in June 1950. MATS converted C-54, C-74, and C-97 transports into long-range medevac aircraft, carrying cargo or personnel westward toward the war zone, and returning eastward with litter and ambulatory patients.

On West Coast bases, these patients would be taken to the appropriate hospitals by MATS domestic C-54 or C-47 aeromedical evacuation aircraft. Over 66,500 Korean War patients were transported by MATS between June 1950 and December 1953.

But when compared to the number of patients transported worldwide by MATS aeromedical evacuation aircraft, which reached a peak of over 131,000 during a one-year period from July 1950 through June 1951, the scope of the total medevac mission becomes apparent.

The organization of the 1706th ATG (AE), headquartered at Brooks AFB, Texas, as a formal aeromedical evacuation group enabled MATS to streamline this mission. And, in an Air Force organizational change authorized by Air Force Headquarters in August 1956, the various MATS air evacuation groups and squadrons converted to 'constituted' groups and squadrons. Effective 8th November 1956, the 1706th Air Transport Group, Light (Aeromedical Evacuation), became the 1st Aeromedical Transport Group, Light, with its various Air Transport Squadrons becoming Light Aeromedical Transport Squadrons.

The second formalized MATS mission involved ferrying aircraft, which had been made a portion of MATS' original mission in June 1948. The Berlin Airlift saw MATS ferrying units shuttling airlift transports to and from reconditioning sites in the United States.

The 1708th Ferrying Group was formed out of the original 1737th Ferrying Squadron late in 1952 at Kelly AFB, Texas. The group's three squadrons and numerous detachments ferried thousands of aircraft worldwide to operating units and MDAP nations, as well as domestically to Air National Guard and Air Force Reserve squadrons.

Finally, in September 1951 transition training of flight and ground crews for MATS and other commands was formalized by the establishment of the Continental Division's 1707th Air Transport Group, Heavy, (Training), at Palm Beach AFB, West Palm Beach, Florida. The three squadrons of the group provided transition training on all four-engined transport aircraft as well as the B-50 and SA-16 types until the late 1950s.

A similar picture of growth and decline during the 1950s existed for the MATS aircraft inventory. In 1950, MATS possessed about 600 total aircraft, including aircraft from its transport division as well as from its Air Rescue Service, Flight Service, Airways and Air Communications Service, and Air Weather Service. This number gradually increased to a high of nearly 1,300 aircraft in 1955, but from 1956 to the early 1960s the total number of MATS aircraft declined. This trend reflected a move toward acquiring more efficient aircraft types, as several hundred C-47s and C-54s were replaced by a generally smaller number of larger and faster C-97, C-118, C-121, C-124, C-131 and C-133 aircraft.

While a complete accounting of all of the internal restructurings, squadron/group/wing changes, and transport route transfers and revisions is outside the scope of this book, there were many changes that occurred within MATS during the decade of the 1950s that deserve mention.

5.3 Strategic Air Command Support

As important as MATS' daily transport operations were, they were considered as only training for its main 'D-Day' mission: airlifting men and materiel for the striking forces of the Strategic Air Command.

From one-to-six formal SAC support movements were scheduled each month, with MATS units airlifting SAC personnel, supplies and equipment from their home base to a temporary overseas base, providing en route support and control team personnel as needed, then reversing the move to return the SAC unit to its home base. These SAC support missions might involve the airlift of from several dozen to thousands of personnel, and from several tons to over 100 tons of cargo to bases in North Africa, Europe, the Pacific or Far East, all under simulated wartime conditions.

5.4 Air Photographic and Charting Service

On 16th April 1951, the Air Photographic and Charting Service (APCS) was transferred from the Office of the Air Force Chief of Staff to MATS. The APCS was responsible for the production and distribution of aeronautical charts and air target materials, and performed aerial mapping photography and aerial electronic geodetic surveys for the Department of Defense.

On 1st October 1952, the 3935th Mapping and Charting Squadron was activated at Offutt AFB, Nebraska. The unit subsequently was assigned to the 55th SRW, Strategic Air Command, at Forbes AFB, Kansas, and operated two C-45s. On 1st October 1953, the 3935th MCS was redesignated as the 1355th MCS and was transferred to the Air Photographic and Charting Service. The unit moved to West Palm Beach AFB, Florida, where it flew fifteen newly-modified photo-mapping RC-45Gs.

In a reorganization, the 1370th Photo Mapping Group was formed at West Palm Beach AFB on 5th April 1954. The group assumed control of the 1355th MCS as well as the 338th SRS, which also had moved from Forbes AFB and was redesignated as the 1371st MCS, the unit operating photo-mapping RB-50Fs. On 1st May 1954, the APCS assumed the mapping and charting functions of the 55th SRW at Forbes AFB, and on 8th July the 1355th MCS was redesignated as the 1372nd MCS (Aerial Photographic). The 1370th PMG expanded again on 1st October 1958, when it gained the 1375th MCS. This squadron operated the RB-50, but on 11th March 1959, the unit received its first RC-130A. By the end of June the 1375th MCS had gained a total of 12 of the photo-recon Hercules and field operations were begun in New York and Iceland. The 1375th MCS achieved its operational readiness on 1st March 1960, and its Aerial Survey Team (AST) detachments began photo and geodetic survey operations in South and Central America, North Africa, Greece and Vietnam. The 1370th PMG was upgraded to wing status on the 1st January 1960.

5.5 Iceland Air Defense Force

In May 1951, an agreement was signed between MATS and the government of Iceland to share facilities at Keflavik International Airport. As the Icelandic Government had been promised US fighter aircraft for its air defense, this put MATS, as the only Air Force presence on the island, into the strange position of having jurisdiction over a series of fighter squadrons. Between September 1952 and July 1961, when the US Navy assumed the responsibility, the Military Air Transport Service provided for Iceland's air defense with F-51Ds from the 192nd/435th Fighter-Bomber Squadrons, F-94Bs from the 82nd FIS, and F-89C/Ds from the 57th FIS.

Photographs on the opposite page:

Top: **By August 1954, when this Atlantic Division C-54G, 45-510, was photographed at Selfridge AFB, Michigan, there were only about 200 Skymasters in MATS service.** Norm Taylor Collection

Bottom: **This Atlantic Division C-97A, 48-399, was the third of 50 C-97A Stratofreighters delivered to MATS, beginning in October 1949.** Bob Pickett, courtesy of Norm Taylor

5.6 Flight Service

In a move to reduce costs and standardize flight services within the Air Force, the Flight Service was absorbed by the AACS on 1st October 1956. The point-to-point flying aids within the continental United States were merged and standardized with similar world-wide aids operated by the AACS. The AACS also assumed eleven new functions, including flight clearance authority, inflight advisory services, and handling aircraft movement messages and flight plans.

5.7 Airways & Air Communications Service

The Airways and Air Communications Service was instrumental in developing and implementing a number of new aircraft navigational aids and communications systems throughout the 1950s, including the very high frequency, omni-directional ranges (VOR), the Tactical Aid to Navigation (TACAN), UHF air-ground communications, long-range, high frequency single-side-band (SSB) communications, and several precision approach radar systems.

On 28th December 1953, the Air Force authorized six four-engined transports, 54 two-engined transports, and one single-engined fighter-type aircraft for accomplishing the AACS' flight checking mission. Seven B-25s had earlier been assigned to the AACS, but the aircraft were not suited for the flight checking mission and presented maintenance and logistic problems as well, and so were used sparingly.

Beginning in 1954, the AACS formed flight checking squadrons at 14 locations whose mission was to conduct in-flight performance evaluations of navigational aids and radars. Specially-equipped AC-47D and AC-54s evaluated newly-placed facilities and made periodic checks on them to ensure that radiation pattern tolerances were maintained and that AACS controllers were proficient. By mid-1954, however, only 41 AACS aircraft were available for this mission. The AACS had requested a T-33A to perform the high altitude, high-speed operational penetration check mission, but had instead received in turn an F-51, F-80B and F-80C. None of these aircraft were equipped with UHF radios, however, nor could they carry additional equipment and an observer.

Toward the end of the decade, AT-29 and T-33A check aircraft were received which performed high altitude NAVAID checks, with the AACS flight checking fleet numbering nearly 90 aircraft at the time. A single B-47B also was flown by the AACS out of Tinker AFB from 1955 to 1961, for a special high altitude flight check program.

Left: **RC-130A, 57-512, was one of 12 Hercules flown by the 1375th MCS, 1370th PMG. The airplane is over Colombia, where it was operated by Aerial Survey Team 2 at Bogota.** Air Force

Center: **F-89C, 51-5767, of the 57th FIS at Keflavik International Airport in January 1955. This MATS squadron provided for Iceland's air defense from 1955 to 1961.** Air Force, courtesy of Larry Davis

Below: **MATS Flight Service Beech C-45G, 51-11658, in the mid-1950s, before the organization was absorbed by the Airways and Air Communications Service.** Courtesy of Robert Parmerter

In 1958, the Federal Aviation Authority Act transferred flight inspection responsibilities to the FAA, although the transition took several years to accomplish. By the early 1960s, the task of managing these widespread communications networks had grown to the point where the Air Force Communications Service, AFCS, was established as a major command on 1st July 1961, and the organization was detached from MATS.

5.8 1700th Test Squadron (Turbo-Prop)

By the early 1950s, it was evident that the piston engine was reaching its zenith for low to medium altitude aircraft applications. The turbojet, with its ever-increasing efficiencies at high air speeds and altitudes, was being planned for a future generation of jet transport aircraft. In the interim, the turboprop engine seemed a logical combination to provide transport aircraft with relatively high speeds at medium to high altitudes. The Air Force embarked on an evaluation program in 1954 to convert several already-existing types to turboprop power: two Convair YC-131Cs to establish the reliability of the new Allison YT56 engine and propeller for its intended use on the production C-130 Hercules, and two Boeing YC-97Js and two Lockheed YC-121Fs, to be equipped with the Pratt & Whitney T34 engine and propeller for the new Douglas C-133 Cargomaster.

In July 1954, a conference was held at MATS Headquarters to plan the activation of a service test squadron that would conduct the evaluations of these three aircraft types. The Service Test Squadron (Turbo-Prop) Provisional was formed at Kelly AFB, Texas, on 5th September, but the unit was redesignated as the 1700th Test Squadron (Turbo-Prop), 1700th ATG, Medium, Continental Division, MATS, on 1st December 1954.

The two YC-131Cs were the first aircraft to be converted and delivered, in January 1955, and were the first to complete their test program in December, six weeks ahead of schedule. The YC-97Js were delivered in September 1955 and completed their accelerated test program in November 1956, also six weeks ahead of schedule. The two YC-121Fs were delivered to the 1700th Test Squadron (Turbo-Prop) in February and April 1956 and completed their test program in June 1957. All six test aircraft established new records for speed on both continental and intercontinental flights, although the two YC-121Fs, the fastest of the three types, suffered a series of problems with cracked propellers and propeller pump housings and with re-skinning a portion of the upper wing surfaces, and reportedly were among the noisiest passenger aircraft ever to fly.

5.9 1708th Ferrying Group

Also based at Kelly AFB and attached to the Continental Division of MATS was a unique group whose function harkened back to the ATC's original mission, that of ferrying aircraft. The 1950s saw a remarkable surge in the types and numbers of new aircraft designs purchased. The 1737th Ferrying Squadron was formed at Kelly AFB in March 1950 to ferry aircraft between the manufacturers' plants and operating squadrons, and to ferry in-service aircraft to various IRAN (Inspect and Repair As Necessary), remanufacturing or retirement sites.

Although many aircraft were transported overseas by ship, by late 1952 the demand for air ferrying services had increased to the point where the 1708th Ferrying Group was formed at Kelly AFB (redesignated as the 1708th Ferrying Wing on 20th October 1955). At the same time, the 1737th Ferrying Squadron relocated to Dover AFB, Delaware, and two new ferrying squadrons were formed: the 1738th FYS at Long Beach Municipal Airport (discontinued on 1st July 1956, due to safety considerations), and the 1739th FYS at Amarillo AFB, Texas. In 1953, the three squadrons were reorganized so that the 1737th FYS and 1738th FYS had responsibility for ferrying all single-engine jet and conventional aircraft, and the 1739th FYS ferried all multi-engined aircraft. The 1708th FYG also had detachments, often consisting of only one officer and one enlisted man, scattered around the world along its ferry routes, such as Labrador, Iceland, Greenland, Scotland, England, Germany, Alaska and Japan.

On a personal as well as an organizational level, the job of ferrying these aircraft was extremely trying. Each ferry pilot was required to be proficient in flying from three to six aircraft types, but some were qualified on over a dozen. Often, training schools for a particular aircraft were nonexistent, and pilots had to undergo on-the-job training at a base where the aircraft was being operated, at the manufacturer's, or at his home base using aircraft diverted from their ferry routes for a few days.

Accidents due to the pilot's unfamiliarity with his aircraft or a field being transited, were all too common. The aircraft being ferried often caused problems, as they either were fresh from the factory and so had not been thoroughly flight tested, or were service or battle weary. The ferry routes flown were likely to be off-the-beaten-path, so that even if the pilot were lucky enough to land his aircraft in need of maintenance at an Air Force base, it was questionable whether the base would have spare parts for his particular airplane. Because of all these factors, a three-day trip might stretch into three weeks, and a two-week mission into months before the ferry pilot returned to his home base. In 1956, it was estimated that the average ferry pilot would spend two years TDY out of a three-year tour of duty. The 1708th FYW was keenly aware of low morale among its pilots as well as their families, and considerable effort was spent ensuring short tours of duty with these ferrying squadrons.

Each ferry squadron, as well as group headquarters, had a small number of aircraft assigned to it for pilot checkout and proficiency, and it was not unlikely to see a MATS Continental Division tail band or the 1708th FYG shield on squadron or group T-33, F-84, F-86, F-100, B-25 or B-26 aircraft. As an example, the three 1708th FYW squadrons had the following aircraft during 1956 for pilot proficiency, checkout, or administrative use:

1737th FYS	*1738th FYS*	*1739th FYS*
4 T-33A	9 T-33A	2 TB-25N
8 F-84F	1 F-84F	1 TB-26B
1 RF-84F	4 F-86F	1 B-26C
2 F-84G	6 F-100A	1 TB-26C
1 VC-47D	4 F-100D	1 B-57B
	1 VC-47A	1 C-47A
		1 C-54D
		1 C-119C
		2 C-119G
		1 SA-16A

U.S. AIR FORCE
MILITARY AIR TRANSPORT SERVICE
A ACS
49029

U.S. AIR FORCE
AACS
272503

CONTINENTAL
22762
S. AIR FORCE
CALIFORNIA EASTERN

5.10 1254th Air Transport Group (Special Mission)

When the 1254th ATS was formed in October 1948 to transport governmental and Washington, DC-based military VIPs, the 'Crown Jewel' in its fleet was the Presidential aircraft, VC-118, 46-505, the 'Independence'. The squadron also operated a small number of VIP C-47s and C-54s, to be joined in 1950 by six C-121As modified with VIP accommodations.

On 1st August 1952, the 1254th ATS was upgraded to the 1254th ATG (SM), consisting of the 1298th ATS, operating long-range aircraft at Washington National Airport, and the 1299th ATS at Bolling AFB, flying the shorter-ranged types.

During the 1950s, these Special Missions squadrons flew a number of interesting VIP-configured aircraft beyond their initial stable of VC-47, VC-54, VC-118, VC-121 and Presidential VC-118 'Independence', VC-121A 'Columbine II' and VC-121E 'Columbine III' aircraft.

For medium-range VIP missions, Convair VC-131s and VT-29s were operated, to be joined in 1961 by Lockheed VC-140Bs. A single Fairchild C-123B was operated by the Special Missions Group, reportedly to transport the Presidential limousine across the country to motorcades and speaking engagements.

For shorter-range flights, several Aero Commander L-26s were used to ferry President Eisenhower and his staff as well as other governmental VIPs. For local hops, the 1254th ATG(SM) used two modified Bell VH-13Js, at least three Sikorsky VH-19s and one Piasecki H-21B, the latter two types painted in a special medium blue, white and red VIP scheme. Most of these aircraft carried the 1254th ATG(SM) emblem on their fuselages: an eagle superimposed over a globe, contained within a shield carrying the motto, 'Experto Crede', or 'Trust One With Experience'.

The Special Missions group joined the jet age on 12th May 1959, when the 1298th ATS Det.1 accepted the first of three Boeing VC-137As at Andrews AFB. The three VC-137As were joined at Andrews AFB by the Presidential VC-137C in October 1962. The new jet transports were used almost immediately to establish intercontinental records. In July 1959, the first VC-137A carried Vice-President Nixon to the Soviet Union, making the 4,800 mile New York-to-Moscow flight in just under nine hours, breaking a record set only two weeks previously by an Aeroflot Tu-114. The Presidential VC-137C set a Washington-to-Moscow record in May 1963, flying the 5,000 mile route in a little over 8½ hours. Meanwhile, the 1254th ATG(SM) had been upgraded to wing status on 1st December 1960, and in July the wing headquarters and both the 1298th and 1299th ATS moved to Andrews AFB. Concurrently, the 1298th ATS Det.1 was inactivated, but the 1254th ATW Det.2 remained at Washington National Airport operating the Presidential 'Air Force One' VC-137A.

After the Military Air Transport Service had been superseded by the Military Airlift Command, the 1254th ATW(SM) was inactivated on 8th January 1966, and replaced by the 89th MAW (SM).

5.11 Single Manager Reorganization

In a move to strengthen the airlift mobilization readiness of the Department of Defense, as well as to 'assure greater effectiveness, efficiency and economy' in airlift capability, the Department of Defense directed, on 7th December 1956, that the Secretary of the Air Force be designated as the single manager for airlift service. The Military Air Transport Service was established as the principal airlift agency for all of the military departments.

Under this new directive, MATS retained its Air Rescue Service, Air Weather Service, Air Photographic and Charting Service and Airways and Air Communications Service non-airlift technical services, but its Continental Division gained the following from the Tactical Air Command:

- the 62nd Troop Carrier Wing (Heavy), at Larson AFB, Washington, comprising three troop carrier squadrons;
- the 63rd Troop Carrier Wing (Heavy), Donaldson AFB, South Carolina, comprising seven troop carrier squadrons.

Control of both Larson AFB and Donaldson AFB was transferred to MATS as well. Some internal squadron transfers within MATS also were made to equalize the workload between the three MATS divisions. This reorganization became effective on 1st July 1957, and resulted in the Continental Division's four-engine transport fleet quadrupling from 85 to 336 aircraft, while its personnel strength jumped from 9,500 to over 21,000.

5.12 Operation Deep Freeze

With the acquisition of the 63rd Troop Carrier Wing and its C-124s in 1957, MATS became increasingly involved in what was termed as 'the greatest peacetime logistics program in US history' – 'Operation Deep Freeze'. This operation was the US Navy's logistic support program for America's many scientific investigations in Antarctica, involving dozens of aircraft, a dozen ships, thousands of men, and the transport of tons of supplies and equipment into and out of the Antarctic continent.

MATS units had been supporting 'Operation Deep Freeze' since the first one in September 1956, as Navy MATS R6D-1s belonging to both VR-3 and VR-22 had been flown to New Zealand on 'Deep Freeze' missions. The Tactical Air Command C-124s of the 63rd TCW also had been supporting the Antarctic operations since the initial 'Operation Deep Freeze', when eight specially-equipped C-124s assembled at Christchurch, New Zealand. The aircraft then flew to McMurdo Sound, where they landed on a sea ice runway to load cargo which was air dropped to the various inland scientific stations. Between 1957 and 1963, MATS 63rd TCW C-124s flew 'Operation Deep Freeze' missions as part of Task Force 43 until replaced by the versatile Lockheed C-130 Hercules, although special missions were flown by MATS C-124s to deliver outsize cargo for several years afterwards.

Opposite page, top: **AACS AC-47D, 43-49029, of the 1861st AACS Flight Checking Squadron.** Clyde Gerdes Collection

Opposite page, center: **C-54D, 42-72503, of the Airways and Air Communications Service, displays a one-star placard under the pilot's window in this 1955 photo.** MAP, courtesy of Tom Hildreth

Opposite page, bottom: **Boeing YC-97J, 52-2762, was one of two Stratofreighters re-engined with the T34 and test flown by the 1700th Test Squadron (Turbo-Prop), 1700th ATG, MATS, from September 1955 to November 1956.** Larry Smalley, courtesy of Douglas D Olson

5.13 Cargo Palletization Program

One of the least-known contributions to aviation progress made by MATS is in the area of cargo-handling, specifically in developing 'palletized' loads. In the early 1950s, both Lockheed and Douglas aircraft companies had independently developed systems of pre-loaded plywood cargo pallets for the C-130 and C-133.

When it became evident that even larger cargo aircraft would require a standardized cargo loading, unloading, and tracking system, Douglas Aircraft Company was contracted in 1957 to study future handling requirements under GOR157. By the early 1960s, this study led to the introduction of Materials Handling System 463L, which produced standardized aluminum pallets, loader/unloader trucks, conveyor systems, and a sophisticated method of cargo documentation, all of which was employed in the design of the Lockheed C-141A. However, palletized cargo systems were used to early advantage by MATS in the mid-1960s on the C-124, C-130, C-133 and C-135.

5.14 EASTAF/WESTAF

As part of the Defense Reorganization Act of 1958, Headquarters Air Force reorganized and consolidated its MATS transport operations and placed it in the Industrial Funding Program, whereby each of its 'customer services', the Army, Navy and Air Force, began paying for required airlift services on a cost basis. This reorganization served to not only reduce MATS' operating costs, but it gave the organization more flexibility in that it could purchase as much supplemental commercial overseas air transportation as the requesting services could afford. MATS' long-range policy now shifted to the use of contract commercial aircraft to the greatest extent possible. By the end of the decade, MATS was utilizing commercial carriers for approximately half of its routine Department of Defense personnel and cargo traffic. The Civil Reserve Air Fleet, CRAF, also was available during national emergencies and consisted of over 300 four-engined transports being flown by 23 airlines. A program was begun to re-wire these so that they could be fitted with military communication and navigation equipment should this need arise.

In this reorganization, the headquarters of the Continental Division at Kelly AFB was transferred to Travis AFB, California, in June 1958, where it joined the headquarters of the Pacific Division to become the Headquarters, Western Transport Air Force, or WESTAF. The Atlantic Division at McGuire AFB became headquarters for the Eastern Transport Air Force, or EASTAF. The only remaining vestiges of the old Continental Division were its domestic medevac routes, which continued to be flown by MC-131 aircraft of the 1405th Aeromedical Transport Wing at Scott AFB, Illinois. As part of this consolidation, Headquarters MATS also had moved from Andrews AFB to Scott AFB on 15th January 1958.

The new EASTAF/WESTAF reorganization of MATS transport operations divided the globe in two. The main EASTAF Aerial Port of Embarkation or Debarkation was McGuire AFB, which processed aircraft to Europe and Africa. Other EASTAF aerial ports were Charleston AFB, South Carolina, for flights to or from South America and the Caribbean; McChord AFB, Washington, for traffic to Alaska; Dover AFB, Delaware, for cargo traffic to Europe; and Hunter AFB, Georgia, where an EASTAF troop carrier wing was based. The main WESTAF base at Travis AFB handled traffic over its routes to bases in the Pacific, Japan, Alaska, and across Asia to meet the EASTAF routes in India.

5.15 Navy MATS

Mention has been made of the Navy's participation in the formation of the MATS as well as the Berlin Airlift and the Korean War efforts. A detailed accounting of a particular Navy squadron's activities will be found in Part II under each aircraft type that was operated by it: the C-54, C-118, C-121 or C-130. However, due to the many confusing organizational changes that occurred to these Navy MATS squadrons through the 1950s, an overview of the Navy's participation in MATS may be helpful.

Upon MATS' formation in June 1948 and through the Berlin Airlift, the Navy's contribution consisted of three squadrons of R5Ds: VR-3, which flew its Continental Division routes to Alaska, shifted to the Westover AFB to Frankfurt run during 'Operation Vittles' and transitioned to the R6D-1 (C-118A) in the fall of 1951; VR-6, which flew Atlantic Division routes until the airlift, set the airlift availability, daily utilization and heaviest average load records, and acquired the R6D-1 in November 1952; and VR-8, flying Pacific Division routes westward and to Alaska, and setting Berlin Airlift efficiency and heaviest average load records, traded its C-54s for the new Lockheed R7V-1 in June 1953. Late in the Korean War, these squadrons were joined by VR-7, which was established in April 1953 at Hickam AFB, Hawaii. VR-7 operated the R7V-1 alongside VR-8, briefly supporting the Pacific Airlift into Korea and later flying Pacific Division 'embassy runs' to the Far East. VR-7 Detachment A was formed at Tachikawa AFB, Japan, initially operating the R5D but later converting to the R7V-1/C-121C.

As previously outlined, on 7th December 1956, the Secretary of Defense directed that the Air Force be designated as the single manager for airlift services, with MATS as the principal agency for all military airlift needs. For the Navy, the directive required that all Navy MATS aircraft be transferred to the Air Force, as well as all Navy four-engined land transports then operating with the Fleet Logistic Support Wings (FLOGWINGS), excepting 30 aircraft the Navy was allowed to retain for its internal fleet service and administrative needs. As a result, VR-3 moved to McGuire AFB in July 1957, joining VR-6, which had relocated to McGuire AFB in July 1955, both attached to the Naval Air Transport Wing, Atlantic, MATS. VR-7 and VR-8 moved to NAS Moffett Field, California, in August and September 1957 respectively, where they joined the NATW, Pacific, MATS.

In June 1958, all aircraft operated by VR-3, VR-6, VR-7 and VR-8 were transferred to the Air Force and were given Air Force designations, from R6D-1 to C-118A and R7V-1 to C-121G, as well as Air Force serial numbers. The following month, the R6D-1s flown by VR-22 at NAS Norfolk, Virginia, also were transferred to the Air Force and the squadron operated as part of the NATW, Atlantic, MATS. Thus, for the following five to eight years, these five Navy squadrons flew their Air Force-assigned and marked aircraft under Air Force/MATS operational control.

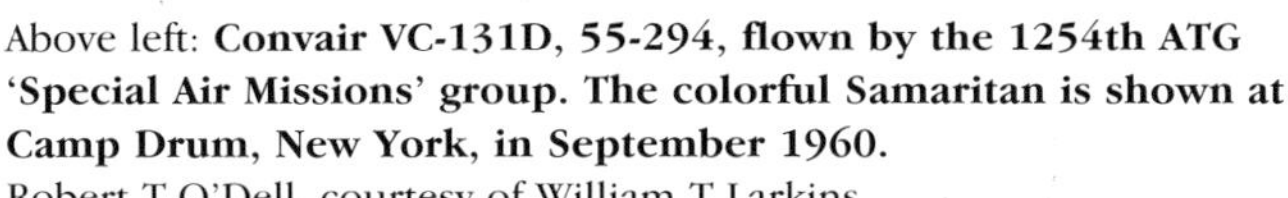

Above left: **Convair VC-131D, 55-294, flown by the 1254th ATG 'Special Air Missions' group. The colorful Samaritan is shown at Camp Drum, New York, in September 1960.** Robert T O'Dell, courtesy of William T Larkins

Above right: **Special Air Missions Boeing VC-137A, 58-6970, was one of three purchased to transport congressional and military VIPs.** Air Force, courtesy of Norm Taylor

Right: **MATS Douglas C-124C, 51-5174, of the 53rd TCS, 63rd TCW, Donaldson AFB, South Carolina, shown at Christchurch, New Zealand, in 1956.** R Smith, courtesy of Norm Taylor

Below: **Operation Deep Freeze C-130E, 62-1815, unloading cargo on the Antarctic continent.** Air Force, courtesy of Clyde Gerdes Collection

These Navy/MATS units often painted their squadron insignia or other Navy-related designs on their aircraft to distinguish them from other Air Force MATS aircraft. When VR-3 and VR-22 converted to the C-130E in August 1963 and the spring of 1964 respectively, the only outward indication of their Navy identity was the acronym 'NATWA' or 'NATWP' painted on the Hercules' forward fuselages, standing for Naval Air Transport Wing, Atlantic, or Pacific, as VR-22 relocated to NAS Moffett Field and WESTAF in the fall of 1965.

5.16 Air Rescue Service

With the end of the Korean War, the Air Rescue Service assumed a global search and rescue mission. The threat of nuclear war dictated that a portion of the ARS mission become the rescue of Strategic Air Command bomber crews from Arctic regions into the Soviet Union, or from the Pacific area surrounding Communist China. Search and rescue within the continental United States also was an Air Rescue Service task. The National SAR Plan of March 1956 defined the Air Rescue Service's responsibilities within the continental US under the administration of the Continental Air Command. However, budget restrictions forced a reduction in the number of ARS squadrons through the 1950s, from 50 squadrons and 8,900 men in 1954 to just ten squadrons and 1,100 men in 1961. In April 1954, Air Rescue Service Headquarters moved to Orlando AFB, Florida.

In September 1958, the Air Rescue Service underwent another reorganization whereby its units and aircraft were organized, trained and deployed to 'support peacetime air operations'. Three Recovery Operation Centers were established in the continental US, Hickam AFB, Hawaii, and at Ramstein AB, Germany, to co-ordinate search and rescue operations, while the number of air rescue squadrons had shrunk to 17.

In spite of these broadened responsibilities, carried out with a shrinking force, the Air Rescue Service continued to provide both Cold War mission and humanitarian support. In February 1953, ARS aircrews flew 198 sorties in SA-16, SH-19, SC-47 and SC-82 aircraft as floods hit the Netherlands. The ARS evacuated 161 persons and delivered over 32,000 pounds of relief supplies during the two-week operation, dubbed 'Operation Humanity'. Similar floods hit Iraq in April 1954, where 59th ARS SH-19s dropped 30,000 pounds of food in 66 sorties to some 4,000 flood victims in the Tigris River Valley. In 1958, during the Lebanon Crisis in July and the Taiwan Crisis in August, the Air Rescue Service deployed its units into these trouble spots, providing SAR coverage for MATS and tactical squadrons operating in the areas.

The Air Rescue Service's aircraft fleet underwent a gradual modernization during the 1950s, in part to meet its global SAR mission by acquiring long-range aircraft with capabilities nearly equal to the bombers and transports then in use. The Second World War vintage OA-10s, SC-47s, SC-82s, SB-17s and SB-29s were replaced by remanufactured Douglas SC-54 Rescuemasters beginning in 1953. The SC-54 carried four MA-1 rescue kits, each containing a 40-person inflatable life raft with provisions, a considerable improvement over the single 14-person wooden life boat carried by the SB-17 and the aluminum A-3 life boat by the SB-29. The introduction of the Grumman SA-16 Albatross in the early 1950s gave the ARS an amphibious capability that the SC-54 lacked, and the Sikorsky SH-19, its main SAR helicopter, and the Piasecki SH-21, used almost exclusively for Arctic rescue, provided the Air Rescue Service with a dependable helicopter SAR fleet as well as increased capabilities.

A demonstration of these capabilities was staged in July 1952 when two Air Rescue Service Sikorsky H-19As flew the Atlantic, making the nearly 3,000 mile crossing in a little over 42 hours flight time. The two aircraft, with the names 'Whirl-O-Way' and 'Hop-A-Long' painted on their noses, made the first crossing of the Atlantic by helicopter, flying from Westover AFB, Massachusetts, to Prestwick, Scotland, with stops in Maine, Labrador, Greenland, and Iceland. Accompanying the helicopters on this flight were an Air Rescue Service SA-16A, SB-17, SB-29 and a C-54 carrying spare parts and maintenance personnel.

The typical Air Rescue Service squadron of the early 1950s might consist of a mix of short-range L-5s and H-5s, medium-range OA-10s, SC-47s or SC-82s, and long-range SB-17s or SB-29s, with units based in Alaska or Arctic regions flying winterized L-5s, L-13s or LC-126s. Later in the decade, the typical squadron was equipped almost exclusively with the SA-16, SC-54 and SH-19, with the SH-21 utilized in Arctic areas.

An interesting exception was Alaska's 10th Air Rescue Squadron, which was under the control of the Alaska Air Command until 1st July 1950, when it was transferred to MATS' Air Rescue Service. The 10th ARS had flights or small detachments positioned at Elmendorf AFB, Lake Hood, Ladd AFB, and Adak Naval Station in the Aleutians. More than just a search and rescue squadron for military and civilian ships and aircraft, the 10th ARS frequently was the only means of survival for isolated Alaskans. On almost a daily basis, a 10th ARS aircraft might be sent to a remote outpost to evacuate a woman to a hospital maternity ward or a native Alaskan to medical care for a serious injury. In 1951, 10th ARS aircraft made numerous paradrops of food and equipment to a scientific expedition located on the western slope of Mount McKinley and to various glacier research camps in the Juneau area.

On 4th November 1952, the 10th ARS was redesignated as the 10th Air Rescue Group, and its detachments became the 71st and 72nd ARS at Elmendorf AFB, the 73rd ARS at Adak NS, and the 74th ARS at Ladd AFB. Due to the withdrawal of the Air Force presence in the Aleutian Islands, the 72nd ARS and 73rd ARS were inactivated in the fall of 1953.

Through the early 1950s, the 10th ARS/ARG operated a fascinating collection of search and rescue aircraft: wheel, ski or float-equipped C-45s, L-5s, L-13s, and LC-126s; OA-10s, SA-16s, SB-17s, H-5s, SH-21s, and one G-15A glider. Unfortunately, the previously-mentioned reductions in the Air Rescue Service caused the inactivation of the 10th ARG in January 1958 and the 71st ARS in March 1960, returning search and rescue responsibilities in Alaska to the Alaska Air Command.

This Air Rescue Service reorganization during 1958 resulted in the activation of the 53rd ARS at Keflavik, Iceland, whose search and rescue responsibilities previously had been performed by an independent air rescue unit. The 53rd ARS, 9th ARG, operated the SA-16, SH-19 and L-20, replacing SB-17s and SC-47s flown by the earlier squadron.

5.17 Air Weather Service

The Air Weather Service underwent a major reorganization in May 1952, whereby it shifted emphasis from a geographical basis to furnishing each major Air Force command with specialized weather information to meet their individual needs. The AWS gathered weather data from the North Pole to the tropics through its 300 weather stations, 24 mobile weather teams, and seven aerial reconnaissance squadrons positioned worldwide. The Air Force Weather Central moved from Andrews AFB to Suitland, Maryland, in January 1955, where it merged with the US Weather Bureau and the Navy's Fleet Weather Central to form the National Weather Analysis Center. The USAF Weather Central at Suitland was closed in December 1957, although its functions were shifted to the Global Weather Central, Offutt AFB, Nebraska. Finally, as part of the June 1958 MATS-wide reorganization, the Headquarters, Air Weather Service moved from Andrews AFB to Scott AFB, Illinois, and by March 1960 all Air Weather Service weather reconnaissance squadrons were placed under the control of the 9th Weather Group at Scott AFB.

The Boeing WB-29 was operated almost exclusively by Air Weather Service reconnaissance squadrons during the early 1950s. Relatively fast and sturdy, the WB-29 nonetheless had been in the Air Force inventory for ten years and suffered from airframe weariness as well as high fuel consumption. The first loss of an AWS hurricane reconnaissance aircraft occurred on 26th October 1952, when a WB-29 crashed with ten crew members aboard while making a low-level penetration of Typhoon 'Wilma' 300 miles east of Leyte.

Due to the considerable damage inflicted on the East Coast of the United States by Hurricane 'Hazel' in October 1954, Congress appropriated funds to improve hurricane forecasting and the Air Weather Service began receiving the Boeing WB-50 in 1955. The 74 WB-50Ds acquired were faster, more stable, were equipped with new doppler radar and airborne temperature-humidity indicators, and had 850 miles longer range than the earlier aircraft, facts which should have made them satisfactory replacements. Unfortunately, between August 1956 and January 1957, the Air Weather Service suffered four major crashes with the WB-50Ds, taking the lives of over 30 aircrew, the worst series of accidents in Air Weather Service history. Subsequently, in November 1957 the Air Weather Service was assigned one Boeing WB-47B converted for weather reconnaissance, to be used during the US Weather Bureau's National Hurricane Research Project. The Air Weather Service eventually replaced the WB-50Ds with the WB-47E and WC-130B/E, but not before experiencing additional crashes with the Superfortress with further loss of life.

Mention should be made of the Air Weather Service's tenuous involvement with the Lockheed U-2's early exploits, first disclosed in an April 1956 press release from the National Advisory Committee for Aeronautics. The U-2s were used to collect 'high level meteorological data', with technical and logistical assistance from the Air Weather Service. The aircraft supposedly were organized into three Weather Reconnaissance Squadrons, Provisional, attached to Air Weather Service Headquarters. While the U-2's exploits, as well as those of the later AWS RB/WB-57Fs, will be covered in more detail within each type's history with MATS, it seems safe to say that 'there is more to this story than meets the eye'.

Below: **Palletized cargo waits to be loaded aboard a MATS C-133B, 56-2014, at Travis AFB, California.** Air Force, courtesy of Clyde Gerdes Collection

Top left: **C-135B, 61-2669, being loaded with palletized cargo by a specialized loading platform pioneered by MATS.** Air Force, courtesy of Clyde Gerdes Collection

Top right: **Rare photo of a C-54D, 42-72633, operated by VR-7 Detachment A at Tachikawa AB, Japan. 'VR-7 Det.A' is painted on the Skymaster's nosewheel door.** Brian Stainer, courtesy of Barry Collman

Above: **This Navy MATS R6D-1, 128431, was flown by VR-3 beginning in 1951.** Navy, courtesy of Robert L Lawson

Left: **Navy Air Transport Squadron Three Flight Orderlies with a Continental Division VR-3 R6D-1, 131615.** Navy, courtesy of Peter Mersky

Bottom left: **MATS Atlantic Division R6D-1, 131618, of VR-6 in 1956. Note the squadron insignia on the Liftmaster's forward fuselage.** MAP

Photographs on the opposite page:

Top: **Navy MATS R7V-1, 131646, flown by VR-7 descends for a landing at Hickam AFB, Hawaii, with Diamond Head and Waikiki Beach in the background.** Navy, courtesy of Robert L Lawson

Bottom: **This Air Force MATS C-121G, 54-4052, shown over NAS Moffett Field, California, in August 1959, is flown by the Navy's VR-7.** Bob Carlisle, courtesy of Robert L Lawson

MILITARY AIR TRANSPORT SERVICE
MATS
PACIFIC DIVISION
131646

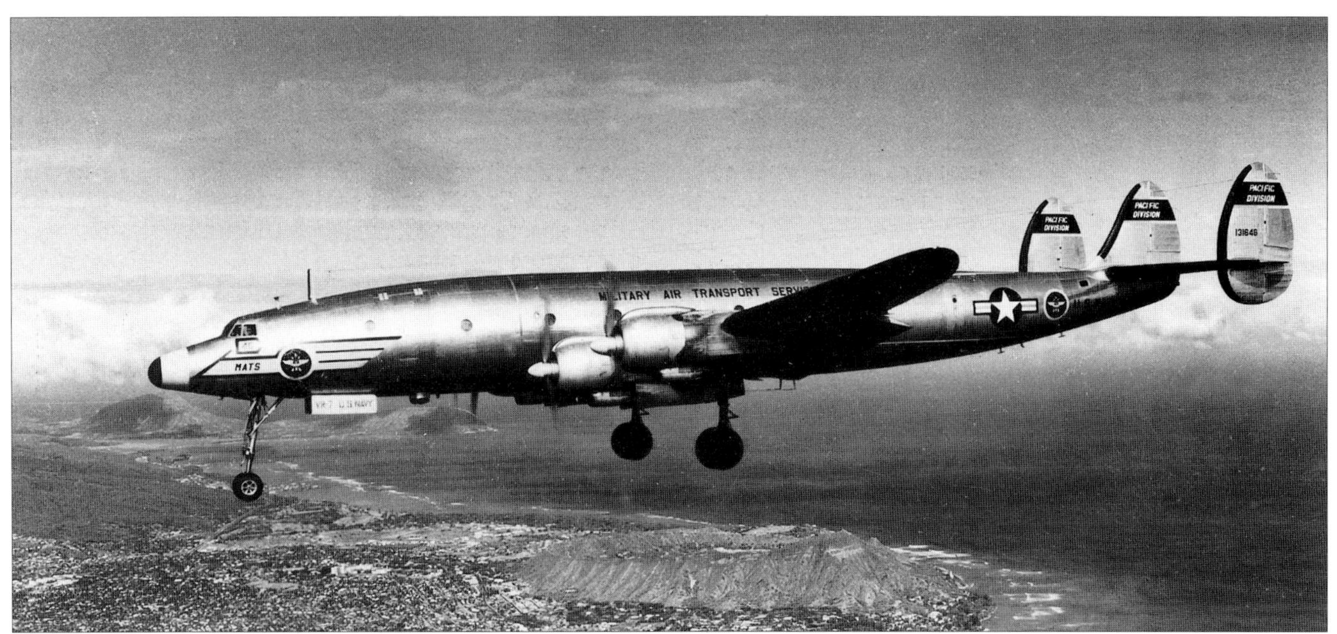

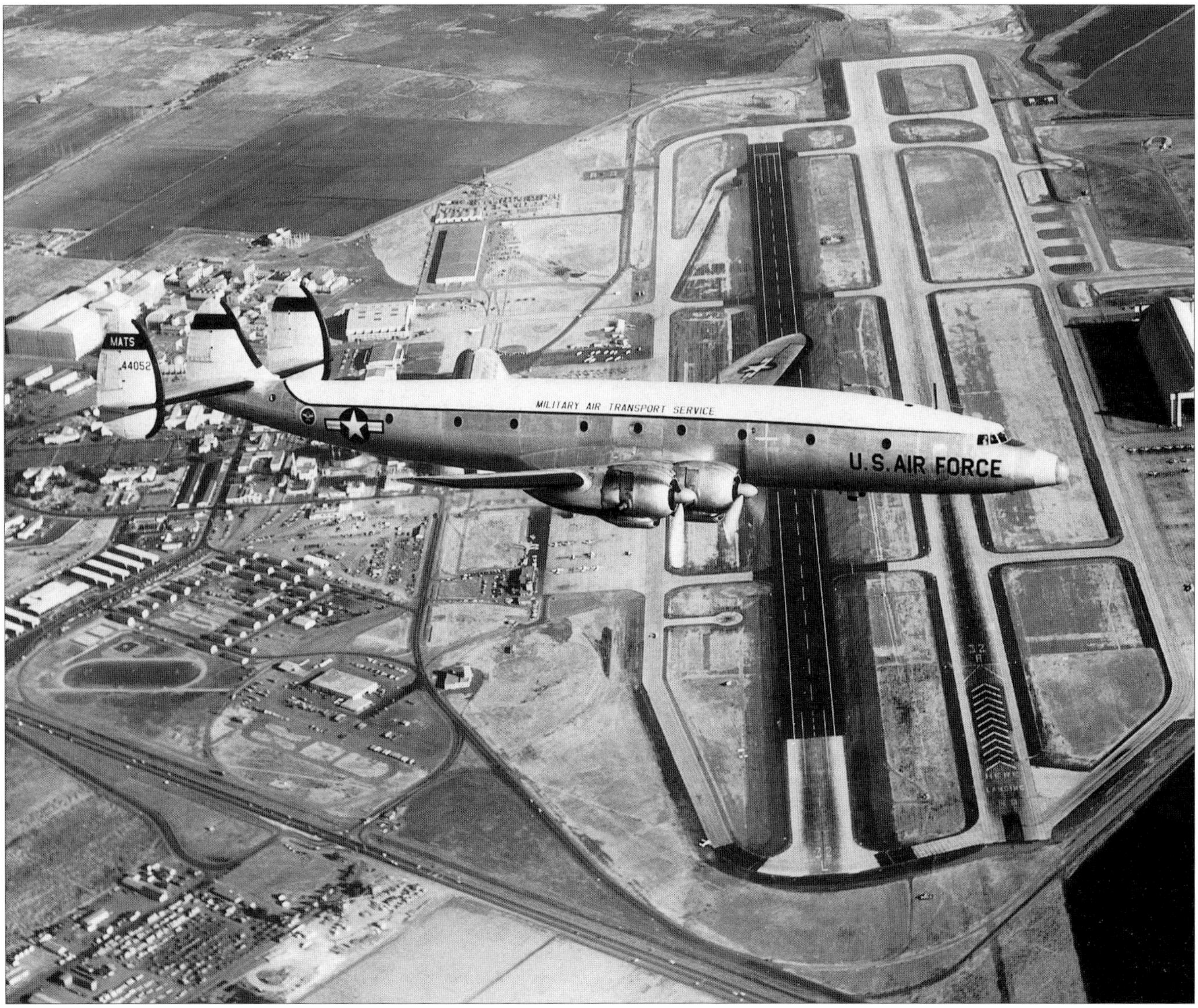
MATS
44052
MILITARY AIR TRANSPORT SERVICE
U.S. AIR FORCE

Top: **Despite the Air Force markings and serial number of this MATS C-118A, 51-17631, the Liftmaster's operator, VR-22, has taken pains to assert its Navy roots: note the squadron insignia on the forward fuselage, 'R6D' below 'Force', and *City of Norfolk* painted on the fuselage. Its former Navy serial number was 131572.** Douglas, courtesy of Matt Rodina

Left: **A 79th ARS SB-29B accompanies a 54th WRS WB-29 with a feathered No.4 engine as the two aircraft approach Anderson AFB, Guam, in 1955.** Richard Slay, courtesy of Robert C Mikesh

Bottom: **An Air Rescue Service SC-47A, 43-15732, of the 3rd ARS in October 1955.** Air Force, courtesy of Matt Rodina

Top: **SC-54D, 42-72566, was capable of air dropping four MA-1 rescue kits, each with an inflatable life raft which could hold 40 persons.** Air Force

Bottom left: **'Hop-A-Long', an Air Rescue Service SH-19A, 51-3893, followed by 'Whirl-O-Way', SH-19A, 51-3894, made the first transatlantic crossings by helicopter in July and August 1952.** Air Force via AAHS Negative Library

Bottom right: **SH-21B, 53-4357, of the 54th ARS at Mud Lake, Goose Bay, Labrador, in February 1959. The SH-21 was the Air Rescue Service's main Arctic rescue helicopter.**
Carl Damonte, courtesy of Wayne Mutza

Above: **Douglas C-47A, 43-15982, an administrative transport with the Air Weather Service at McCarran Field, Nevada, in September 1957.** Courtesy of Clyde Gerdes Collection

Below: **Air Weather Service RB-50D, 49-275, at Logan Airport, Boston, Massachusetts, in February 1958.** Courtesy of Norm Taylor

Chapter 6

Military Air Transport Service 1960 to 1966

Above: **The MATS flight line in the late 1950s at Hickam AFB, Hawaii, with a characteristic mix of C-124, C-118, C-97 and C-121 aircraft.** Air Force

6.1 Jet Modernization Program

> *'Our ability to meet our commitments to more than 50 countries around the globe has been critically impaired by our failure to develop a jet airlift capability'.*
>
> Senator John F Kennedy, 1960

By 1960, it was painfully obvious that the Military Air Transport Service, serving as the main airlift agency for the Department of Defense, was lagging behind the commercial airlines in adopting turbojet-powered transports. While the Boeing 707 had entered service in December 1958, the Douglas DC-8 in September 1959, and the Convair 880 in May 1960, by 1961 the MATS strategic airlift force still consisted solely of propeller-driven transports: 107 C-118s, 56 C-121s, 291 C-124s and 31 C-133s.

During the presidential campaign of 1960, Senator John F Kennedy included in his platform a commitment to acquire jet transports rapidly for the MATS fleet. He was supported by the Air Force Association, which, during their national convention held in San Francisco in September, adopted resolutions asking Congress to authorize funds for new jet transports for MATS, for modernizing other MATS equipment, and for retaining the MATS fleet of medevac aircraft, as the commercial airlines were making overtures to take over this responsibility from MATS. MATS Commander Lt General Joe William Kelly announced to the convention that MATS was planning to buy 18 commercial jets from either Boeing, Douglas or Convair.

In fact, the Air Force already had issued, in May 1960, a Specific Operational Requirement (SOR 182) for an aircraft capable of carrying more than 60,000 lbs over 3,500 nautical miles. It was announced in March 1961 that Lockheed-Georgia had won a design competition with their turbofan-powered C-141 Starlifter. But as the production C-141A would not be available until mid-1965, newly-elected President Kennedy and Lt Gen Kelly made good on their promises by purchasing 45 all-jet C-135s for MATS, with the first Stratolifter delivery occurring in June 1961.

6.2 Transport Operations

The acquisition of these new turbine-powered transports allowed MATS to upgrade its routine airlift capabilities as well as its responses to United Nations interventions and humanitarian missions. From July 1960 to January 1964, for example, MATS transports including the C-135 participated in the United Nations airlift to the Congo, providing 90 percent of all cargo and nearly 80 percent of personnel airlifted, over 63,000 passengers and 18,000 tons of supplies in more than 2,100 flights into the area. In November 1962, MATS C-135s participated in two concurrent crises. The first was in response to an incursion of Chinese Communist forces into India's Assam Valley and Ladakh District. Over a two-week period, twelve MATS C-135s delivered almost 10,000 tons of equipment, small arms, and ammunition in 45 flights into Calcutta after the Indian government had issued a request for military aid. Each C-135 averaged 12,000 miles for the round trip between Western Europe and India. The second crisis involved transporting relief supplies to the island of Guam, which had been hit by Typhoon 'Karen'. C-124s and C-135s from Travis AFB and McGuire AFB, some just back from the Indian arms lift, flew the 6,000 mile round trip to Guam, delivering over 800 tons of emergency supplies and returning with 726 homeless military dependants between 13th and 18th November. Finally, in 1964 MATS began operating 'Junction Run' airlift routes that had been relinquished by USAF-Europe, including flights to the Mediterranean, the Middle East, Africa and South Asia as far as to New Delhi.

One aspect of the MATS transition that was occurring at this time, which will be covered in more detail in the section on the Boeing C-97, is the turnover of dozens of Stratofreighters to Air National Guard units. Between 1960 and 1963, a number of ANG fighter squadrons converted to flying the C-97 as air transport squadrons. Cold War tensions over Soviet attempts to remove the Western Powers from West Berlin prompted President Kennedy to call 64 Air National Guard units to active duty on 1st October 1961, including at least six Air National Guard C-97 squadrons which flew transport missions for the Military Air Transport Service.

6.3 Cuban Crisis

In the fall of 1962, the festering Cold War between the United States and the Soviet Union suddenly erupted into a potential military confrontation. For MATS, the emergency was a test of an ongoing evolution in its airlift mission: from flying routine scheduled operations along standard air routes to becoming a truly global airlift force responding to emergency situations as well as combined armed forces mobility exercises.

On October 22, 1962, President Kennedy announced to the world that aerial reconnaissance photos had shown that the Soviets were placing offensive nuclear-tipped ballistic missiles within Cuba in an attempt to change the strategic balance of world power. In response, Kennedy had directed that US military forces be put on standby alert and that a weapons quarantine was being placed around Cuba to prevent any additional missiles from being shipped to the island. In the following weeks, it appeared that the stage had been set for the beginning of a Third World War, as the military's Defense Condition (DEFCON) status escalated in response to the crisis.

Kennedy's announcement was only a public admission of what had been known for some time, as SAC/CIA U-2s had photographed the Soviet military build-up on Cuba as early as 29th August. The Defense Department began contingency plans on 14th October to deal with a possible military confrontation with the Soviets over the missiles. The Military Air Transport Service began airlifting battle equipment, ammunition and supplies into Florida on 17th October, eventually flying 54 missions into the aerial staging areas of the state. This included an Army artillery unit, consisting of 169 troops and 486 tons of cargo, which was airlifted from El Paso, Texas, to Homestead AFB in two days by 19 MATS transports. From 21st-23rd October, MATS C-124s and C-135s airlifted battle-ready US Marines from their bases on the West Coast to the Naval Station at Guantanamo Bay, Cuba, becoming the first major airlift of Marine Corps forces by MATS.

As MATS responded to the various priority assignments directed by the Joint Chiefs of Staff, it became necessary to grant specific flying waivers to accomplish these missions, including extensions of crew duty time on C-133s, an increase in take-off gross weights for C-124A and C-124C aircraft, an increase in the number of troops authorized to be carried in the C-135 from 84 to 125, an increase in the number of flying hours flown per month by aircrews from 125 hours to 150 hours (330 hours/quarter to 350 hours/quarter), and numerous one-time waivers for over gross weight landings made by MATS C-118s. As it turned out, these waivers were necessary for only ten to fifteen days as the Cuban Crisis quickly de-escalated.

The Cuban build-up also enabled MATS to expedite its planned troop and cargo airdrop and formation flying capabilities. In September 1962, MATS C-124s had made their first formation drop of 2,100 paratroopers at Fort Campbell, Kentucky. After the Cuban Crisis began, MATS C-124s participated in a joint exercise with the Army's Strike Command forces, air dropping 1,600 paratroopers and 84,000 pounds of equipment between 24th October and 2nd November. In order to equip all MATS C-124s with cargo and personnel drop equipment, 'Project Full Speed' was initiated, accomplishing the task in only 20 days. And, on 23rd October, Air Force Headquarters advised MATS that C-124 formation training would resume after completion of the priority missions for the Joint Chiefs of Staff. This formation training program with the C-124 was accomplished between 26th-30th October.

The Cuban Crisis ended on 27th October, almost as suddenly as it had developed. Following a series of communications between President Kennedy and Premier Khrushchev, the Communists agreed to dismantle their Cuban-based missiles and to return them to the Soviet Union, as well as remove a large number of Russian Il-28 jet bombers from the island. For MATS, the crisis proved the efficiencies of the 44 Boeing C-135 Stratolifters used during the airlift, and in the MATS global command and control system and its ability to react to unplanned emergencies.

Photographs on the opposite page:

Top: **Boeing C-135B, 61-2666, was one of 45 Stratolifters delivered as interim jet transports until the C-141 became operational.** Air Force, courtesy of Jack M Friell

Bottom: **These MATS Stratofreighters, C-97Cs 50-691 and 50-701, are from the 146th ATW, California Air National Guard, Van Nuys Airport.** Air Force, courtesy of 1Lt M J Kasiuba

MATS
U.S. AIR FORCE

Above: **Douglas C-124C, 52-1078, loading Marine Corps equipment at NALF Fentress.** Navy, courtesy of Robert L Lawson

Left: **Douglas MC-118A, 53-3269, shown at Malta in June 1965.** Courtesy of Clyde Gerdes Collection

6.4 Vietnam Build-Up

While the massive airlift of men and supplies to the Vietnam War – some two million tons of materiel and two million passengers – flown by the Military Airlift Command between 1966 and 1973 is outside the scope of this book, the airlift's roots began with a small MATS presence in the region. The gradual build-up of men and materiel into Vietnam by MATS, starting at the end of 1961, was balanced by the Department of Defense's policy, begun by late 1963, of contracting increasingly large numbers of civilian air carriers to replace MATS transports on their scheduled routes. By June 1964, the C-124s of the 22nd TCS, 1503rd ATW, at Tachikawa AB, Japan, were the only MATS heavy lift transports based in the Far East. This increased use of commercial air carriers placed the 22nd TCS in the special-mission role on a nearly full-time basis, and its mission emphasis shifted from the Japan-Korea area to that of Southeast Asia, with increasing flights into Vietnam, Thailand and Laos. Between January and May 1963, the number of squadron crews deployed in the Southeast Asia area increased from 4 to 17, and by June the 22nd TCS had 15 crews trained in formation air-drop, a new emphasis spurred by the Cuban Crisis. By 1965, the Vietnam airlift requirements, for men as well as helicopters, bulldozers, and howitzers, increased to the point where 22nd TCS crews began staging out of Tan Son Nhut Air Base in Saigon.

By 1965, the Military Air Transport Service's strategic airlift, troop carrier, and aeromedical evacuation fleet was composed of the following:

C-118	
48th ATS, 1502nd ATW	Hickam AFB, Hawaii
29th ATS, 1611th ATW	McGuire AFB, New Jersey
30th ATS, 1611th ATW	McGuire AFB, New Jersey
38th ATS, 1611th ATW	McGuire AFB, New Jersey
11th AMTS, 1405th AMTW	Scott AFB, Illinois
12th AMTS, 1405th AMTW	McGuire AFB, New Jersey
C-121	
VR-7, NATW Pacific	Tachikawa AB, Japan
C-124	
4th ATS, 62nd ATW	McChord AFB, Washington
7th TCS, 62nd ATW	McChord AFB, Washington
8th ATS, 62nd ATW	McChord AFB, Washington
19th ATS, 62nd ATW	Kelly AFB, Texas
75th ATS, 1501st ATW	Travis AFB, California
85th ATS, 1501st ATW	Travis AFB, California
28th ATS, 1501st ATW	Hill AFB, Utah
50th ATS, 1502nd ATW	Hickam AFB, Hawaii
6th TCS, 1502nd ATW	Hickam AFB, Hawaii
22nd TCS, 1503rd ATW	Tachikawa AB, Japan
9th TCS, 1607th ATW	Dover AFB, Delaware
20th TCS, 1607th ATW	Dover AFB, Delaware
31st ATS, 1607th ATW	Dover AFB, Delaware
3rd ATS, 1608th ATW	Charleston AFB, South Carolina
17th ATS, 1608th ATW	Charleston AFB, South Carolina
14th TCS, 63rd TCW	Hunter AFB, Georgia
15th TCS, 63rd TCW	Hunter AFB, Georgia
52nd TCS, 63rd TCW	Hunter AFB, Georgia (PCS Rhein-Main AB, Germany)
53rd TCS, 63rd TCW	Hunter AFB, Georgia
54th TCS, 63rd TCW	Hunter AFB, Georgia
7th ATS, 63rd TCW	Robins AFB, Georgia
1740th ATS, 1707th ATW	(Operational Training), Tinker AFB, Oklahoma
C-130	
86th ATS, 1501st ATW	Travis AFB, California
41st ATS, 1608th ATW	Charleston AFB, South Carolina
76th ATS, 1608th ATW	Charleston AFB, South Carolina
VR-3, NATW, Atlantic	McGuire AFB, New Jersey
VR-7, NATW, Pacific	NAS Moffett Field, California
VR-22, NATW, Atlantic	NAS Norfolk, Virginia
C-131	
10th AMTS, 1405th AMTW	Kelly AFB, Texas
11th AMTS, 1405th AMTW	Scott AFB, Illinois
12th AMTS, 1405th AMTW	McGuire AFB, New Jersey
13th AMTS, 1405th AMTW	Travis AFB, California
C-133	
84th ATS, 1501st ATW	Travis AFB, California
1st ATS, 1607th ATW	Dover AFB, Delaware
39th ATS, 1607th ATW	Dover AFB, Delaware
C-135	
44th ATS, 1501st ATW	Travis AFB, California
18th ATS, 1611th ATW	McGuire AFB, New Jersey
40th ATS, 1611th ATW	McGuire AFB, New Jersey
C-141	
44th ATS, 1501st ATW	Travis AFB, California
1741st ATS, 1707th ATW	Tinker AFB, Oklahoma (Operational Training)

6.5 Air Rescue Service

After nearly a decade of reductions in force imposed upon the Air Rescue Service, the organization reached its lowest ebb in mid-1961, when it consisted of only 1,059 personnel, ten squadrons and a total of 81 mission-assigned aircraft: 56 SC-54s, 21 SA-16s, and four SH-19s. The Recovery Operation Centers established in 1958 were replaced in August 1961 by Air Rescue Centers, each with a number of dispersed detachments. The mandate to provide global search and rescue gave the service new life, however, in that all rescue operations now were to be consolidated under a single command. Consequently, the Air Force Chief of Staff directed in December 1960 that all of the 70 independent Local Base Rescue units be transferred to the Air Rescue Service. These Local Base Rescue units were spotted worldwide at all major Air Force bases, each providing rescue services in a 75-mile radius of the base with two helicopters and a six-man fire suppression crew. The Kaman H-43s used mainly for this task were equipped with a fire suppression kit which hung beneath the helicopter from a sling, providing 800 gallons of fire suppression foam. Seven types of helicopters were in use by these LBR units, but the Air Rescue Service standardized the fleet by using the H-43s almost exclusively. Thus, on 1st October 1961, these 70 LBR units were absorbed into the Air Rescue Service, adding 17 H-43As, 69 H-43Bs, 58 H-19Bs, and four SH-21Bs to the ARS fleet.

MATS
21787
U.S. AIR FORCE
MATS
21785

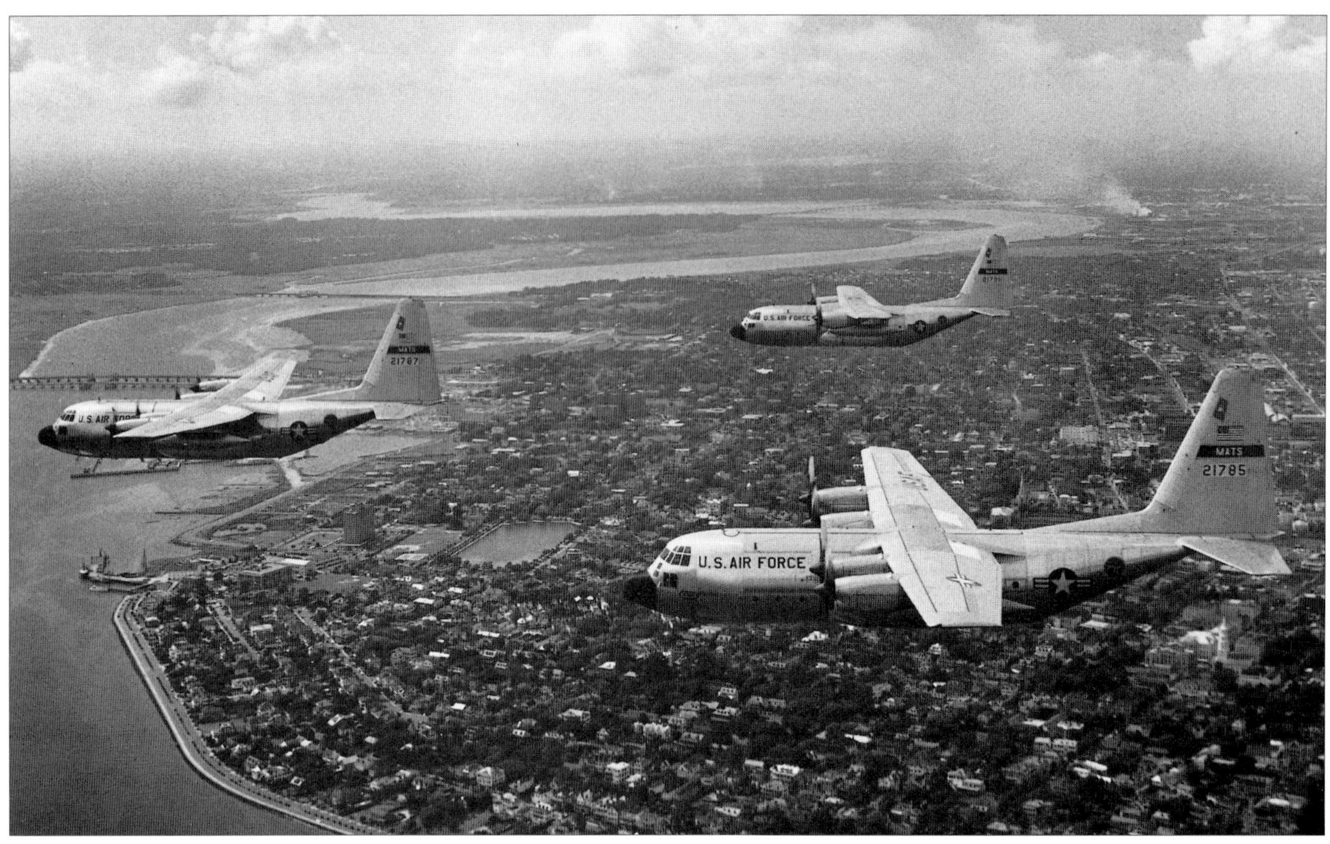

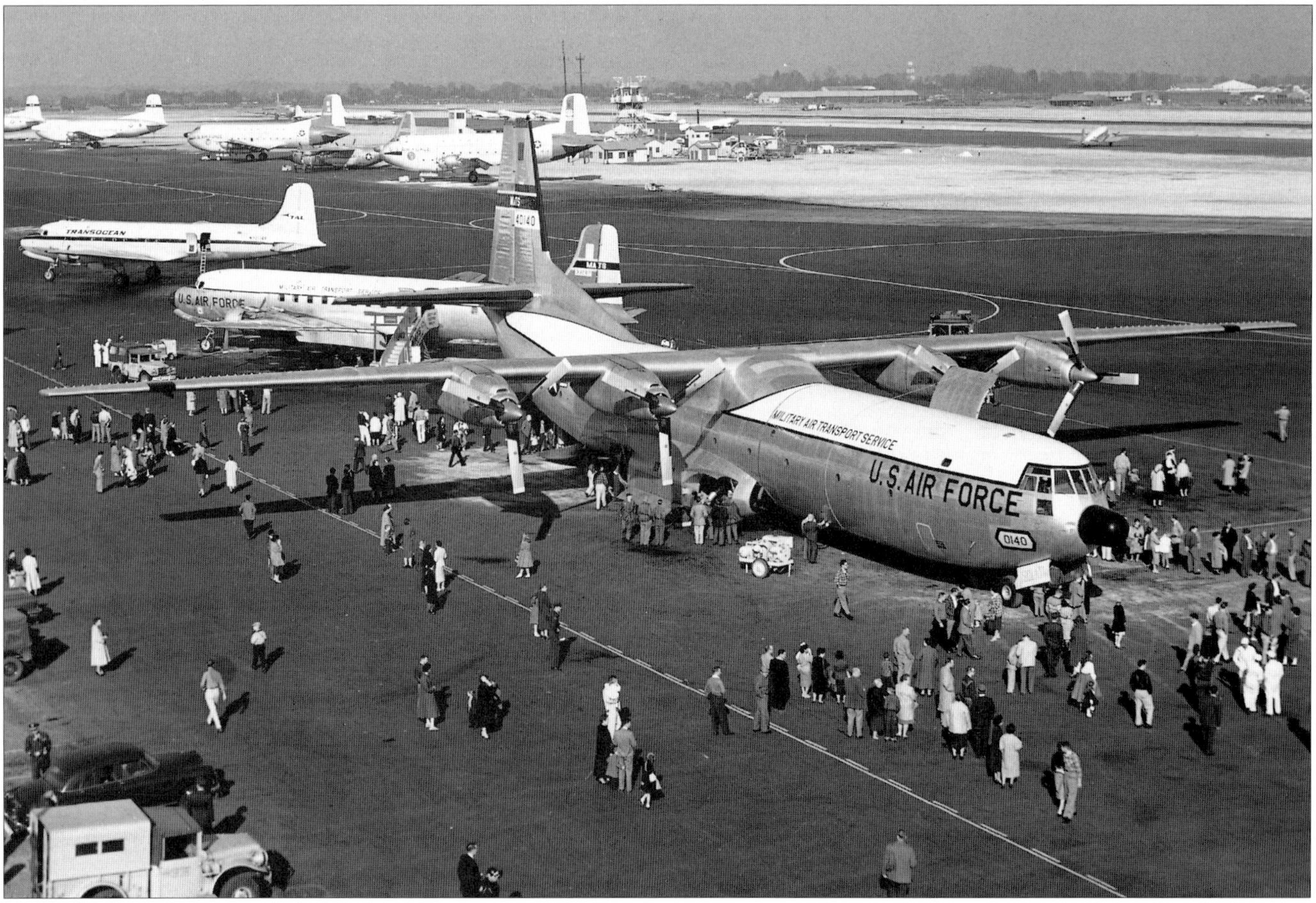
TRANSOCEAN
40140
U.S. AIR FORCE
MILITARY AIR TRANSPORT SERVICE
U.S. AIR FORCE
0140

By late 1964, the Air Rescue Service embarked upon a three-year modernization program to re-equip its squadrons with turbine-powered fixed and rotary-winged aircraft, and the service began to receive the initial examples of the new Lockheed HC-130H and Sikorsky CH/HH-3C (the prefix 'H' having now replaced 'S' in denoting search and rescue aircraft in 1962). In the interim, a number of Boeing KC-97s were reconfigured for the SAR role and were redesignated as HC-97Gs. The Air Rescue Service fleet by 1965 was composed of the following aircraft:

1	C-47	35	HU-16
24	HC-54	1	U-6A
29	HC-97	4	HH-21
16	HC-130	149	HH-43
		11	HH-3

Air Rescue Service squadrons in 1965 were made up of 61 Local Base Rescue units and the following Air Rescue Squadrons:

31st ARS	Clark AB, Philippines
33rd ARS	Naha AB, Okinawa
36th ARS	Tachikawa AB, Japan
41st ARS	Hamilton AFB, California
48th ARS	Eglin AFB, Florida
54th ARS	Goose AB, Labrador
55th ARS	Kindley AB, Bermuda
57th ARS	Lajes Field, Azores
58th ARS	Wheelus AB, Libya
67th ARS	Prestwick AB, Scotland
76th ARS	Hickam AFB, Hawaii
79th ARS	Anderson AFB, Guam

6.6 Air Photographic and Charting Service

Through the early 1960s, the Air Photographic and Charting Service continued to perform its mapping and survey mission, deploying many small Aerial Survey Teams to remote and isolated corners of the world. In July 1961, 138 men, three RB-50s and one C-54 from the 1370th Photo Mapping Wing, Turner AFB, Georgia, made an aerial survey of the Hawaiian Islands, including the Johnston Islands and Midway. In 1964 and 1965, the Ethiopian Government requested that the entire country be photographed and mapped. To accomplish this task, a network of 14 HIRAN (High Precision Ranging and Navigation) sites had to be established so that accurate lines of position could be determined. Three RC-130As from Aerial Survey Team No.4, 1370th PMW, flew the actual photomapping missions during 'Project King's Ransom'. To construct and maintain most of the 14 mountaintop HIRAN sites, however, the APCS was forced to utilize Kaman HH-43Bs from the Air Rescue Service, as the APCS' new CH-3s lacked the Huskie's high-altitude performance. These ARS HH-43Bs and their crews served on a rotating, temporary duty basis from eleven Local Base Rescue units in Europe, Turkey and from Kindley AB, Bermuda. The Huskies flew personnel and supplies to mountaintop HIRAN sites from 4,000 to 12,500 feet high. Despite some of the most primitive conditions imaginable – living in tents, isolation, high winds, tropical sun, eating C-rations, and even local bandits who captured two US Army men (later released unharmed) – the project was completed without incident.

During the Cuban Crisis of October 1962, the Air Photographic and Charting Service developed a streamlined motion picture camera pod for combat and reconnaissance aircraft. The forward and rearward-looking 16mm cameras were mounted on the center bomb shackles of six Tactical Air Command F-100s to obtain over-the-target photo-documentation of weapons employment. High-speed, low-altitude tests also were made with the pods attached to the RF-101 Voodoo. In December 1964, the new camera pods were used on TAC aircraft to provide the first high-altitude, sideview instrumentation photography during launches of Mariner III and IV and Atlas Centaur missiles. After refinement, the capabilities of these pods soon would be evident over the battlefields of Vietnam.

By 1965, the APCS was composed of the 1370th PMW at Turner AFB and its two squadrons: the 1371st MCS flying the RB-50F, RC-54 and RC-118A, and the 1375th MCS operating the RC-130A, CH-21B and CH-3B, the 1372nd MCS (Aerial Photographic) having been disbanded in March 1960. A new era was dawning as the launching of the geodetic satellite Anna in 1962 began the age of satellite geodesy.

On 1st October 1965, the geodetic and cartographic missions of the APCS were reassigned to a special wing reporting directly to Headquarters MATS. Finally, in the reorganization of MATS on 1st January 1966, the Air Photographic and Charting Service was re-named the Aerospace Audio-Visual Service (AAVS).

6.7 Air Weather Service

The first half of the decade saw the Air Weather Service consolidate several of its missions and complete the transition from the WB-50D to newer turboprop and jet-powered weather reconnaissance aircraft.

For the first time since 1951, all weather reconnaissance units had been placed under the control of one headquarters when the 9th Weather Group was organized at Scott AFB, Illinois, in March 1960. In 1961, the 9th WG was redesignated as the 9th Weather Reconnaissance Group and it relocated to McClellan AFB, California. The organization was upgraded to wing status on 8th July 1965.

In August 1961, the Air Force designated the Air Weather Service as the 'single manager' for aerial sampling missions for the Department of Defense. As a result, the AWS gained a balloon sampling program and its CH-21B helicopter recovery aircraft and a rather mysterious RB-57 high-altitude sampling mission. On the negative side of the single manager concept, the Air Weather Service field units were required to relinquish their support aircraft, mostly C-47s and C-54s, to their host bases.

Opposite page, top: **Lockheed C-130Es, 62-1785/1787/1791, were part of an initial allotment of 99 C-130Es to MATS as interim transports prior to the arrival of the C-141.** Air Force, courtesy of Clyde Gerdes Collection

Opposite page, bottom: **This C-133A, 54-140, on display at Tachikawa AB, Japan, dwarfs the MATS C-118A and Transocean Airlines DC-4 in the background.** Air Force

The balloon sampling mission, which was attached to the 59th WRS at Goodfellow AFB, Texas, was moved to Tinker AFB, Oklahoma, on 8th May 1964, when the Air Weather Service consolidated all of its balloon support activities under Detachment 1, 6th WS (Mobile), 4th WG, at Tinker AFB.

With the acquisition of the WB/RB-57s, the Air Weather Service's aircraft-related missions could be divided into two categories: daily synoptic and hurricane and typhoon weather reconnaissance over Western Atlantic and Pacific waters; and aerial sampling missions, including nuclear weapons fission products, on a worldwide basis. Hurricane reconnaissance missions over the Atlantic and Caribbean were flown from Ramey AFB, Puerto Rico, by Detachment 2, 53rd WRS, using the WB-50D and WC-130B aircraft, and from Kindley AB, Bermuda, by Det.3, 55th WRS, in 1960; Det.7, 9th WG in 1961; the 53rd WRS in 1962; and Det.1, 53rd WRS in 1963, all operating the WB-50D. During the latter part of 1963, the 53rd WRS moved to Hunter AFB, Georgia, where they transitioned to the newly-converted WB-47E for the 1964 storm season. As the WB-47Es were suitable only for high-altitude reconnaissance, 56th WRS WB-50Ds were flown on low-altitude reconnaissance and storm-penetration missions during 1964. By May 1965, the first WC-130Es, capable of both low and high-altitude storm penetrations, were placed into service with the 53rd WRS at Ramey AFB and the 54th WRS at Anderson AFB, Guam.

The first of ten WC-135Bs began to be received by the Air Weather Service in mid-1965. These were assigned to the 53rd WRS at Hunter AFB, Georgia, and to the 55th WRS at McClellan AFB, California. The introduction of the WC-130B/E, WB-47E and WC-135B enabled the last Air Weather Service WB-50D, from the 56th WRS at Yokota AB, Japan, to be retired to Davis-Monthan AFB, Arizona, in September 1965. In their ten years as Air Weather Service weather reconnaissance aircraft, the WB-50Ds had suffered 13 accidents taking the lives of 66 crewmen.

The delivery of the first RB-57F in June 1964 was not the first exposure the Air Weather Service had had with the Martin bomber, as the WB-57B, WB-57C, and RB-57D all had been flown by the AWS since at least the early 1960s for high altitude weather reconnaissance as well as for collecting samples of nuclear debris. No doubt, important meteorological information was collected by these WB-57s, as well as by WU-2s flown by/for the Air Weather Service, but it appears certain that their primary mission was that of gathering intelligence for the Central Intelligence Agency and other government entities.

By 1965, the Air Weather Service was composed of the 9th WRG, headquartered at McClellan AFB, California, and the following weather reconnaissance squadrons:

53rd WRS, Hunter AFB, Georgia	WB-47E
54th WRS, Anderson AFB, Guam	WB-50D
55th WRS, McClellan AFB, California	WC-130B/E
	WB-47E
	RB-57F
56th WRS, Yokota AB, Japan	WB-50D
	WC-130B/E
	RB-57F
57th WRS, Avalon AS, Australia	RB-57B/C
58th WRS, Kirtland AFB, New Mexico	RB-57F

6.8 MATS to MAC

On 1st January 1966, the Military Air Transport Service was redesignated as the Military Airlift Command. This was much more than a simple name change, and the transition had its roots in the presidential election of 1960.

Since 1961, Secretary of Defense Robert S McNamara and his staff, primarily Dr Harold Brown, Director of Defense Research and Engineering, and Charles J Hitch, Assistant Secretary of Defense (Comptroller), had forced the services to consider the overall national defense needs rather than continue to compete against each other for defense dollars. The services also were made to treat each new weapon that was wanted as a total 'program package', and to produce five-year cost projections for each new weapon system.

As a result, McNamara's Department of Defense made a number of across-the-board cancellations of programs long-sought by both the military and Congress: the Navy's Missileer fighter and the Eagle long-range air-to-air missile; the nuclear powered aircraft program; the Air Force's B-70 Valkyrie strategic bomber; the Mobile Minuteman ICBM; and the Army's Nike Zeus anti-missile missile. McNamara also made the unification of various activities one of his priorities, as the Defense Intelligence Agency, the Defense Communications Agency, and the Defense Supply Agency were formed to avoid redundancy. Likewise, the Air Force's Tactical Air Command and the Army's Strategic Army Command were combined to form the US Strike Command.

Fortunately for the Military Air Transport Service, building up the nation's strategic airlift capability had a high priority in the Defense Secretary's mind. Even before the 1964 presidential election, one stated objective of the Department of Defense was to quadruple, by 1968, the airlift capability that existed in 1961. And so in 1965, the Air Force directed that the Military Air Transport Service would be redesignated as the Military Airlift Command, placing the new organization on an equal level with the other Air Force combat commands.

On 1st January 1966, the newly-designated Military Airlift Command reorganized its components: the Eastern Transport Air Force became the Twenty-First Air Force; the Western Transport Air Force was redesignated as the Twenty-Second Air Force; the Air Rescue Service became the Aerospace Rescue and Recovery Service (ARRS) under the Twenty-Third Air Force; and the Air Photographic and Charting Service was transformed into the Aerospace Audio-Visual Service (AAVS). The Air Weather Service retained its name and mission virtually intact.

The new Military Airlift Command became a more streamlined, cost-effective and capable strategic airlift force, leading to today's Air Mobility Command. But these strengths are built upon the proud history of the dedicated men and women who organized, flew and maintained the many aircraft which proudly bore the colorful blue and yellow markings of the Military Air Transport Service.

Top left: **'Whirl-O-Way', one of two Air Rescue Service SH-19As to fly the Atlantic in 1952, prepares to land at Reykjavik, Iceland, in 1960.** Courtesy of Baldur Sveinsson

Top right: **Kaman HH-43B, 62-4523, was one of 149 Huskies to equip over 60 Air Rescue Service Local Base Rescue units worldwide in 1965.** Courtesy of Clyde Gerdes Collection

Centre: **HC-54D (former SC-54D) Rescuemaster, 42-72696, of the 67th ARS, at Prestwick AB, Scotland, in September 1963. In the background is 42-72624 of the same unit.** Norm Taylor

Bottom: **HC-54D, 42-72564, shown at Elmendorf AFB, Alaska, in March 1964. By 1965, 24 Rescuemasters were still being flown by the Air Rescue Service.** Norm Taylor

Above: **Air Photographic and Charting Service RC-130A, 57-517, was one of 16 used for aerial survey and mapping. The aircraft is shown at Elmendorf AFB, Alaska, in May 1962.** Courtesy of Norm Taylor

Left: **C-130E, 63-7872, one of over one hundred of this model to equip MATS.** Courtesy of 1Lt M J Kasiuba

Below: **The Air Rescue Service gained 16 search and rescue Hercules before the end of 1965. The first of these, HC-130H, 64-14852, is shown at Edwards AFB in 1965.** Duane Kasulka, courtesy of Norm Taylor

Above: **Convair C-131D, 54-2815, of 1299th ATS(SM), 1254th ATW(SM), at Nellis AFB, Nevada, on 7th October 1960.** Douglas D Olsen

Left: **Fog-bound 55th WRS WB-50D, 49-304, at Scott AFB, Illinois, in May 1962, has the colorful day-glo bands painted on some of these aircraft.** Courtesy of Norm Taylor

Below: **RB-50E, 47-122, at Papua New Guinea, in January 1964, was formerly a SAC photo recon aircraft but was acquired by the 1370th PMW of the APCS.** Courtesy of Clyde Gerdes Collection

Above: **The Air Weather Service acquired 34 WB-47Es in 1963 to replace the ageing WB-50D. WB-47E, 51-5218, of the 55th WRS is shown at McClellan AFB, California, in October 1965.** Douglas D Olson, courtesy of Paul D Stevens

Below: **The end of an era: a MATS RB-50F, 47-142, awaits the chopping blade-equipped crane in the background at Davis-Monthan AFB, Arizona, in January 1969.** Norm Taylor

Part Two

MATS Aircraft in Color

Right: **Douglas C-47 Skytrain in pre-MATS era yellow markings standardized for domestic Air Transport Command aircraft.** Air Force, courtesy of Dana Bell

Below: **Cargo being loaded aboard Bu7101, a Naval Air Transport Service Consolidated PB2Y-3R, operated under contract by Pan American Airways, in the pre-MATS era.** PAA, courtesy of Thor Johnson

Above: **Consolidated-Vickers SA-10A 44-33939 of the 4th Rescue Squadron, at Hamilton Field, California, in the fall of 1948.** William T Larkins via David Menard

Below: **Grumman SA-16B Albatross 51-7180 of the Air Rescue Service, MATS.** Grumman via Wayne Mutza

Above: **Grumman SA-16A Albatross 51-11, and the all-black B-17 behind it most probably were attached to the 581st ARCW of the Air Resupply and Communications Service, MATS.** R McNeil via Wayne Mutza

Below: **Grumman SA-16B Albatross 51-57 of the 53rd ARS, Keflavik, Iceland.** Chessington via Larry Davis

Above: **Boeing SB-17G Flying Fortress 44-83706 in non-standard Air Rescue Service markings in Korea in 1953.** Harry Sievers via Jack M Friell

Left: **Boeing SB-17 Flying Fortress flown by the 5th Air Rescue Squadron at Selfridge AFB, Michigan.** via Lionel N Paul

Below: **North American TB-25N Mitchell 44-31178 at Midway Airport, Chicago, September 1955, carrying MATS fleet number '673'.** David Menard

Above: **Boeing SB-29B Superfortresses 44-84084 and '094 head the 5th RS, Flight 'C' line at Maxwell AFB, Alabama, in 1950.** Robert C Mikesh

Right: ***The Flying Nightmare*, B-29A 44-62264 of the 581st ARS, 581st Air Resupply and Communications Wing, Clark AB, in the Philippines, 1953. Note the Thirteenth Air Force emblem on the fin.** Bob Brice

Bottom: **SB-29B 44-84078 flown by the 52nd ARS at Harmon AB, Newfoundland, in the early 1950s.** Ken Hiltz

Above: **Boeing B-47B Stratojet, 51-2120, nicknamed *Sweet Marie*, became the AACS' second high-altitude flight check aircraft in June 1956.** US Air Force via James A Moyers

Below: **Boeing RB-50E, 47-122, of the Air Photographic and Charting Service, MATS.** via Jack M Friell

Above: **Boeing WB-50D Superfortress, 48-60, of the Air Weather Service at Alconbury, England, May 1959.** via Jack M Friell

Below: **Boeing WB-50D Superfortress, 48-108, Air Weather Service, MATS.** Robert C Mikesh

Air Weather Service Martin RB-57F 63-13292, with RB-57C 53-3832 in the background. US Air Force via Robert L Lawson

Above: **Beech RC-45G Expediter 51-11805 of the 1372nd Mapping and Charting Squadron (Aerial Photographic) at West Palm Beach AFB, Florida.** US Air Force, courtesy George M Horn

Right: **Curtiss SC-46D Commando 44-78542, as flown in the early 1950s by the 3rd Rescue Squadron, Misawa, Japan.** J Chessington, courtesy David Menard

Below: **Crowds line up to inspect a MATS Douglas C-74 Globemaster past a gleaming MATS C-47, during a September 1949 air show.** Courtesy Lionel N Paul

Above: **Douglas C-47D Skytrain 43-49281 served as a VIP transport for a four-star general.** William Balogh via David Menard

Left: **MATS was still operating nearly 50 Skytrains when C-47, 45-881, was photographed in November 1957.** Air Force

Below: **Douglas AC-47D Skytrain 43-48892 of the Airways and Air Communications Service, MATS, at Bovingdon, UK, May 1960.** Jack M Friell

MATS Pacific Division Douglas C-54 Skymaster flown by the 100th ATS, Tokyo, Japan, in 1953. Harry Sievers via Jack M Friell

Douglas C-54E Skymaster 44-9065 at Quito, Ecuador, in May 1954. Len Burke, courtesy of Harry Gann

Above: Navy/MATS R5D-3, 56540, at Westover AFB, Massachusetts, in 1949. Note the podded radar/navigation gear under the forward fuselage. Courtesy of Lionel N Paul

Below: **Douglas HC-54G Skymaster, 45-608, one of only a few ARS SC-54s not modified by Convair Fort Worth to SC-54D standard, April 1963.** Jack M Friell

Above: **Douglas C-54E Skymaster, 44-9055, lifts off with MATS C-97, C-124 and C-133s in the background.** Len Burke, courtesy Harry Gann

Below: **Douglas VC-54G, 45-627, carrying a one star general's placard at Portella, Lisbon, Portugal, August 1965.** Jack M Friell

Above: **Douglas C-74 Globemaster, 42-65409, of MATS Atlantic Division.** via Lionel N Paul

Below: **Fairchild C-82A Packet, 44-23031, in 1955 wearing the US civil registration N4833V, but still in the markings of the 1st Installation and Maintenance Squadron, AACS.** George Cull

Above: **Boeing C-97A Stratofreighter, 48-402, Pacific Division of MATS at Itazuke AB, Japan, in 1953.** Beecroft

Right: **Boeing C-97A Stratofreighter, 49-2607, over San Francisco Bay.** US Air Force

Below: **Boeing C-97A Stratofreigher, 48-416, at Paris' Orly Airport in June 1963.** via Jack M Friell

Above: **Boeing HC-97G Stratofreighter 53-217 flown by the 76th ARS, at Danang, Vietnam, in May 1965.** David Menard

Below: **Douglas C-118A Liftmaster, 53-3235, over the California desert.** Douglas Aircraft via Harry Gann

Above: **Douglas MC-118A Liftmaster, 53-3244, of the 1405th AMTW at Scott AFB, Illinois.** Jack M Friell

Below: **C-118A, 53-3290, with fluorescent orange conspicuity markings at Frankfurt, Germany, in July 1962.** Jack M Friell

Below: **Douglas C-118A Liftmaster, 51-7654, *Star of London*, flown by Navy MATS VR-22, at Harewood, New Zealand, in November 1961.** 'Bunny' Darby via Jack M Friell

Above: **Lockheed C-121A Constellation 48-616, of MATS' Atlantic Division, at Westover AFB in September 1949.** Lionel N Paul

Below: **Lockheed C-121A Constellation, 48-611, shares the ramp with a BOAC Boeing Stratocruiser at London's Heathrow Airport.** Nelson Hare

Douglas C-124A Globemaster II 51-133, 85th ATS, 1501st ATW, Pacific Division, MATS, Korea in 1953. Harry Sievers via Jack M Friell

Above: **Douglas C-124C, 52-950, MATS' 63rd Troop Carrier Wing, photographed in England in the early 1960s.** Jack M Friell

Below: **Douglas C-124C Globemaster II 52-1060 of the 1607th ATW, Dover AFB, Delaware, in May 1961.** Jack M Friell

Above: **A pair of 1501st ATW C-124C Globemaster IIs cruise above the snow capped mountains of California.** Douglas, courtesy of Harry Gann

Below: **The final Globemaster II built, C-124C, 53-052, is shown in MATS' red day-glo markings at Harewood, New Zealand, in November 1961.** 'Bunny' Darby, courtesy of Jack M Friell

Above: **Lockheed C-130E Hercules, 62-1786, of the 1608th ATW, undergoing an engine change at RAF Mildenhall, England, in October 1965.** Jack M Friell

Right: **Lockheed HC-130H, 64-14853, carrying the insignia of the Air Force Flight Test Center, Edwards AFB, California, in June 1965.** Jack M Friell

Below: **Lockheed HC-130H Hercules, 64-14862, at Eglin AFB, Florida, in 1965.** US Air Force via Norm Taylor

Above: **Convair C-131A Samaritan, 52-5790, serving as a medevac transport, at Northolt, England, September 1964.** Jack M Friell

Below: **Convair C-131A Samaritan, 52-5788, of the 1405th AMTW was used for aeromedical evacuation.** Jack M Friell

Above: **Douglas C-133B Cargomaster, 59-529, of the 1501st ATW, Travis AFB, California.** US Air Force via Norman Taylor

Below: **Douglas C-133A Cargomaster, 56-2011, shown at Andrews AFB, Maryland, in May 1962.** Robert C Mikesh

Above: **The first production Boeing C-135A Stratolifter, 60-369, over the Puget Sound in 1961.** Boeing via Alwyn T Lloyd

Below: **Boeing C-135B Stratolifter, 61-2663, powered by TF33 turbofan engines.** via Alwyn T Lloyd

Below: **MATS C-135A Stratolifter, 61-328, photographed at London Heathrow in May 1962.** Jack M Friell

Above: **Lockheed VC-140B 61-2490, flown by the 1254th ATW, shown at Andrews AFB in September 1962.** Robert C Mikesh

Right: **Lockheed C-141A, 63-8075, the first of over 100 production Starlifters for MATS/MAC.** Jack M Friell

Below: **C-141A Starlifter, 63-8090, of the 1501st ATW, Travis AFB, California, in June 1965.** Jack M Friell

Above: **Northrop F-89C Scorpions of the 57th FIS attached to MATS in 1955-1956 as part of the Iceland Air Defense Force, at Keflavik, Iceland.** via Larry Davis

Left: **Sikorsky H-5G, 48-539, of the 3rd Rescue Squadron in 1949.** J B Chessington via David Menard

Below: **Sikorsky VH-19B Chickasaw, 51-3942, of 1254th ATG(SM), Andrews AFB, MD, at NAS Anacostia, Maryland, in May 1957.** Warren Shipp via Douglas D Olson

Above: **Sikorsky SH-19B Chickasaw, 52-7552, of the 52nd ARS at Harmon AB, Newfoundland, in 1954.** Ken Hiltz

Right: **Kaman HH-43B Huskie, 62-4535, in Ethiopia in 1965 during support operations for 'Project King's Ransom'.** John Christianson

Below: **Piasecki H-21B, 52-8682, of the 1254th ATG(SM), Andrews AFB, Maryland, at NAS Anacostia, Maryland, in May 1957.** Warren Shipp via Douglas D Olson

Above: **Kaman HH-43B Huskie, 62-4523, at Le Bourget, Paris in June 1965.** Jack M Friell

Below: **Sikorsky CH-3C, 63-9683, of Detachment 15, Eastern Air Rescue Center, at Patrick AFB, Florida, off Cape Kennedy in 1965.** US Air Force via Wayne Mutza

Above: **De Havilland Canada L-20A Beaver, 52-6122, of the 52nd ARS, Harmon AB, Newfoundland, in 1954.** Ken Hiltz

Right: **Aero Commander U-4A, 55-4637, flown by the 1299th ATS, 1254th ATW(SM), from Andrews AFB, at Hampton, Virginia, in May 1963.** Ken Hampton

Below: **Sikorsky CH-3C, 61-4225, at Patrick AFB, Florida, in 1965.** Carl Damonte, courtesy of Wayne Mutza

Above: **Convair T-29B, 51-5122, in April 1963.** Jack M Friell

Left: **Lockheed T-33A, 53-5883, operated by the 1501st Flight-line Maintenance Squadron, MATS, as evidenced by the tip-tank inscription and fin badge.** Steve Brown via David Menard

Below: **Convair T-29D, 52-5832, in July 1965, converted to a VIP transport by MATS.** Jack M Friell

Above: **North American T-39A Sabreliner, 61-650, serving as a VIP transport for the 1405th Air Base Wing at Scott AFB, Illinois, May 1963.** Robert C Mikesh

Below: **Cessna U-3A, 58-2170, at McGuire AFB, New Jersey, in May 1965.** Stephen Miller

We make no apology for concluding our color section with this fine aerial shot of Douglas C-124C Globemaster II, 52-1035, of the 1501st ATW, Travis AFB, California. This aircraft is featured on the cover of this book. Air Force, courtesy of Jack M Friell

Part III

AIRCRAFT

Boeing SB-17G, 43-39457, carrying the A-1 wooden lifeboat. Air Force

Chapter 7

Amphibians

7.1 Consolidated SA-10A Catalina

Beginning in 1941, 56 Consolidated OA-10 Catalinas, which originally had been built as Navy PBY-5s, were transferred to the Army Air Corps for search and rescue missions. In 1944, the Army Air Forces received 230 PBY-5A amphibians with retractable landing gear which had been ordered by the Navy as the PBV-1A. These aircraft, designated as OA-10As, were built by Canadian Vickers, and the first delivery occurred in 1945. A further 75 OA-10Bs, equivalent to the Navy PBY-6A with a taller tail, were ordered and delivered in 1945 by Consolidated's New Orleans factory.

By the time of the Air Rescue Service's formation in March 1946 and its assignment to the Air Transport Command on 1st April, only 12 OA-10As were operational due to military budget cuts. Upon the formation of MATS and its acquisition of the Air Rescue Service in June 1948, 19 Catalinas were in the inventory, now redesignated as SA-10As.

By 1949, the Air Rescue Service was operating a high of 24 SA-10As, but these would all be retired and replaced by newer aircraft by 1952.

Top: **Consolidated-Vickers SA-10A, 44-33924, near Hamilton AFB, California, in June 1948.** William T Larkins

Above: **SA-10A, 44-33939, of the 4th Rescue Squadron, Flight A, at Hamilton AFB, California, in the fall of 1948.** William T Larkins

7.2 Grumman SA-16 Albatross

The Albatross was designed, beginning in April 1944, as a replacement for the Navy's Grumman JRF Goose. Two XJR2F-1 prototypes were ordered in November 1944, and the Pelican, as it initially was called, made its first flight on 1st October 1947. While the Navy took delivery of a relatively small number of production UF-1s as utility amphibians, the Air Force eagerly sought the Albatross as a replacement for the ageing OA-10s and SB-17s flown in the search and rescue role by the Air Rescue Service. Between 1949 and 1965, the SA-16/HU-16 Albatross served as the backbone of Air Rescue Service search and rescue operations, equipping virtually every squadron and providing a versatility unequalled by other aircraft.

SA-16A

Twenty Air Force SA-16As were ordered in May 1948 as part of a larger Navy contract for UF-1 and PF-1 amphibians. The SA-16A's first flight was made on 20th July 1949. Subsequent contracts brought the total to 290 SA-16As, which were delivered between July 1949 and December 1953.

The Albatross was a large airplane, spanning 80 feet and grossing 30,000 pounds. The main cabin could accommodate ten passengers or 12 litter patients and one attendant, although in practice the ARS crews found that many more survivors could be fitted into the airplane during emergency situations. Underwing racks usually carried two 295-gallon drop tanks, which extended the SA-16A's range to over 2,600 miles. Mid-way through the SA-16A's production run, the wing-mounted APS-31 search radar was relocated to the nose in a 'thimble' radome. Also, for use by Alaska and Greenland-based ARS squadrons, the Air Force procured 154 'triphibian' ski conversion kits for the SA-16A. The kit consisted of a 15 foot long centerline ski which attached to the hull, and swivelling skids which could be bolted to the wing floats, enabling the airplane to land and take off from snow or ice.

The introduction of the SA-16A into the inventory came none too soon, as the start of the Korean War on 25th June 1950, gave the ARS an opportunity to prove its merits. The 3rd ARS, operating within Korea with its headquarters and four flights based in Japan, received its first SA-16As in July 1950, a month after the war's start. These patrolled the Tsushima Straits between Japan and Pusan, Korea, making their first open sea rescue of a Navy pilot within a week of arriving. By the end of 1950, the SA-16As had rescued 26 airmen from the sea surrounding Korea.

In the fall of 1950, the 3rd ARS moved its SA-16As into Korea itself, flying strip alert missions from Wonsan, Seoul and, in November, from Taegu Airfield. As the war progressed, SA-16As were operated by the 3rd ARS and MATS' 581st Air Resupply and Communications Wing, based on Cho-do and Paengyong-do Islands off the North Korean coast, rescuing allied airmen as well as, for the 581st ARCW, inserting and extracting agents along the coastal mud flats. Despite often poor weather, high seas, and icing problems during water take-offs in the extreme Korean winters, the SA-16As were credited with saving 81 American and allied aircrewmen during the war.

Air Rescue Service SA-16As also performed heroic rescues away from the war zone during the early 1950s. In July 1952, one ARS SA-16A from the 58th ARS at Wheelus AB, Libya, responded to the distress calls from the crew of a British transport aircraft that had ditched in the Mediterranean. After locating the survivors and realizing that the choppy seas would be too rough for a safe take-off, the pilot surveyed his crew which gave approval, then landed the Albatross. An astounding 32 survivors were brought aboard the SA-16A and given blankets, hot food and drink. While the survivors were soon transferred to a British destroyer, the aircrew remained with the Albatross for the following three days until it was taxied and towed into port. This scenario was repeated on 23rd July 1954, when a Cathay Pacific DC-4 was shot down off Hainan Island over international waters by Communist Chinese fighters. An SA-16A from the 31st ARS at Clark AB, Philippines, rescued nine survivors of the airliner's crash.

The SA-16A also was operated by MATS' 1707th Training Squadron (Amphibian), a transition training unit located at Palm Beach International Airport, Florida. Between 1952 and 1959, the 1707th TS (Amph) flew as many as a dozen Albatrosses in the training role. An additional SA-16 was flown in 1956 by the 1739th Ferrying Squadron at Amarillo AFB, Texas, the Albatross being used as a check out and proficiency trainer for the squadron's multi-engine ferry pilots.

SA-16B

In order to overcome some operational deficiencies of the SA-16A, Grumman began the design of an improved Albatross in April 1955 as a modification of the SA-16As. The resulting SA-16B had a significant performance improvement through a 16ft 8in increase in its wingspan, the use of cambered leading edges on the wing, a 206-gallon fuel tank built within each wing float, larger aileron and horizontal tail surfaces, and a taller tail as well as other minor improvements. A total of 86 SA-16As were modified to the SA-16B standard, either through a Grumman modification program, or as each SA-16A became due for its IRAN (Inspect and Repair As Necessary) cycle.

Using the improved HU-16B (as the SA-16B was redesignated in 1962), two crews from the 48th ARS, Eglin AFB, Florida, set two world class records in March 1963: flying an average speed of 153.65 mph over a 1,000 km closed course while carrying a 5,000-kg payload, and carrying the same payload to a record height of 19,747 feet.

The Albatross was used for search and rescue missions early in the Vietnam War when two HU-16Bs from the 33rd ARS, Naha AB, Okinawa, were deployed to Korat RTAFB, Thailand, in June 1964. The aircraft performed airborne rescue control during 'Yankee Team' operations in Laos, teaming with Kaman HH-43Bs and Douglas A-1s to locate, co-ordinate, and direct the rescue of downed airmen. Three HU-16Bs from the 31st ARS, Clark AB, Philippines, also were sent to Danang AB in South Vietnam during June for search and rescue missions in the Gulf of Tonkin. These HU-16Bs were replaced by September 1967 by the Douglas HC-54 and Lockheed HC-130. By 1965, the HU-16 was being phased out in favor of newer aircraft, although it still filled an important role with the following squadrons:

33rd ARS, Naha AB, Okinawa
41st ARS, Hamilton AFB, California
48th ARS, Eglin AFB, Florida
54th ARS, Goose AB, Labrador
55th ARS, Kindley AFB, Bermuda
58th ARS, Wheelus AB, Libya

Above: **Grumman SA-16A, 51-04?, at Boise, Idaho, in August 1952.** William T Larkins

Left: **SA-16A, 51-7195, has its landing gear lowered to provide stability in the water.** Air Force, courtesy of Wayne Mutza

Bottom: **SA-16B, 51-7200, the first SA-16A to be modified to an SA-16B, carries the insignia of the Air Force Flight Test Center at Edwards AFB, California.** Courtesy of Robert Esposito

Chapter 8

Bombers

8.1 Boeing B-17 Flying Fortress

Design of the Boeing B-17 was begun in 1934, and first flight of the prototype Model 299 was made in July 1935. Following 13 service test YB-17s, over 12,000 Flying Fortresses were accepted by the Army Air Forces and were used as one of two main AAF heavy bombers during the Second World War. Only a few hundred B-17s equipped the Strategic Air Command when it was formed in 1946, and most of these aircraft were quickly scrapped as newer designs became operational.

TB-17H/SB-17G

Approximately 130 B-17Gs were converted for the Air-Sea Rescue role as B-17Hs and TB-17Hs toward the end of the Second World War. These aircraft carried a Higgins A-1 self-righting lifeboat fastened to their bellies by cables attached to the airplane's bomb shackles. This boat was able to accommodate twelve persons, although as many as 36 were carried in tests.

In 1948, some 25 B-17H/TB-17Hs were in the Air Rescue Service inventory, and all were redesignated as SB-17Gs. In the September 1949 Air Rescue Service reorganization, seven Air Rescue Service squadrons were formed worldwide, the ARS having acquired the SAR units based in Hawaii, the Far East and Europe earlier in the year. Each squadron had one headquarters-based Flight A and, in most instances, three deployed Flights – B, C and D. All flights were equipped with from one to four SB-17Gs as well as other SAR aircraft types.

The A-1 airborne lifeboat carried by the SB-17G weighed approximately 3,200 pounds when loaded with provisions, was made of laminated mahogany and birch plywood with 20 watertight compartments, and was 27 feet long and 7½ feet in beam. When survivors had been located, the SB-17G pilot flew the airplane into the wind at 1,500 feet and 120 mph. When directly over the survivors, the boat was released. As the boat fell away, a static line attached to the keel of the SB-17G's bomb-bay catwalk would deploy three standard 48-foot cargo parachutes, while a 200-yard rocket line fired behind the boat. As the A-1 struck the water, two rocket-propelled 200-yard lines were projected from the sides of the boat. The collapsed parachutes acted as sea anchors, holding the boat in position while the survivors floated downwind to grasp the boat or its sidelines.

Top: **Crewmen maneuver an A-1 practice drop boat beneath SB-17H, 43-37652, of ARS Detachment 8 at McChord Field, Washington.** Gordon S Williams, courtesy of Scott A Thompson

Left: **SB-17G, 44-83754, of the 5th Rescue Squadron Flight A landing at Lowry AFB, Colorado, in 1950 with 'MATS' under its left wing.** Robert L Lawson

Center: **One of the last operational Air Rescue Service SB-17Gs, 44-83700, photographed late in 1955. Note MATS insignia below bulged scanner's window.** Air Force, courtesy of Clyde Gerdes Collection

Bottom: **B-25J, 44-30457, probably was converted to a TB-25N for its service as a proficiency trainer by MATS.** Air Force

Once aboard the boat, the survivors released the parachutes, started the two air-cooled four-stroke engines or hoisted the boat's sails, and navigated using an area map which had been placed aboard showing the position of the crew and the desired route to be taken. The A-1 lifeboat was supplied with food, water and clothing for transporting 12 people for approximately two weeks. Thirty desalination kits also were provided, and a device was attached to the cylinder heads of the engines which produced two gallons of distilled water for every gallon of fuel used.

Air Rescue Service use of the SB-17G reached a high in 1949, when 66 aircraft were in its inventory. This number steadily declined during the early 1950s as early SC-54s and the SB-29B 'Super Dumbo' became operational. During the Korean War, the SB-17G was used by both the 2nd ARS in the Philippines and Okinawa, and the 3rd ARS, headquartered at Johnson AB, Japan.

These SB-17Gs often carried defensive machine guns as they orbited offshore over the Sea of Japan and Yellow Sea. By 1955, only four Air Rescue Service SB-17Gs were on hand, including SB-17Gs 44-83511 and 44-83700, and all were transferred out by the end of the year.

A small number of SB-17Gs were used for air-sea rescue training in the late 1940s by the 5th Rescue Squadron. And, on 21st January 1950, the 2156th Air Rescue Unit was activated at MacDill AFB, Florida, taking over SAR training with the SB-17Gs as well as other ARS aircraft.

RB/WB-17

The Boeing B-17 was used for weather reconnaissance by the Army Air Forces Weather Wing beginning in 1944, reaching a high of 22 aircraft in 1945. Upon MATS' formation in 1948, the Air Weather Service possessed ten RB-17s, although this number quickly declined to two-to-four aircraft beginning in 1949 as the WB-29 became operational. The last WB-17 (as the aircraft were redesignated on 30th August 1950) was retired by the Air Weather Service in 1955.

VB-17/TB-17G/H

A small number of TB-17s were used as administrative and training aircraft by the Military Air Transport Service during the late 1940s. In the fall of 1948, the Atlantic Division of MATS operated four training B-17s beginning in September, while up to four administrative B-17s were flown beginning in the same month. Sixteen of these TB/VB-17s were flown by MATS in 1948, the last being retired in 1950.

8.2 North American B-25 Mitchell

North American Aviation Co began the design of the B-25 in 1938 in response to an Army Air Corps specification for a twin-engined medium attack bomber. The NA-40 which resulted featured twin tails and a crew of three, with the pilot and co-pilot seated in tandem under a long 'greenhouse' canopy. The prototype NA-40-1, powered by 1,100 hp P&W R-1830 Twin Wasp engines, made its first flight in January 1939, but disappointing performance resulted in a switch to 1,350 hp Wright Cyclones. While the NA-40-2's performance improved with these engines, the airplane was destroyed during tests at Wright Field and a further redesign effort produced the NA-62, with 1,700 hp R-2600 engines and a revised fuselage housing the pilot and co-pilot in side-by-side seats. The NA-62/B-25 made its first flight in August 1940, and the Air Corps placed an order for 184 B-25s. Only 24 B-25s were built, however, before a switch was made to the B-25A, 40 of which were constructed, and 120 B-25Bs, to complete the contract.

The first of over 1,600 B-25Cs began to be delivered at the end of 1941, followed by nearly 2,300 B-25Ds built at North American's Dallas, Texas, plant. Over 400 B-25Gs and one thousand B-25Hs were built, these airplanes carrying a 75mm cannon in the nose and, in the B-25H, side blisters for machine guns. The final production model of the Mitchell was the B-25J, which reverted back to the transparent nose housing a bombardier's station, although a number of B-25Js later were built with an eight-gun 'solid' nose.

In 1943, ten B-25Ds were converted by North American to photo reconnaissance F-10s, featuring additional bomb-bay mounted fuel tanks and cameras installed in the rear fuselage and in chin fairings for tri-metrogon photography. In the early 1950s, 47 TB-25Ns were produced by Hayes Aircraft Corp of Birmingham, Alabama, by converting B-25Js to multi-engine proficiency trainers.

The Military Air Transport Service acquired two B-25s when it was formed in June 1948, but it is not known whether these aircraft were operated as TB-25 proficiency trainers or as VB-25 staff transports. The Airways and Air Communications Service was assigned seven B-25s in 1953 to be used as facilities checking aircraft. However, the Mitchells presented maintenance and logistic problems and were not considered suitable for this mission. Also, the basic design of the B-25 was not deemed appropriate. The AACS had designed a portable console which would provide a facilities checking capability for future aircraft. Due to the B-25's cockpit design, however, this console would have had to be placed in the aft compartment where the pilot would not have had access to it in flight.

TB-25J/N

In 1953, MATS gained over 40 TB-25Js as multi-engine pilot proficiency trainers. Many of these aircraft were assigned to the 1360th Air Base Group, Orlando AFB, Florida, which became Air Rescue Service Headquarters in April 1954, and to MATS Headquarters at Andrews AFB. These latter TB-25Js originally had been assigned to the 1050th Air Base Wing/1401st Air Base Wing at Andrews AFB, which were attached to Headquarters US Air Force Command, but the unit was reassigned to MATS in August 1952.

Most of these aircraft later were modified to TB-25Ns by Hayes Air Craft Corporation at their Birmingham, Alabama, modification center. These TB-25Ns continued their MATS service at Andrews AFB until October 1957, when the 1401st ABW was assigned back to Headquarters US Air Force Command.

Several TB-25s were flown by the 1708th Ferrying Group as multi-engine proficiency trainers. Beginning in mid-1953, the 1708th FYG Headquarters or the 1708th FYG Detachment 12 at Kelly AFB, Texas, were flying two TB-25s, while the 1708th FYG's multi-engine ferrying squadron, the 1739th FYS, Amarillo AFB, Texas, was using two TB-25Ns for proficiency training.

Left: **TB-25N, 44-30628 (fleet number 602) photographed at St Louis, in 1956.**
R Burgess, courtesy of Robert Esposito

Center: **TB-25N, 44-30425 (fleet number 669) with an over-size MATS insignia.**
Robert Esposito collection

Bottom left and right: **North American F-10, 43-3374, of the Air Photographic and Charting Service, MATS, at Davis-Monthan AFB in December 1957. Note nose camera ports for tri-metrogon camera.**
Courtesy of Norman Avery

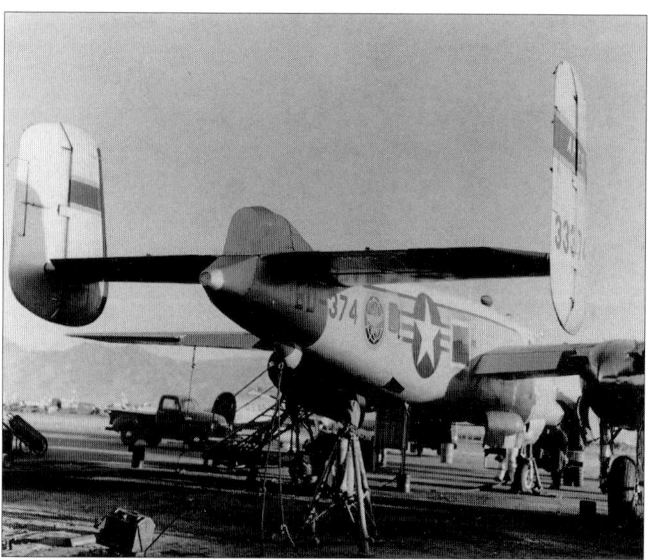

F-10

As mentioned, ten B-25Ds had been converted to photo reconnaissance F-10s by North American in 1943. Several of these aircraft survived to be operated into the early 1950s by MATS' Air Photographic and Charting Service. At least one F-10, 43-3374, was flown from Buckley Field to Talara, Peru, to fly mapping and charting missions. This airplane was rescued from the scrapyard at Davis-Monthan AFB in 1958, when it was flown to the North American plant to be reworked to resemble Jimmy Doolittle's B-25B for the Doolittle Raiders' reunion in Las Vegas. This airplane now rests in the Air Force Museum collection.

In 1954, MATS was operating a high of 58 B-25s of several models. By 1958, all Mitchells had been transferred or retired from MATS service.

8.3 Douglas B-26 Invader

The Douglas Invader was designed to meet a 1940 Army Air Corps requirement for a fast, low-level attack aircraft and medium altitude precision bomber. In June 1941, three prototype XA-26s were ordered, the first flying on 10th July 1942. The initial production model, the A-26B, featured six 50-caliber machine guns in the nose with two remotely-controlled turrets amidships, each with two 50-caliber guns. The A-26B carried a crew of three: pilot, navigator/radio operator, and gunner. Douglas built 1,355 A-26Bs at its Long Beach, California, and Tulsa, Oklahoma, factories. The A-26C featured a transparent 'bombardier' nose, and a widened fuselage and dual controls for the co-pilot, who also acted as bombardier. Nearly 1,100 A-26Cs were built at Long Beach and Tulsa beginning in 1945. The Invader was used in both the European and Pacific Theaters during the Second World War, and for night interdiction and reconnaissance during the Korean War. The Invaders were redesignated as B-26s in June 1948.

Upon the formation of MATS in June 1948, at least one B-26 was being flown by the 535th Air Base Group, Fort Pepperell, Newfoundland, an organization reassigned to MATS in the same month. By 1949, four B-26s were flown by MATS at various locations as proficiency trainers and 'base hacks'.

The 1739th Ferrying Squadron, 1708th Ferrying Group, Amarillo AFB, Texas, operated the Invader from approximately 1951 to 1958. By August 1953, the unit had two B-26s used for pilot checkout and familiarization training and occasionally as administrative transports. These aircraft, a TB-26B and TB-26C, provided important training to ferry pilots, as many Far East Air Force B-26s were being returned to the continental United States (CONUS) as new Tactical Air Command B-57 Canberras replaced them beginning in 1956.

Returning these service-weary B-26s presented problems to their ferry pilots as only a few aircraft had HF radios and LORAN sets installed, and the aircraft had to be led by MATS C-124s or B-29s. And, despite the installation of long-range ferry tanks, the long overwater flights had to be delayed often due to adverse winds. None of the aircraft were equipped with de-icing or anti-icing equipment or cockpit heat. Because of this, the ferrying crews of some USAF-Europe B-26s returning across the North Atlantic in the winter of 1955 suffered frostbite. A new MATS policy was implemented by the 1708th Ferrying Wing in July 1956, directing that the ferrying of B-26s across the North Atlantic would only take place from May through October.

The 1739th Ferrying Squadron at Amarillo AFB retained three B-26s through 1957. By the following year, all of the squadron's Invaders were gone as the B-26 had been retired from the Tactical Air Command.

8.4 Boeing B-29 Superfortress

As the airplane which brought the Second World War to the Japanese homeland, and finally ushered in the Atomic Age with missions over Hiroshima and Nagasaki, the Boeing B-29 Superfortress has been described as the most influential airplane in the history of aviation. Between April 1941 and May 1946, 3,970 Superfortresses were built in five models, with subsequent modifications producing photo-recon, search and rescue, weather reconnaissance and aerial refueling versions.

SB-29B

Toward the end of the war, a number of B-29s were modified to perform the search and rescue role, carrying rescue and survival equipment while accompanying B-29 bombers on their flights to and from Japan. Upon the formation of MATS in 1948, only three SB-29s served with the Air Rescue Service. By 1950 this number had grown to seven, but by 1952 nineteen SB-29s were flying with ARS squadrons. These SB-29As and SB-29Bs were equipped with a search radar, its antenna housed in a thimble-shaped radome behind the nosewheel doors, combination observation/gunner's blisters on the fuselage sides, and increased fuel capacity giving the airplane a 15-hour endurance. The SB-29 carried a 15-man aluminum A-3 lifeboat on its belly. This 3,000 lb boat could be dropped by parachute to survivors, providing food, water, a sail and enough fuel for its air-cooled engines to give it a 900 mile range.

The SB-29s played a significant role during the Korean War with the 2nd ARS, based in the Philippine Islands and on Okinawa, and with the 3rd ARS in Japan. Squadron SB-29s followed bomber flights across the Yellow Sea and Sea of Japan, orbiting offshore until the bombers returned from their missions and trailing the last bomber out.

37th ARS SB-29s also escorted FEAF Bomber Command B-29s on night bombing missions when Communist night fighters became a threat. The SB-29s continued to serve with the Air Rescue Service through the mid-1950s, with roughly 15 aircraft on hand in 1955. By the end of 1956, these 'Super Dumbos' had all been replaced by the Douglas SC-54D, partly due to the SB-29's high fuel consumption.

RB/WB-29

The RB-29 had been used for weather reconnaissance by the AAF Weather Service since 1946, participating in weather recon and atomic fallout sampling missions during the atomic bomb tests in Nevada, and at Bikini and Eniwetok Atolls in the South Pacific. Air Weather Service RB-29s made the first weather recon flights over the North Pole in March 1947, and the first low-level and night penetrations of a hurricane were made by an AWS RB-29 in October 1947.

When the Air Weather Service was assigned to MATS in June 1948, some 67 RB-29s equipped its weather reconnaissance squadrons worldwide. Each squadron was responsible for flying specific routes on mostly overwater missions lasting up to 16 hours. To distinguish these, each route was given the name of a bird, often with an added qualifier to denote route variations. 'Lark', 'Stork', 'Ptarmigan', 'Loon Charlie', 'Buzzard Hotel', 'Gull Papa', and 'Falcon Alpha' applied to specific weather recon flight tracks. By the early 1950s, these flights were being made by WB-29s (RB-29s being redesignated as WB-29s on 30th August 1950) from the following squadrons:

53rd WRS, Kindley AB, Bermuda, and RAF Burtonwood, England
54th WRS, Anderson AFB, Guam
55th WRS, McClellan AFB, California, and Hickam AFB, Hawaii
56th WRS, Yokota AB, Japan
57th WRS, Hickam AFB, Hawaii
58th WRS, Eielson AFB, Alaska
59th WRS, Ladd AFB, Alaska, and Kindley AFB, Bermuda

Air Weather Service RB/WB-29s made invaluable contributions to the Korean War effort, with the first wartime weather recon mission being flown over Korea within 24 hours of the outbreak of hostilities. An Air Weather Service RB-29 led the first B-29 strike against North Korea from Japan on 13th July 1950, earning its pilot, 1Lt Fred R Spies, an Oak Leaf Cluster to his Distinguished Flying Cross. In February 1952, the first WB-29 crews to complete 50 combat missions, from the 56th WRS, were transferred to the United States. In fact, the 56th WRS and its WB-29s was the only Air Force unit to have had an aircraft over enemy-held territory every day of the war between June 1950 and June 1952, accumulating some 750 combat missions in the process. One AWS WB-29 pilot from the 514th Reconnaissance Squadron (VLR) Weather, Captain Charles R Cloniger, was awarded the Distinguished Flying Cross in September 1950. Despite having to feather one engine on his WB-29, Cloniger continued the recon mission and determined the position and intensity of a typhoon, knowing that the return of this vital information would be used to plan loading operations in preparation for the Inchon invasion.

Air Weather Service WB-29s were involved in another highly classified mission: worldwide detection of atomic explosions. The Air Force Office of Atomic Detection (AFOAT) had been established in the late 1940s to co-ordinate US efforts to detect and evaluate fission products from foreign nuclear explosions. Air Weather Service RB/WB-29s were given the assignment as they already were performing routine weather reconnaissance flights in the areas of interest, and could accomplish the atomic detection mission with only minor variations in their flight tracks. It was an Air Weather Service RB-29, flying a routine weather recon track from Japan to Alaska on 3rd September 1949, that had detected the radiation cloud which later was confirmed to have come from the detonation of Russia's first atomic bomb. Testing of classified Atmospheric Measuring Equipment (AME), carried on AWS WB-29s, began in October 1950. The Atomic Energy Detection System (AEDS) was established in 1952, and Air Weather Service WB-29 squadrons were deployed to intercept atomic debris in areas surrounding the Soviet Union where it was likely to be found. The system was successful, as an AWS WB-29 detected the explosion of Russia's first hydrogen bomb on 12th August 1953.

Air Weather Service use of the WB-29 reached a peak in 1954, when 80 aircraft were on hand. However, by March 1954 the WB-29 was beginning to show signs that its days with the Air Weather Service were numbered, as most of the dozen aircraft flown by the 54th WRS were not available for the typhoon season due to excessive airframe corrosion.

In nine years of service, the WB-29s suffered eight crashes taking the lives of 58 crewmen, the first occurring on 26th October 1952, when all ten men aboard a 54th WRS WB-29 were lost while making a low-level penetration of 'Typhoon Wilma', 300 miles east of Leyte. The WB-29s began to be replaced by the WB-50 in November 1955, and by late 1957 the last two AWS WB-29s were retired.

B-29

A small number of B-29s were operated by the newly-organized Air Resupply and Communications Service, MATS, as psychological warfare/propaganda and agent insertion aircraft during the Korean War. These jet-black B-29s were modified by removing all guns except the tail turret, and by installing a 'Joe hole' in the airplane's belly through which agents could be dropped behind enemy lines.

Three ARCS wings were organized at Mountain Home AFB, Idaho: the 580th ARCW in April 1951, the 581st ARCW in July 1951, and the 582nd ARCW in September 1952. The 581st ARCW was the first wing to deploy when it moved to Clark AB, Philippines, in July 1952, later relocating to Kadena AB, Okinawa. 581st ARCW B-29 missions included agent drops over North Korea and Communist China, psychological warfare leaflet drops over enemy-held territory, and drops of leaflets warning civilians of impending bomb attacks. It was on one of these latter missions that an ARCS B-29, piloted by Col John K Arnold, Commander of the 581st ARCW, was shot down near the Yalu River by three Communist MiGs on 12th January 1953. Eleven of the 14 crewmen survived the ordeal, only to be interned in China as spies for the next 2½ years. On 3rd August 1955, Col Arnold and his crew became the last American POWs of the Korean War to be released by the Communist Chinese. By this time, however, the Air Resupply and Communications Service had been detached from MATS (on 1st January 1954), and its B-29s had slipped into obscurity.

2.5 Boeing B-47 Stratojet

The Boeing Aircraft Co began studies for a jet bomber as early as 1943, but the design of the Model 450, which became the B-47, was initiated in October 1945. Following extensive design changes, the Air Force ordered two prototypes in May 1946, the first of which made its maiden flight on 17th December 1947. Following an initial production contract for ten B-47As, 380 B-47Bs were built with deliveries to the Strategic Air Command beginning in mid-1951. Utilizing three production lines spread across the country, over 1,600 B-47E and RB-47E Stratojets were constructed by Boeing, Douglas and Lockheed between January 1953 and February 1957. At its peak in 1957, Strategic Air Command had some 1,800 Stratojets in service, including

Above: **TB-26B, 44-34650, of MATS' Continental Division photographed at Wold-Chamberlain Field.** Logan Coombs, courtesy of Douglas D Olson

Left: **MATS Continental Division Douglas TB-26B, 44-34622, has a transparent bombardier's nose.** Courtesy of David Menard

Below: **SB-29B, 44-84078, of the 3rd ARS** *en route* **to the Sea of Japan with an aluminum A-3 lifeboat.** Air Force, courtesy of NASM

the final production version, the RB-47K, of which 15 were built for weather or photo reconnaissance.

B-47B/ETB-47B

Since the late 1940s, the Airways and Air Communications Service had been conducting operational flight checks of navigational aids, Ground Controlled Approach (GCA) and Instrument Landing System (ILS) installations, and airport control tower procedures at its numerous facilities scattered around the world. These checks were accomplished in large part by AACS AC-47s and AC-54s. As faster and higher-flying jet aircraft became operational during the early 1950s, it became evident that procedures for conducting high-speed and high-altitude operational flight checks would have to be established.

On 12th November 1953, the Air Proving Ground Command published a test directive containing three objectives:

- to evaluate current air traffic control facilities and procedures used by high-speed and high-altitude aircraft, and to recommend new procedures, if required;
- to determine the space patterns and capabilities of the current ground navigational aids at altitudes of 20,000 feet and above;
- to determine whether there was a requirement for regularly-scheduled high-altitude flight checking and, if so, to develop special high-altitude flight checking procedures to supplement the low-level methods then in use by the AACS.

The Air Proving Ground Command began this program in 1954 with assistance from the SAC and the AACS, but by December 1954 the project was suspended with only nine of the 35 scheduled project missions completed due to the project aircraft being reassigned to a higher priority project. In June 1955, the remaining missions of the project were assumed solely by the 1800th AACS Wing, at Tinker AFB, Oklahoma, with a target completion date of 1st August 1956.

A B-47B, 50-017, modified as an ETB-47B by the installation of an APS-23 radar, a modified flight checking panel with two recorders, and various additional modifications, was delivered to the wing by the Air Proving Ground Command on 7th June 1955. However, the airplane, with the nickname 'The Navaider' painted on its nose, was immediately grounded at Tinker AFB for an acceptance inspection. The project languished for the next five months due to poor weather, maintenance and supply problems on the B-47, and due to the project's B-47 aircraft commander spending 'considerable time' in performing his administrative duties as Chief of the Office of Flight Operations, and in attending the transition school with his co-pilot at McConnell AFB, Kansas, until mid-October.

The flight checks eventually performed by the AACS ETB-47B were flown at 20,000 feet, 30,000 feet, and 40,000 feet for navigational facilities, while actual approaches and landings were made to check airfield ILS and GCA performance. At the same time, AACS AC-47s and C-45s were used to make comparative flight checks. Checks were made to both Air Force facilities, such as at Eglin AFB and MacDill AFB, Florida, Tinker AFB, Oklahoma, Davis-Monthan AFB, Arizona, and McGuire AFB, New Jersey, and at CAA facilities in Arizona, Oklahoma and Kansas. However, due to continuing poor weather, maintenance and supply problems, by the end of June 1956 the high-altitude project was considered only 41 percent complete.

A further blow to the program came on 21st June 1956, when the ETB-47B was transferred to a different program and its test gear was removed. A replacement B-47B, 51-2120, was gained on the same day, although this airplane required two months to be inspected and instrumented for the high-altitude project. B-47B, 51-2120, nicknamed 'Sweet Marie' and 'The Sooner', completed the project and became the AACS' high-altitude flight check aircraft for the following six years. On 9th October 1962, after the AACS had been renamed the Air Force Communications Service and was detached from MATS, the airplane was transferred to the 340th Bomb Wing, Whiteman AFB, Missouri, and AFCS C-140As assumed the high-altitude flight check mission.

WB-47B

A single B-47B was assigned to the Air Weather Service in November 1957, in conjunction with the US Weather Bureau's National Hurricane Research Project, or 'Project Stormfury'. B-47B, 51-2115, was transferred from the Strategic Air Command and was modified for weather reconnaissance by General Precision Laboratories. The Stratojet conducted hurricane research beginning in 1957, flying out of Pinecastle AFB, Florida (renamed McCoy AFB in May 1958). By 1961, the WB-47B was being flown by the 55th WRS, McClellan AFB, California, performing high-altitude cloud photography in a program to determine the accuracy of the weather satellite Tiros II. This AWS Stratojet was retired in 1963, becoming a training aid for Air Training Command student mechanics at Amarillo AFB, Texas.

WB-47E

By the early 1960s, the Air Weather Service's fleet of weather reconnaissance aircraft still included 43 ageing WB-50Ds. The first of five converted WC-130Bs would not become available until late 1962, and the eagerly-awaited WC-130E was not slated to become operational until 1965. The B-47Es then being retired from SAC, however, were immediately available, still had time on their airframes, and performance-wise could do twice the job at less cost than the accident-prone WB-50Ds.

Photographs on the opposite page:

Top left: **SB-29B, 44-84054, of the 5th Rescue Squadron Flight C at Maxwell AFB, Alabama.** Courtesy of Clyde Gerdes Collection

Top right: **SB-29B with spartan Air Rescue Service markings.** Courtesy of Clyde Gerdes Collection

Center: **RB-29, 45-21717, of the 308th WRG at Fairfield-Suisun AFB, California, in September 1948. The Air Weather Service insignia is on the airplane's tail.** William T Larkins

Center left: **Air Weather Service WB-29A, 44-62225, photographed at McClellan AFB, California, in February 1955.** Air Force

Center right: **B-47B, 51-2120, was the second B-47, acquired in June 1956, by the AACS for a special high-altitude flight check program.** Air Force, courtesy of Clyde Gerdes Collection

Bottom: **WB-47E, 51-2373, of the 55th WRS, McClellan AFB, photographed in October 1965.** Douglas D Olson

484054

WEATHER AIR SERVICE
521717
WEATHER RECONNAISSANCE

U.S. AIR FORCE

U.S. AIR FORCE

U.S. AIR FORCE
WEATHER
012373

Above: **WB-47B, 51-2115, was originally acquired by the Air Weather Service to conduct hurricane research during 'Project Stormfury' in 1957. The airplane is shown at Scott AFB in May 1961.** David Ostrowski, courtesy of Paul Stevens

Left: **MATS Air Weather Service WB-50D, 48-108, of the 53rd WRS, taxying at Hunter AFB, Georgia.** Clyde Gerdes collection

Below: **RB-50E, 47-122, was possibly the only RB-50E flown by the Air Photographic and Charting Service.** Air Force

Between March and November 1963, 34 WB-47Es were converted by the Lockheed-Georgia Company and delivered to the Air Weather Service, with the 55th WRS, McClellan AFB, California, receiving the first airplane on 20th March. Other units receiving the WB-47Es in 1963 were the 53rd WRS, Hunter AFB, Georgia; the 54th WRS, Anderson AFB, Guam; the 56th WRS, Yokota AB, Japan; and the 55th WRS, Detachment 1, Eielson AFB, Alaska. The 57th WRS, Hickam AFB, Hawaii, began operating its WB-47Es in 1965.

The converted WB-47Es were equipped with the AMQ-19 Meteorological System, which included a new doppler navigator and computer; highly accurate temperature, pressure and dewpoint measuring instruments; data handling, storage and communications sub-systems; and an APS-64 search radar used for storm detection and navigation. The WB-47Es were flown above 18,000 feet along standard AWS routes, recording observations every 150 miles and releasing dropsondes every 450 miles. The three-man crew consisted of the pilot, co-pilot/meteorological operator, and the navigator, who also had a battery of weather indicators and recorders at his station.

In addition to conducting daily synoptic weather flights, these WB-47Es performed special weather reconnaissance flights in satellite and missile recovery areas and for early manned space flights, and air sampling missions for the Atomic Energy Commission and other government agencies. The Stratojets also flew high-altitude hurricane and typhoon reconnaissance missions, although storm penetration flights were forbidden due to structural concerns. In fact, the only known major WB-47E accidents during its service with MATS occurred on 23rd November 1963, when a 55th WRS Stratojet crashed while landing at Lajes Field, Azores, and in April 1964 when a 55th WRS, Det.1, WB-47E crashed at Eielson AFB, Alaska. By 1965, 32 WB-47Es still served the Air Weather Service with the 53rd WRS, 55th WRS, and the 57th WRS, although the Stratojets were to be retired by October 1969.

8.6 Boeing B-50 Superfortress

While the B-50 bore a strong resemblance to the B-29 Superfortress, having initially been placed into production as the B-29D, the B-50 shared only one-quarter of its components with the earlier aircraft. Major differences included a switch to 3,500 hp Pratt & Whitney R-4360 Wasp Major engines in revised nacelles, a taller fin and rudder, strengthened landing gear, and a 20 percent increase in the airplane's gross weight. Following the B-50A's first flight on 25th June 1947, some 425 B-50s were built in four basic models, although most of these aircraft underwent later conversions to perform photographic and weather reconnaissance and aerial tanker missions.

RB-50E/RB-50F

In 1951, 43 RB-50Bs, which previously had been modified for the Strategic Air Command's 91st SRW, were again modified: 14 becoming RB-50E photo-recon aircraft; 14 to RB-50F photo-mapping platforms; and 15 designated as RB-50G electronic reconnaissance aircraft. The photo-mapping aircraft were assigned to SAC's 338th SRS (Medium, Photographic-Mapping), at Ramey AFB, Puerto Rico, moving to Forbes AFB, Kansas, late in 1952. On 1st May 1954, the mapping and charting functions of the parent 55th SRW were transferred to MATS, and the RB-50Fs moved to Palm Beach AFB, Florida, as part of the newly-organized 1370th Photo Mapping Group. The 1370th PMG moved its headquarters to Turner AFB, Georgia, in February 1959 (and was upgraded to wing status in January 1960), its RB-50Fs ranging far and wide while deployed with 1371st MCS Aerial Survey Teams to various parts of the world on photo-mapping missions.

On 1st October 1965, the 1370th PMW was detached from the APCS and assigned directly to MATS. The last RB-50F was flown from Turner AFB to retirement at Davis-Monthan AFB, Arizona, in May 1966. As a matter of pure conjecture, at least one photo-recon RB-50E, 47-122, has been photographed in APCS colors, and probably was acquired from the Strategic Air Command by the 1370th PMW as a replacement aircraft.

WB-50D

The saga of the WB-50D's use by the Air Weather Service could be likened to a Greek tragedy. The Air Weather Service first coveted the B-50 for the weather reconnaissance role late in 1950, but Air Staff indicated that the new airplanes were not then available as weather reconnaissance occupied a rather low position on the Air Force mission food chain. Two years later, the Air Weather Service was given a choice: the B-50 or the B-47. Following a study of the relative merits of the two aircraft, the AWS determined that the B-50 would be expensive to convert and maintain, but that the B-47 also would be expensive to modify and could not penetrate storms safely. The Air Weather Service much preferred accepting new C-130 Hercules' modified for the weather recon mission, but when it learned that these aircraft would not be available for four or five years, it reluctantly chose the B-50. A contract was signed on 8th April 1955, with Lockheed Air Services chosen to do the modifications. What followed was a comedy of errors between Lockheed Air Services and the Air Weather Service, with the AWS accusing Lockheed of foot-dragging and poor work, and Lockheed in turn accusing the AWS of causing delays by constantly changing the specifications.

This resulted in the Air Weather Service accepting the converted WB-50Ds still in need of considerable maintenance to make them airworthy. Once in service, the 69 converted WB-50Ds proved to be maintenance nightmares, with excessive oil leakage and consumption, leaking exhaust stacks, ignition problems, and outright engine failures all too common. A second concern was for pilot transition training, as former WB-29 pilots appeared to be underestimating the not-so-subtle differences between the B-29 and the B-50. The net result was that, between 31st August 1956, the date of the first WB-50D crash, and the last airplane's retirement in the fall of 1965, 13 crashes took the lives of 66 aircrewmen, the worst accident record in Air Weather Service history.

In spite of these shortcomings, the WB-50D was the mainstay for Air Weather Service weather reconnaissance squadrons from 1956 to 1963 and beyond, even after the AWS began to receive the first WC-130s. During the Cuban Crisis of October 1962, WB-50Ds from the 53rd WRS at Kindley AB, Bermuda, supplemented by three aircraft and crews from the 55th WRS at McClellan AFB, California, made the twice-daily weather recon flights around Cuba, covering 3,350 miles during each circuit.

Above left: **RB-50F, 47-162, flying with the Aerial Survey Team at Papua New Guinea, in January 1964.** Courtesy of Clyde Gerdes Collection

Above right: **This RB-50F, 47-121, was photographed in October 1965 at McClellan AFB after the 1370th PMW had been assigned directly to MATS.** Douglas D Olson

Left: **WB-50D, 49-300, of the 55th WRS, McClellan AFB, California.** Courtesy of Robert Esposito

Below: **TB-50A, 46-007, carrying the insignia of the 55th WRS.** Peter M Bowers, courtesy of Larry Davis

By 1965, only two weather recon squadrons were still operating the WB-50D: the 54th WRS at Anderson AFB, Guam, and the 56th WRS at Yokota AB, Japan. The last Air Weather Service WB-50D was flown to Davis-Monthan AFB from Yokota AB on 14th September 1965.

TB-50A

Anticipating the planned conversion, in November 1955, from the WB-29 to the WB-50, the Air Weather Service acquired a small number of TB-50s in the fall of 1954 to cross-train its aircrews. Possibly one of these aircraft, TB-50A, 46-007, had the insignia of the 55th WRS, McClellan AFB, California, displayed on its forward fuselage.

The 1742nd ATS, Palm Beach AFB, Florida, began a formal training program on the B-50 on 1st January 1956, functioning as the Continental Division's Transition Training Unit on the type. The squadron operated up to four WB/TB-50s at least through 1957.

Finally, early in 1956 the 1707th ATW, Heavy (Training), at Palm Beach AFB, was given the responsibility for base support for the US Weather Bureau's National Hurricane Research Project. Two Air Weather Service TB-50s used in the project were received in July 1956, to be joined by a 55th WRS WB-47B in November 1957. It is possible that the previously mentioned 55th WRS TB-50A was based at Palm Beach AFB for this latter project.

8.7 Martin B-57 Canberra

The Martin B-57 was a direct adaptation of the English Electric Canberra bomber, with Martin establishing a production line at its Baltimore, Maryland, plant in 1951 to build eight B-57As and 67 RB-57As patterned after the Canberra B.2. Martin then redesigned the airplane's cockpit to seat two in tandem, following standard American practice, as well as giving the airplane a rotary bomb bay, wing-mounted machine guns or cannon, and re-engining the airplane with the 7,220 lb thrust J65. The resultant airplane, designated as the B-57B, entered service with the Tactical Air Command beginning in January 1955, and 202 aircraft of this model were built. The B-57C was built as a dual-control transition trainer for TAC, 38 being constructed, and 68 B-57Es were built as target tugs, although these aircraft could easily be converted back to bombers.

RB-57D

Twenty RB-57Ds were built between 1955 and 1957 by reducing the original B-57B contract and designing a new 106-foot span wing around the basic B-57B fuselage of these aircraft. While these 20 Canberras were all designated as RB-57Ds, they were built in three distinct models, some being one-place aircraft, some having aerial refueling provisions, and all being equipped with differing sensor system packages. The RB-57Ds were powered by two 10,500 pound thrust J57s, giving them a service ceiling well in excess of 55,000 feet.

The RB-57Ds were placed into service between November 1955 and March 1957. Details of their use are still largely unknown, but a small number seem to have been operated by the 58th WRS, Kirtland AFB, New Mexico. At least one RB-57D was painted in Air Weather Service markings, but its use in 'Project Bordertown' clandestine perimeter flights of the Soviet Union may explain its true mission as well as its all-black undersurfaces.

B-57E

At least one B-57E was operated in 1956-1957 by the 1739th Ferrying Squadron, 1708th Ferrying Wing, at Amarillo AFB, Texas. The airplane was used for pilot checkout and proficiency training for squadron ferry pilots.

RB/WB-57B/C/E

In August 1961, the Air Force designated the Air Weather Service as the single manager for aerial sampling missions for the Department of Defense. By gathering samples from foreign nuclear explosions, considerable information about the weapons' characteristics could be gleaned by analyzing their fission products. The Air Weather Service had been involved with this mission, to one degree or another, since at least 1946 with its RB-29s, and since the mid-1950s with RB-57s and possibly the U-2 flown by the 55th WRS, Detachment 1, at Eielson AFB, Alaska, and the 57th WRS, at Avalon AF, Australia.

In short order, the 1211th Test Squadron (Sampling) was organized on 16th August 1961, at Kirtland AFB, New Mexico. This was followed on 12th October 1961, by the activation of the 55th WRS, which was organized on 8th January 1962, at McClellan AFB, California; on 8th February 1962, by the activation and organization of the 57th WRS at Kirtland AFB; and by the organization of the 54th WRS at Anderson AFB, Guam, on 18th April 1962. All of these squadrons were assigned to the 9th Weather Reconnaissance Group, MATS, with their primary mission being variously described as 'sampling the atmosphere for radioactive nuclear particles', 'air testing (and) hot sampling after nuclear explosions', and 'aerial atmospheric sampling through photo and visual reconnaissance'.

These units operated several models of the B-57: the WB-57B, NB-57B, RB-57B, RB-57C and WB-57E, all equipped with wingtip-mounted pods for the collection of airborne debris from nuclear explosions. The aircraft were used on Christmas Island in 1962 to sample nuclear debris during 'Operation Dominic', the last American atmospheric nuclear detonation. The 1211th Test Squadron (Sampling) was redesignated as the 58th WRS on 8th June 1963, at Kirtland AFB, while the 57th WRS had moved to Avalon AF, Australia, on 30th September 1962, and then to Hickam AFB, Hawaii, on 15th September 1965.

RB/WB-57F

The Air Force came to the realization early in 1962 that it needed a new high-altitude reconnaissance platform that would combine the RB-57D's payload carrying abilities with the U-2's high-altitude performance. On 27th March 1962, the Air Force signed a contract with General Dynamics for a study into modernizing the B-57 into a more capable reconnaissance platform. This was followed on 2nd October by Air Force authorization for General Dynamics to build two RB-57Fs under the Air Force's new 'Big Safari' procurement policy of expediting new projects by eliminating the usual bureaucratic red tape. Consequently, the RB-57F made its first flight on 23rd June 1963, and the first two aircraft entered service performing CIA-directed missions in February 1964. By March 1967, 21 RB-57Fs were built using the fuselages, horizontal stabilizers and landing gear from either RB-57A, B-57B or RB-57Ds. The RB-57F's 16,000 pound thrust TF33 turbofan engines, along with its detachable underwing J60 turbojets which produced an additional 3,000 pounds of thrust each, gave the airplane a service ceiling of over 68,000 feet, with an absolute maximum altitude of nearly 74,000 feet and a range of 4,000 miles.

Following the first two RB-57Fs, most of the remaining aircraft were operated as aerial samplers and photo reconnaissance platforms by the 58th WRS, beginning in June 1964, at Kirtland AFB or at one of its detachments at East Sale, Australia; Mendoza, Argentina; Eielson AFB, Alaska, or Albrook AFB, Panama. The 9th Weather Reconnaissance Wing's Detachment 3 also flew the airplane in the early 1960s out of Yokota AB, Japan.

Air Weather Service/MATS figures show that a high of 38 RB/WB-57s of various models were flown in 1962. In mid-1964, when the first RB-57Fs became operational, this number had dropped to 19, but by mid-1965 as many as 26 RB/WB-57s were being operated by the Air Weather Service.

Above: **Air Weather Service WB-57E, 55-4245, with wingtip air sampling pods.** Courtesy of Robert C Mikesh

Left, second down: **While this RB-57D, 53-3980, carries MATS Air Weather Service markings, it is a single-seat version used in 'Project Bordertown' perimeter intelligence flights.** General Dynamics, courtesy of Jay Miller

Left, third down: **WB-57B, 52-1506, with wingtip-mounted sampling pods at Andrews AFB in October 1962.** Robert C Mikesh

Bottom left: **NB-57B, 52-1496, of the 4926th Air Test Squadron, a MATS Air Weather Service unit, photographed at East Sale, Victoria, Australia, in November 1961.** John Hopton, courtesy of Robert C Mikesh

Opposite page, top: **RB-57F, 63-13503, was operated as both a photo-reconnaissance platform and as an aerial sampling aircraft by the Air Weather Service.** Air Force, courtesy of 1Lt M J Kasiuba

Right: **RB-57C, 53-3944, in May 1965.** Courtesy of Robert C Mikesh

Below: **RB-57F, 63-13291, had a service ceiling in excess of 68,000 feet.** Air Force, courtesy of 1Lt M J Kasiuba

Chapter 9

Cargo / Transports

9.1 Beech C-45 Expediter

More than 4,000 C-45s were built for the Army Air Forces between 1940 and 1944 and used as light transports, navigator and bombardier trainers, and photo reconnaissance aircraft. Many of these C-45s were still operated by the Air Force in the late 1940s, but from mid-1948 through 1952 the Military Air Transport Service possessed only about a dozen C-45s, including two JRBs flown by Navy MATS squadrons, serving as utility transports and proficiency trainers.

SC-45F

At least eight C-45s were flown by the Air Rescue Service in the search and rescue role between 1948 and 1952. Several of these aircraft were operated in Alaska with the 10th Rescue Squadron, on floats or skis as well as wheel-equipped undercarriage.

C-45G/H

The Beech design proved to be so versatile that the Air Force chose to remanufacture 900 C-45s beginning in 1951. MATS received 90 of these six-seat aircraft between April 1952 and June 1954, in either the C-45G or C-45H versions. The C-45G was equipped with R-985-AN-3 engines and Aeroproducts propellers, while the C-45H had R-985-AN-14B engines and Hamilton Standard props. Andrews AFB received the largest number of these remanufactured C-45s (27), probably used by Headquarters MATS for personnel transports as well as proficiency trainers. From 1953 through the late 1950s, the C-45G/Hs were flown at nearly all MATS bases as light transports ('base hacks') and proficiency trainers, with the largest number on MATS' inventory occurring in 1953 with 50 aircraft. By 1959, all of the MATS transport/utility C-45Gs and C-45Hs had been retired from service.

RC-45G/RC-45H

Between May and July 1953, 17 C-45Gs were delivered to Kelly AFB where they were converted to RC-45G vertical photo-mapping aircraft. Each airplane's belly skin was removed and replaced by glass panels covered by bomb-bay doors. The lower fuselage was reinforced and camera mounts were installed. The cockpit floor underneath the pilots' feet was replaced by thick safety glass, so that the pilots could view downward between their legs to line up the camera in the rear fuselage with the 'target' area to be photographed.

As these RC-45Gs became available, they were assigned to the 3935th Mapping and Charting Squadron (Domestic), which had been activated at Offutt AFB, Nebraska, on 1st October 1952, as part of the 55th SRW, 15th Air Force. Exactly one year later, the squadron was redesignated as the 1355th Mapping

Opposite page: **C-45F, 44-47161, one of the few early MATS C-45s shown Mitchell Field, Milwaukee, Wisconsin, in May 1953.** Leo J Kohn Collection

Top: **Beech C-45G, 51-11740, over Andrews AFB, Maryland, in November 1957.** Air Force

Right: **Air Photographic and Charting Service RC-45G, 51-11876, of the 1355th MCS, at Arriccia, Italy, in 1953.** Air Force, courtesy of George M Horn

Bottom: **C-45H, 52-10825, was one of 26 C-45Hs used by the Airways and Air Communications Service for flight checking navigational aids.** David Menard, courtesy of Robert Parmerter

and Charting Squadron and was reassigned to the Air Photographic and Charting Service, MATS, at West Palm Beach AFB, Florida. On 5th April 1954, the 1355th MCS was assigned to the newly-organized 1370th Photo Mapping Group at West Palm Beach AFB, and on 8th July 1954, the squadron was redesignated as the 1372nd Mapping and Charting Squadron (Aerial Photographic).

With the 1355th/1372nd MCS, the RC-45Gs were used (along with one squadron single-control Beech F-2, the photo-recon variant of the C-45) on visual, vertical photo-mapping missions within the United States and on deployment to Canada, Central and South America, Spain, Italy, Portugal, and French Morocco. As many of these photo missions were flown above 15,000 feet, the aircraft were equipped with an oxygen system. Occasionally, the RC-45Gs were used for oblique aerial photography of military installations and before-and-after photos of atomic explosions.

Late in 1958, the 1372nd MCS moved to Turner AFB, Georgia, and all but two of the RC-45Gs (51-11846 and 51-11902) were converted to RC-45Hs. By mid-1960, all of the RC-45G/Hs had been replaced by the RC-130A. The Beeches were flown to Davis-Monthan AFB, Arizona, for retirement or sale to civilian owners, while the 1372nd MCS was disbanded.

(A)C-45H

The Airways and Air Communications Service used a number of aircraft types in the early 1950s for flight checking AACS-operated electronic navigation aids and ground-air communications facilities. In December 1953, Air Force Headquarters had authorized the AACS six 4-engined transports (AC-54s), 54 two-engined transports (AC-47s and C-45Hs), and one single-engine fighter aircraft to accomplish this mission. However, as of mid-1954, only 41 flight check aircraft were available, including five AC-54s, 23 AC-47s, and approximately a dozen C-45Hs.

The AACS much preferred to obtain the new Convair C-131 for its twin-engine flight check aircraft, but had to settle for additional AC-47s instead. The C-45Hs were considered unsuitable for this flight check mission due to the low output of their generators. A project completed in July 1954 supplied ten C-45Hs to the AACS with larger-capacity generators, and by the end of 1957, 26 C-45Hs were being operated by the AACS by various flight checking squadrons across the country. By 1960, all of these C-45Hs had been replaced by the AC-47 and AT-29, the trainer version of the C-131.

9.2 Curtiss C-46 Commando

At the end of the Second World War, the Air Transport Command possessed over 760 C-46 Commandos, used for troop and cargo transport mainly in the Pacific Theater. By 1946, only a handful remained with the ATC, most aircraft having been transferred to the Troop Carrier Command. When MATS was formed in 1948, approximately ten C-46s were retained through 1950 as utility transports at various MATS bases.

Two additional C-46s were operated in the early 1950s by the 1739th Ferrying Squadron, 1708th Ferrying Group, at Amarillo AFB, Texas. These Commandos were used for familiarization and proficiency training, and as 'squadron hacks' until 1955.

SC-46D

During 1949 and 1950, two Commandos were flown by the Air Rescue Service in the Far East: SC-46D, 44-78420, was flown by the 2nd Rescue Squadron at Kadena Field, Okinawa, and SC-46D, 44-78542, was operated by the 3rd Rescue Squadron at Misawa, Japan. A rare color photograph of the latter airplane appears on page 73.

The two squadrons used these SC-46Ds on shorter-range rescue missions over the Yellow Sea and the Sea of Japan. The aircraft retained an overall weathered olive drab paint scheme, and carried the standard Air Rescue Service black-bordered yellow bands on the rear and center fuselage, with yellow wingtips.

Below: **Curtiss SC-46D, 44-78420, flown by the 2nd ARS, at Kadena Field, Okinawa, in the early 1950s.** A W George, courtesy of David Menard

Above: **A weary-looking SC-47D, 45-1012, flown by Detachment 6, Air Rescue Service, out of Biggs Field, Texas, photographed near Hamilton Field, California, in June 1948.** William T Larkins

9.3 Douglas C-47 Skytrain

More C-47s were operated by the Army Air Forces during the Second World War than any other transport. Various models of the Skytrain served with the ATC, NATS and MATS continuously from 1941 through 1965 and beyond, equipping at one time or another virtually every MATS group or wing in numerous roles.

Following the maiden flight of the first DC-3/DST (Douglas Commercial Three/Douglas Sleeper Transport) on 15th December 1935, over 400 DC-3s were built for airline use. In 1940, the Army Air Corps placed its first orders for the military version, the C-47, powered by 1,200 hp P&W R-1830s and built at the new Douglas plant at Long Beach Airport, California. Over 950 C-47s were built at Long Beach before a switch was made to the C-47A, this model having a 24-volt electrical system rather than 12-volt. Nearly 2,900 C-47As were built at Long Beach, while the Douglas Tulsa, Oklahoma, factory contributed another 2,099. The need for better high-altitude performance to carry cargo over 'The Hump' from India to China led to the development of the C-47B, with supercharged R-1830 engines. The Long Beach and Tulsa factories built a total of over 3,200 C-47B/TC-47Bs. Following the end of the war, the remaining C-47Bs had their two-speed superchargers removed and became C-47Ds.

At war's end, over 1,000 C-47s were in the Army Air Forces' inventory, but most of these were quickly liquidated so that, by the formation of MATS on 1st June 1948, only 242 C-47s were on hand for mostly domestic, short-range transport flights, 'depot feeder' runs, proficiency training or administrative uses, including three Navy R4D Skytrains operated as part of its contribution to MATS. Indicative of the three MATS transport divisions at the time, the Atlantic Division possessed 31 C-47A, 4 C-47B, and 59 C-47D types, with Westover AFB having the lion's share of these aircraft. By the end of June 1948, according to MATS' records, the total number of C-47s serving as transports had been cut to 143 aircraft.

Over the following 17 years of MATS' existence, the number of C-47s flown slowly dwindled as the C-54 took over the C-47's transport duties. The start of the Berlin Airlift in June 1948 drew some of the MATS C-47s to the European Theater for 'Operation Vittles' flights, but most Skytrains were withdrawn from the airlift by October as the C-54 was the favored aircraft to make these flights. By 1955, only about 50 C-47s were being operated by MATS, and as MATS became the Military Airlift Command in 1966, only seven tired C-47s remained active.

MC-47

Through the early 1950s, MATS used the C-47 mainly for the domestic air evacuation mission, flown by the 1731st ATS, Scott AFB, Illinois; 1732nd ATS, Westover AFB, Massachusetts; 1733rd ATS, Travis AFB, California; 1734th ATS, Brooks AFB, Texas; 1735th ATS, Brookley AFB, Alabama; and the 1736th ATS, at Brooks AFB, with most squadrons operating seven aircraft in 1953. By April 1954, however, the C-131 Samaritan began to replace these MC-47s for the domestic medevac role.

SC-47

The Air Rescue Service operated as many as 33 SC-47s upon its formation in 1946. By June 1948, when the ARS was absorbed by MATS, the number of SC-47s had shrunk to about 15 aircraft. But by 1955, nearly 80 C-47s had been converted to the search and rescue role, although they passed from the scene quickly as the SA-16A Albatross and the SC-54D Rescuemaster became operational. In 1958, 30 Air Rescue Service SC-47s were retired leaving one aircraft which was disposed of the following year.

AC-47D

The Airways and Air Communications Service had been flying the C-47 as an administrative aircraft since its inception, but in 1953 some 26 C-47s were modified by Hayes Aircraft Co as AC-47D flight checking aircraft with, among other electronic additions, a prominent nose radome. By mid-1956, the AACS was flying one AC-47A, 21 AC-47Ds, five C-47A and three C-47D administrative and support aircraft at various widespread locations. One administrative VC-47A was gained by mid-1957, but by 30th June 1961, just before the AACS was detached from MATS as the Air Force Communications Service, this airplane had been relinquished and at least nine administrative C-47Ds were being flown by AACS units.

RC-47A/D

An unknown number of C-47s were converted as photographic reconnaissance RC-47A or RC-47D aircraft flown by the Air Photographic and Charting Service. These aircraft could be distinguished by fairings in the lower rear fuselage containing flat glass panels for camera installations. Little is known about either the modifications made to these aircraft or their mission.

Below left: **Continental Division VC-47D, 45-917, at Logan International Airport, East Boston, Massachusetts, in July 1950.** Leo J Kohn

Below right: **Ski-equipped SC-47B, 43-48765, of the 52nd ARS, shown at BW-1 in February 1953. Note RATO bottles beneath fuselage.** Ken Hiltz

Bottom: **As the torn insignia on the door indicates, this C-47D, 45-917, shown at LaCrosse, Wisconsin, was converted to an air evacuation transport by the Continental Division of MATS.** Bob Stuckey, courtesy of Douglas D Olson

Top left: **AC-47D, 43-48783, one of 26 operated by MATS' Airways and Air Communications Service for flight checking navigational aids, is shown at Haneda Air Base, Japan, in 1953.** Chalmers Johnson, courtesy of Douglas D Olson

Top right: **RC-47D, 43-49565, in Air Rescue Service colors with numerous antennae, photographed at Los Angeles in October 1952.** Courtesy of Leo J Kohn

Center: **AC-47D, 43-48892, in May 1960 with the colorful orange day-glo scheme of the Airways and Air Communications Service.** MAP

Right: **RC-47D, 43-49190, awaiting a new engine at Scott AFB, Illinois, in May 1958.** Norman Taylor

Bottom right: **RC-47D, 43-49522, formerly flown by MATS' Air Photographic and Charting Service, is shown derelict at Ryan Field, Tuscon, Arizona, in 1976. Note camera port at lower rear fuselage.** MAP

9.4 Douglas C-54 Skymaster

The Douglas C-54 Skymaster became the Air Transport Command's main long-range transport from 1943 onwards, earning a reputation for reliability and safety unequalled by other aircraft. Following the Second World War, the Skymaster served as MATS' primary long-range transport during the Berlin Airlift and the Korean War. And, through the 1950s, the C-54 proved its versatility in the medevac, electronic airways check, and search and rescue roles.

In 1935, the Douglas Santa Monica Division design team headed by Arthur Raymond created the DC-4E, a four-engined, tricycle-geared, and triple-tailed civil airliner, designed in collaboration with United Air Lines and financed by four additional airlines. However, the airplane, which made its first flight in June 1938, proved to be too complex and uneconomical for airline use. A redesign effort was begun in May 1939 which produced a smaller, lighter, and faster DC-4A. Both United and American Air Lines ordered this model in 1940, but none had been completed by the time the United States had entered the Second World War in December 1941.

The Army Air Forces took delivery of the first 24 airplanes beginning in March 1942, designating them as C-54s, which essentially were civil airliners powered by 1,350 hp R-2000 engines with seating for 26 passengers. A militarized model, the C-54A, featuring a strengthened floor, a large cargo door and uprated engines, was the next model to be built: 52 at the Santa Monica factory and 155 at a new Douglas plant in Chicago, Illinois. The C-54B, with seating for 50 and increased fuel capacity in the wings, came next on the two production lines, with 220 being constructed. The Chicago factory ended its Skymaster production with 350 C-54Ds, powered by R-2000-11 engines. Meanwhile, Douglas Santa Monica produced 75 combination passenger-cargo C-54Es with increased fuel capacity and 76 C-54Gs with 1,450 hp R-2000 engines and seating for up to 50 passengers.

The Air Transport Command flew the C-54 over its worldwide routes during the last three years of the Second World War, making nearly 80,000 ocean crossings with the loss of only three aircraft, only one of which was fatal. At war's end, the ATC had some 700 Skymasters in its inventory, but post-war demobilization reduced these to only 302 C-54s by mid-1947.

When the Military Air Transport Service was formed in June 1948, it inherited 234 C-54s from the ATC. Less than a month after the start of the Berlin Airlift in June 1948, MATS committed 81 C-54s to the effort. By the fall of 1948, over 150 MATS C-54s would be participating in 'Operation Vittles', including 24 R5Ds from the Navy MATS squadrons VR-6 and VR-8. The Berlin Airlift produced one short-term modification to the C-54, as 38 C-54Es were stripped of all non-essential equipment to serve as C-54M coal haulers, with an increased payload of 2,500 lbs to a maximum of 35,000 lbs. By the end of 1949, MATS possessed only 144 Air Force C-54s and 39 Navy R5Ds.

MC-54M

The Korean War which began in June 1950 gave the C-54 a new opportunity to prove its value, as MATS Skymasters soon were flying the Pacific Airlift in support of the war. At the airlift's peak, over 100 MATS C-54s were involved in transporting personnel and cargo westward. In 1951, 30 C-54Es were converted to MC-54M aeromedical evacuation aircraft, each with accommodation for 30 stretcher patients and their attendants. These MC-54Ms featured vibration-proof stretcher slings, improved cabin soundproofing, individual ventilation controls, a complete medical station, and an electrical stretcher lift capable of loading or unloading two stretcher patients at a time. Foam rubber mattresses also replaced the old air mattresses that would expand and contract with changes in air pressure.

By the end of 1953, there were 231 C-54s of all models in the MATS inventory, and an additional 22 Navy R5Ds. This number steadily declined over the remainder of the decade as the C-54s were replaced by more modern aircraft in the transport role. By 1960, there were only sixteen MATS C-54s being operated, and by the end of 1965 only nine C-54s remained.

SC-54D

From 1950 to 1954, four C-54Ds were in use by the Air Rescue Service as search and rescue aircraft, with at least one operated by Alaska's 10th Rescue Squadron Flight D and one by the 53rd ARS at Keflavik, Iceland. While both of these aircraft were painted in full ARS markings, it appears that no special modifications were made to the C-54s for the search and rescue mission, other than a search radar mounted beneath the forward fuselage of the 10th ARS Skymaster.

In 1954, 38 C-54Ds were modified by Convair Fort Worth as Air Rescue Service SC-54D search and rescue aircraft. These 'Rescuemasters' featured an APS-42 search radar mounted in the nose, large circular observation blisters in the aft cabin for two scanner positions, an anti-skid brake system, and internal storage for flares and rescue equipment, including four MA-1 rescue kits which could be deployed using a chute leading outside through an auxiliary cargo door. Each MA-1 rescue kit contained a 300 pound inflatable life raft which could hold up to 40 persons.

These SC-54Ds became available to the ARS in 1955, and by 1958 42 Rescuemasters were being operated, indicating that the earlier SC-54s were still in use. In 1962, 40 SC-54s were in the ARS inventory, being redesignated as HC-54s in the new triservice classification system. By the end of 1964, 39 HC-54s were being flown by the following squadrons:

31st ARS	Clark AB, Philippines
33rd ARS	Naha AB, Okinawa
36th ARS	Tachikawa AB, Japan
41st ARS	Hamilton AFB, California
48th ARS	Eglin AFB, Florida
54th ARS	Goose AB, Labrador
55th ARS	Kindley AB, Bermuda
57th ARS	Lajes Field, Azores
58th ARS	Wheelus AB, Libya
67th ARS	Prestwick AB, Scotland
76th ARS	Hickam AFB, Hawaii
79th ARS	Anderson AFB, Guam

AC-54

In December 1953, the Airways and Air Communications Service was authorized the use of six four-engined transports to perform the facilities flight checking mission, evaluating the performance of navigational aids and radars. Six C-54Ds subsequently were modified as AC-54Ds by the substitution of four

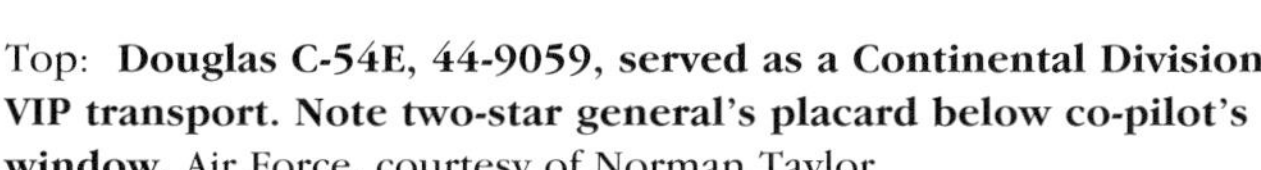
Top: **Douglas C-54E, 44-9059, served as a Continental Division VIP transport. Note two-star general's placard below co-pilot's window.** Air Force, courtesy of Norman Taylor

Center left: **MATS Continental Division C-54D, 42-72543, photographed at Selfridge AFB, Michigan, in May 1953.** William Balogh, courtesy of Norman Taylor

Center right: **Navy MATS Continental Division R5D-3, 56504, flown by VR-3, is shown landing at NAS Moffett Field, California, in April 1951.** William T Larkins

Right: **Staff transport C-54A, 42-107451, displays a two-star placard.** MAP

300-amp generators for the usual 100-amp units, a search radar fitted to the nose, the installation of a facilities flight check recording system, and a data recorder operator's station within the cabin.

By 1955, these six AC-54Ds were being operated by the following AACS units:

1800th AACS Wing	Andrews AFB, Maryland
1855th AACS Flight	Elmendorf AFB, Alaska
1856th AACS Flight	Harmon AB, Newfoundland
1857th AACS Flight	Rhein-Main AB, Germany
1862nd AACS Flight	Hickam AFB, Hawaii

By mid-1957, the 1800th AACS Wing's AC-54D had been reassigned to the 1861st AACS Flight at Tachikawa AB, Japan. By the end of the year, one AC-54D had been replaced by an AC-54B for the 1861st AACS Flight, while one C-54G was being flown by the Continental AACS Area at Tinker AFB, Oklahoma, and one C-54G by the 1857th AACS Flight at Rhein-Main AB. At the time of the AACS' detachment from MATS and its establishment as the Air Force Communications Service on 1st July 1961, the organization was still operating six AC-54s and one C-54G.

VC-54D/G

While at least several standard C-54s were flown as staff transports, a number of C-54s were converted to VIP aircraft and were operated by MATS Headquarters and selected MATS Division/Group/Wing headquarters as well as by the 1254th ATG (SM) at Washington National Airport and later at Andrews AFB, Maryland. Details of their use as VIP aircraft, however, are not known.

Left: **MC-54E, 44-9031, flown by the 1405th AMTW, MATS.** Courtesy of Clyde Gerdes Collection

Below: **SC-54D, 42-72566, one of 38 Skymasters modified in 1954 for the search and rescue role flown by the Air Rescue Service, MATS.** Convair, courtesy of Robert Archer

Bottom left: **VC-54M, 44-9047, assigned to the 375th Aeromedical Airlift Wing, Scott AFB, Illinois, shown in May 1960.** B Burgess, courtesy of Norman Taylor

Bottom right: **VC-54E, 44-9083, flown by the 1254th ATW(SM) at Andrews AFB, Maryland.** Courtesy of Clyde Gerdes Collection

Seven UC-64 Norsemen were flown by MATS when it was formed in 1948. UC-64A, 45-41749, takes off from Chandler Lake, Alaska, in the late 1940s. Air Force

9.5 Noorduyn C-64 Norseman

The rugged Norseman was a Canadian design built by Noorduyn Aviation of Montreal. Following service trials with seven YC-64s in 1942, the Army Air Forces ordered over 700 C-64As as utility aircraft operating on wheels, skis or floats. The Air Transport Command flew a number of these C-64s during the Second World War in the utility role as well as for Arctic search and rescue missions.

When the Military Air Transport Service was formed in June 1948, it inherited seven utility UC-64As and one Norseman flown by the Air Rescue Service for Arctic search and rescue, although this airplane's squadron and location are not known. At least one UC-64A is known to have flown during the late 1940s and early 1950s with the 10th Air Rescue Squadron at Ladd AFB, Alaska. It is possible that this airplane came into the MATS fold in July 1950 when the Air Rescue Service absorbed the 10th ARS.

9.6 Douglas C-74 Globemaster

The C-74's design was begun immediately after the Japanese attack on Pearl Harbor on 7th December 1941, as Douglas engineers saw the need for a truly global Army Air Corps transport capability. Using the DC-4 then entering production, Douglas expanded the design in an attempt to produce a 'no frills' transport capable of accommodating most Army equipment and entering production without delay. The Army Air Corps was contacted early in 1942 to determine their interest in the airplane and, after several months of negotiations, a contract was signed for 50 C-74s. However, the C-74's production was delayed due to the higher priority the Army Air Forces placed on building the Douglas A-26 Invader, and the first C-74 was not completed until July 1945, with the first flight occurring on 5th September. Post-war cutbacks reduced the Globemaster's contract to 14 aircraft, C-74s 42-65402/65415, although only twelve became operational after 42-65403 crashed during a company test flight and 42-65405 was destroyed during static tests at Wright Field.

The twelve remaining C-74s began operations with the Air Transport Command on 9th September 1946, first at Memphis, Tennessee, then at Morrison Field, West Palm Beach, Florida,

Above: **Douglas C-74 Globemaster, 42-65408, 1260th ATS, 1601st ATG, Brookley AFB, Alabama, Atlantic Division, MATS, in 1949.** Air Force

Right: **Continental Division C-74s, 42-65409/65410, prior to loading 31st Fighter Escort Wing maintenance personnel for a mass transpacific flight of F-84G Thunderjets to Yokota AB, Japan, in July 1952.** Air Force

finally with the 31st ATS and 32nd ATS at Brookley Field, Alabama, in the spring of 1947. When the Military Air Transport Service was formed on 1st June 1948, the two C-74 squadrons were redesignated as the 17th ATS and 19th ATS, 521st ATG, Brookley AFB, attached to the Atlantic Division of MATS.

For a time, the C-74 Globemaster was the largest land-based transport in the world, and was one of the first aircraft to use the mammoth 3,250 hp Pratt & Whitney R-4360 Wasp Major engine. With a gross weight of 145,000 lbs and a 6,800-cubic-foot main cabin, the C-74 could carry up to 125 passengers. After a gross weight of 165,000 lbs was approved, the airplane could carry over 50,000 lbs of cargo with a 2,100 mile range, or a maximum of over 72,000 lbs of cargo at a reduced range. Though not particularly fast, cruising at 260 mph, the Globemaster's six integral wing tanks had a capacity of 11,100 gallons of fuel, which gave the airplane a remarkable 7,200 mile ferry range. Two travelling electric cranes ran nearly the entire length of the 75-foot-long cabin on overhead rails, and could function as a freight elevator through a detachable section of the cabin floor aft of the wing.

The Berlin Airlift, which began in June 1948, gave MATS the opportunity to test the C-74's capabilities, although only one Globemaster, 42-65414, participated directly in the airlift. On 11th August, the C-74 was flown to Westover AFB, finally arriving at Frankfurt's Rhein-Main airfield, in Germany, on the 14th. On the 17th, 42-65414 landed at Berlin's Gatow airfield carrying 20 tons of flour, and for the next six weeks flew 24 missions into the city, delivering 1,234,000 pounds of supplies.

Several airlift records were set by 414 during Operation Vittles, as the Globemaster averaged over 38,000 pounds of cargo for these missions. On Air Force Day, 18th September, the C-74 flew six round trips into Berlin hauling a total of 250,000 pounds of coal, setting a new Airlift Task Force utilization record by flying 20 hours during the 24-hour effort. The Globemaster participated in a unique way during the construction of a new airfield at Tegel, in the French sector of Berlin. Large construction equipment was needed to build new runways, but the equipment, including a rock crusher, was too big even for the Globemaster to accommodate. Consequently, the machinery was cut into pieces by welding torch at Rhein-Main, loaded aboard the C-74, and flown into Tegel for reassembly.

C-74, 42-65414, returned to Brookley AFB on 26th September after six weeks of Vittles flights. The Globemaster had performed admirably during its airlift operations, but it became clear that the need for a single C-74 was not great enough to justify continued flights into Berlin. Although the Russians reportedly complained that the Globemaster could be used as a bomber (via the open elevator well), the fact that the runways were not stressed for the Globemaster's weight, and that the C-74 was incompatible with the airlift's tight air corridor scheduling, were other factors considered in its withdrawal.

DIVISION
265410
CONTINENTAL
DIVISION
265409
MILITARY AIR TRANSPORT SERVICE

On 4th October 1948, regularly-scheduled C-74 flights to Germany were begun. Called 'The Goliath', this once-a-week flight carried much-needed C-54 engines and parts for the airlift's main haulers. The flights originated at Brookley AFB, with stops at Westover AFB and the Azores before ending at Frankfurt, Germany. By February 1949, the tempo of these 'Goliath' flights had increased to 16 per month.

Other regularly-scheduled MATS C-74 flights at this time were the 'Panamanian', from Brookley AFB to Albrook Field in the Canal Zone, and the 'Puerto Rican' from Brookley AFB to Ramey AB, Puerto Rico, and return.

The C-74 Globemasters set a number of records during their service with MATS. Early in November 1948, a MATS first was achieved by an Atlantic Division C-74 when the first non-stop transatlantic flight was made between Westover AFB and Shannon, Ireland, covering 2,950 statute miles. On 16th May 1949, a C-74 carried 75 passengers plus a crew of 12 to England, at the time the largest military passenger load to fly the Atlantic. Six months later, on 25th November, the Berlin Airlift C-74, dubbed 'The Champ' by its crew, flew the Atlantic with a record 103 people aboard, setting down at RAF Marham, England, 24 hours after take-off from Brookley AFB.

In October 1949, the C-74s were reassigned to the Continental Division of MATS, flying with the redesignated 1260th ATS, 1703rd ATG, Brookley AFB, Alabama. Early in 1950, the C-74s were assigned two new regularly-scheduled routes – 'The Hawaiian', a once-weekly round-trip flight between Brookley AFB and Hickam AFB, Hawaii, with one stop made at Fairfield-Suisun AFB, California, and 'The Jonathan', a thrice-weekly flight between Brookley AFB and Anchorage, Alaska, with intermediate stops made at Kelly AFB, Texas, McClellan AFB, California, and McChord AFB, Washington.

The North Korean attack against the Republic of Korea on 25th June 1950, began another supporting phase of the C-74's career. From 1st July to December, the Globemasters logged over 7,000 hours in flights to Hawaii, hauling troops and high-priority cargo westward toward the Korean War and returning eastward with wounded GIs. In December alone, 40 flights were made to Hawaii by the C-74s as they flew on an 'in commission' basis, rather than on a set schedule. In seven months, from July 1950 through to January 1951, the Globemasters moved 2,486 patients, 550 passengers, and 128,000 pounds of cargo from Hawaii to the mainland, while hauling just under a million pounds of cargo westward.

During the early 1950s, the 1260th ATS functioned as a 'utility squadron', dispatching its C-74s on regularly-scheduled or special flights as the need arose. Consequently, Globemaster missions ranged throughout Europe, North Africa, South America and the Middle East. And, while utilization rates for the C-74 averaged over ten hours per day, the highest of any aircraft in the 1703rd ATG, its maintenance manhours climbed due to a shortage of parts and an influx of untrained maintenance personnel. By 1955, the C-74's maintenance manhour requirements were so high, and the utilization rates so low, that the 6th ATS (as the 1260th ATS had been redesignated) was merged with the 3rd ATS in June 1955 to facilitate the transition of its crews from the C-74 to the 3rd ATS' C-124s. On 1st November 1955, the C-74s finally were placed in flyable storage at Brookley AFB, and by March 1956 all had been flown to Davis-Monthan AFB, Arizona, for retirement or sale to civilian owners.

9.7 Fairchild C-82 Packet

Fairchild's Aircraft Division designed the C-82 Packet, beginning in 1941, to provide straight-in ramp loading of Army trucks, tanks, howitzers and supplies. The airplane's twin-tail booms enabled large trucks to back up underneath the horizontal stabilizer, loading or unloading cargo through the Packet's opened clamshell rear doors onto the low cargo hold floor. The prototype XC-82 made its first flight in September 1944, and by the end of the Second World War a handful of production C-82As had been delivered to the Air Transport Command. Following post-war production cancellations, a total of 220 C-82As and three C-82Ns were built by the time production ended in September 1948.

Between 1948 and 1951, Military Air Transport Service figures show that as many as six C-82s were operated, although details of their service have been elusive. In an early MATS history, it is claimed that the C-82As were used as transports as well as by the Air Weather Service and the Airways and Air Communications Service.

From 1953 to 1954, the 1st AACS Installation and Maintenance Squadron, Tinker AFB, Oklahoma, did operate two C-82As, 44-23026 and 44-23031, using the Packets to transport squadron personnel and equipment for the installation and maintenance of AACS air traffic control facilities in the United States. C-82A, 44-23031, has been photographed in 1956 in the Stockton/Hayward, California, area after it had been retired and sold to a civil owner to be refurbished as a crop sprayer. Newly-registered as N4833V, the Packet still carried its mostly-intact AACS paint scheme including a large AACS emblem on its nose. It is interesting to note that this particular aircraft had its undersurfaces – wings, horizontal stabilizer and lower fuselage – painted black.

Left: **C-74, 42-65408, in the final scheme with reflective white fuselage top to reduce cabin temperatures.** Air Force

SC-82A

The Air Rescue Service modified as many as 18 C-82As as search and rescue or support aircraft between 1948 and 1953. Units which flew these SC-82As include the 4th Rescue Squadron, Flight A, at Hamilton AFB, and the 4th Rescue Squadron, Flight B, at March AFB, California; the 9th Rescue Squadron, Flight D/58th Air Rescue Squadron, Wheelus Field, Libya; and the 66th ARS, Manston, England and the 67th ARS, Sculthorpe, England, each with one Packet, both of which were retired in August 1953. Air Rescue Service SC-82As participated in humanitarian flights as well, such as the 'Operation Haylift' and 'Operation Snowbound' missions in the Western United States in 1949, and during floods in the Netherlands in February 1953.

Two additional Air Rescue Service C-82As were assigned between 1949 and 1953 to the 2156th Technical Training Unit at MacDill AFB, Florida. The aircraft were used in direct support of the Air Rescue Service Pararescue and Survival School, for parachute jump training and for transporting instructors, pararescue students and equipment to jump training areas surrounding MacDill AFB and West Palm Beach International Airport (where the unit moved in May 1952). The Packets also moved classes to desert training areas at Palm Springs and 29 Palms, California; Arctic training bases at Lowry AFB, Colorado, Mountain Home AFB, Idaho, and Goose Bay, Labrador; and to jungle survival training sites in Florida. The C-82As flown by the 2156th TTU were unmodified Packets, and were painted in standard Air Force markings.

Top: **Fairchild SC-82A, 44-22978, of the 4th Rescue Squadron, Flight A, Air Rescue Service at Hamilton Field, California, in March 1949.** William Balogh, courtesy of David Menard

Lower left: **C-82A, 44-23031, registered as N4833V at Stockton, California, in 1956. The Packet retains most of the markings of the 1st AACS Installation and Maintenance Squadron at Tinker AFB.** Clay Jansson

Lower right: **SC-82A, 44-23029, in standard Air Rescue Service markings circa 1953.** MAP

Top: **Boeing C-97A, 48-399, of the Pacific Division, MATS, in late 1949.** Boeing/Gordon Williams, courtesy of Robert L Lawson

Above left: **C-97A, 49-2605, of MATS' Pacific Division at the Dayton Airport in September 1953. Note the open cargo door on the right side and the open rear clamshell doors.** Warren Shipp, courtesy of Douglas D Olson

Above right: **C-97C, 50-696, of the 146th ATW, California ANG, Van Nuys Airport, California.** California ANG, courtesy of 1Lt M J Kasiuba

Left: **C-97G, 53-349, of the 109th ATS(H), 133rd ATW, Minnesota ANG.** Courtesy of Lionel N Paul

9.8 Boeing C-97 Stratofreighter

Boeing Airplane Company engineers took full advantage of the design work done on the B-29 Superfortress when, in 1942, they proposed a transport version of the airplane to the Army Air Forces. The Boeing C-97 Stratofreighter used the wings, tail assembly, engines, landing gear, and lower fuselage of the B-29, while a new, pressurized upper fuselage was designed in a weight-saving 'double-bubble' arrangement. Including later use of converted HC-97Gs by the Air Rescue Service, the Military Air Transport Service operated over one hundred Stratofreighters between 1948 and 1966.

YC-97

A contract for three XC-97s was signed in January 1943, with the prototype's first flight occurring on 15th November 1944. To demonstrate the Stratofreighter's prowess, this airplane made a highly publicized 2,323 mile cross-country flight two months later while carrying a 20,000 lb payload, averaging a remarkable 383 mph.

On 6th July 1945, the Army Air Forces ordered an additional ten YC-97 service test aircraft, 45-59587/59596, the first six of which were delivered beginning on October 11 to the Air Transport Command as cargo transports. The ATC operated these six YC-97s on a regularly scheduled freight run between California and Hawaii. The remaining four YC-97s and subsequent Stratofreighter models incorporated the features of the B-50 Superfortress, including the type's more powerful R-4360 engines and a taller vertical stabilizer. Three of these aircraft, designated as YC-97As, were completed as troop carriers and were flown by non-ATC commands.

YC-97B

The last airplane in the YC-97 series was built as a plush personnel transport and designated as YC-97B, 45-59596. The rear clamshell loading doors were deleted, and the main cabin had accommodation for 80 passengers in airline-type seats, separate men's and women's dressing rooms, a small lounge in the lower rear fuselage, and circular airline-style windows. The YC-97B was accepted by the Military Air Transport Service on 31st January 1949, and was used on Pacific Division flights between California and Hawaii.

C-97A

On 24th March 1947, less than two weeks after the first flight of the B-29-based YC-97, the Army Air Forces ordered 27 B-50-based C-97As, 48-397/423. The C-97A could carry a 53,000 lb payload or 134 troops, and this model was equipped with a chin-mounted APS-42 weather-avoidance radar. In December 1948, an additional 23 C-97As, 49-2589/2611, were ordered, these aircraft featuring a cargo door on the right side of the forward fuselage. The C-97A made its first flight on 16th June 1949, and MATS began accepting the type in October. By 1950, MATS was operating over 20 C-97s of various models.

C-97C

Fourteen C-97Cs, 50-690/703, were ordered with strengthened floors, uprated R-4360 engines, and other minor changes. These aircraft were equipped as MC-97C medevac transports, carrying up to 79 stretchers and four attendants. MATS accepted these aircraft between February and December 1951, and used them on Pacific Airlift flights during the Korean War, returning casualties from Japan to California for further treatment.

C-97K

In order to meet a continuing need for additional MATS transports, 26 KC-97Gs in the 1952 and 1953 serial number blocks were converted to C-97Ks beginning in the mid-1950s. All aerial refueling related equipment was removed, with the exception of the refueling boom operator's pod in the lower rear fuselage. The airplane's cargo doors were sealed and passenger seats were installed for MATS passenger-carrying missions.

Most of the above mentioned passenger-cargo C-97 Stratofreighters served with Pacific, Continental and Atlantic Division air transport squadrons through the 1950s, with a high of nearly seventy aircraft in MATS service in 1952. In the spring of 1954, MATS participated extensively in the evacuation of casualties after the French defeat at Dien Bien Phu during the French Indochina War. While C-124s transported the casualties from Saigon to Tokyo, MATS C-97s flew these men from Tokyo to Travis AFB, California, then on to Westover AFB, Massachusetts, and finally to Algeria and France.

A small number of C-97s were flown by the Continental Division of MATS as transition trainers. These aircraft were operated until the late 1950s at Palm Beach International Airport/West Palm Beach AFB, Florida, by the 1740th ATS, Detachment A 1742nd ATS.

As MATS C-97s began to be replaced by more modern transports, beginning in 1960 these Stratofreighters were transferred to Air National Guard units across the country. Six Air National Guard fighter squadrons converted to the C-97 in 1960, and by 1962 all 48 C-97s in the MATS inventory had been transferred to ANG transport squadrons.

In June 1961, Cold War tensions mounted when the Russians called for Western withdrawal from West Berlin. As thousands of East Berliners fled the city, the Communists responded by constructing the infamous Berlin Wall. President John Kennedy countered this move by announcing the mobilization of 64 Air National Guard units. On 1st October 1961, six ANG C-97 squadrons were called to active duty to supplement MATS during the Berlin Crisis:

109th ATS(H), 133rd ATW	Minnesota ANG
115th ATS(H), 146th ATW	California ANG
195th ATS(H), 146th ATW	California ANG
125th ATS(H), 125th ATG	Oklahoma ANG
133rd ATS(H), 157th ATG	New Hampshire ANG
139th ATS(H), 109th ATG	New York ANG

These Air National Guard C-97 squadrons painted their Stratofreighters in MATS colors, and for the following eleven months flew transport missions to the Far East, South America and Europe from points of embarkation at Dover AFB or Travis AFB. Following an easing of tensions, these squadrons were demobilized on 31st August 1962, and returned to state control. However, two MATS Air National Guard wings, following their demobilization, volunteered for MATS missions during the Cuban Crisis. The 133rd ATW, Minneapolis, Minnesota, and the 146th ATW, Van Nuys, California, flew their Stratofreighters on 29 missions to Greenland and South America carrying 266 tons

Top: **YC-97Js, 52-2693 and 52-2762, were re-engined with P&W T34 turboprops intended for the Douglas C-133.** Air Force courtesy of Norman Taylor

Lower left: **HC-97G, 52-2783, one of approximately 30 Air Rescue Service Strato-Rescuers converted in 1963-1964 by Fairchild Hiller Corp.** Courtesy of Clyde Gerdes Collection

Lower right: **C-97C, 50-692 of the Atlantic Division, was one of 14 such examples built, and shows the airplane with arctic red markings.** David W Menard, via Chris Salter

of cargo. A third MATS Air National Guard unit, the 125th ATG, Oklahoma Air National Guard, flew one of their C-97s on a MATS-sponsored two-week, 21,000 mile mission in November 1962, delivering 14 prize breeding cattle to Afghanistan. By 1965, MATS was supervising five reserve and 25 Air National Guard squadrons.

YC-97J

In the early 1950s, the Air Force began establishing requirements for turboprop-powered transport aircraft. The Lockheed C-130 Hercules and the Douglas C-133 Cargomaster designs eventually were accepted for production. In the interim, the Air Force needed test aircraft to gain flight experience with the engines intended to power these new transports. Two Lockheed C-121s and two Boeing C-97s were chosen to be modified as flying test beds for the Pratt & Whitney T34 turboprops intended for the C-133. KC-97Gs 52-2693 and 52-2762 were re-engined with 5,700 hp P&W YT34-P5s equipped with three-bladed Curtiss Turboelectric propellers.

Following conversion, the first airplane was flown to Edwards AFB for preliminary flight tests. Aircrews from the 1700th Test Squadron (Turbo-Prop), 1700th ATG, Kelly AFB, an organization established by MATS specifically to flight test these new turboprop engines, were sent to Edwards AFB in August 1955 for familiarization and indoctrination in turboprop flight procedures with the aircraft. The first YC-97J was flown to Kelly AFB on 14th September, and the second airplane on the 29th, to begin the accelerated service test program with the stated goal of accumulating 4,150 flying hours by 31st December 1956.

During the first three months of operations with the YC-97Js, the 1700th Test Squadron (Turbo-Prop) was visited by numerous Air Force, CAA and aircraft industry representatives who participated in flights and observed their operations. On 26th January 1956, YC-97J 52-2693 flew from Kelly AFB to Rhein-

Main AB, Germany, with stops at Dover AFB, Harmon Field, Newfoundland, Prestwick in Scotland, London and Paris *en route* to Frankfurt. The flight from Harmon to Prestwick was made in slightly over six hours, four hours better than a normal MATS flight over this route.

Several semi-scheduled cargo missions with the YC-97Js were flown in March 1956 from Kelly AFB to Ramey AB, Puerto Rico, via Charleston AFB, South Carolina, with Brookley AFB, Alabama an intermediate stop on the return flight. Average flight time for these runs was 16 hours, nine hours less than normal. The first transpacific crossing by a YC-97J was begun on 2nd March 1956. The airplane made the 18,000 mile round trip to Tokyo in 50 hours 46 minutes flying time, averaging nearly 355 mph, despite having to shut down one engine due to a propeller malfunction on the flight from Guam to Tokyo, and another propeller mishap occurring on the flight from Tokyo to Midway Island which forced the airplane to return.

In April, deterioration of the engine tail pipes forced the suspension of flight operations with the YC-97Js during May 1956, until the modified tail pipes were received late in the month. Following installation of the new tail pipes, the two YC-97Js broke a combined flight record that had been set the previous year by the two 1700th Test Squadron YC-131C Turboliners. On 30th May, the two YC-97Js flew a total of 46 hours 35 minutes during one calendar day, averaging only 28 minutes during the three refueling stops made by each airplane.

On 15th November 1956, the YC-97J flying hour program was considered completed six weeks ahead of schedule, with a total of 3,240 hours flown. Although problems had developed with the propeller systems, starters and fuel control systems, exhaust pipes, and cracks discovered on the airplanes' flaps and flap wells, the test program proved the suitability of the T34 engine and Curtiss propeller combination for use on the C-133.

Following completion of the test program, both YC-97Js continued to fly MATS transport missions with the 1700th Test Squadron, such as airlifting Hungarian refugees to the United States during the crisis in Hungary. On 17th January 1957, the aircraft were flown to Tinker AFB, Oklahoma, for overhaul and reassignment to other commands.

HC-97G

In 1963, the Air Rescue Service was searching for an interim replacement for its ageing HC-54D Rescuemasters before the new Lockheed HC-130Hs were to become operational. As a number of KC-97Gs were ending their usefulness as aerial tankers, approximately 30 of these aircraft were converted to HC-97G Strato-Rescuers by the Aircraft Service Division of the Fairchild Hiller Corporation. The division was a logical choice to accomplish these conversions as it had been performing IRAN (Inspect and Repair As Necessary) work on KC-97s at its St Augustine, St Petersburg and Crestview, Florida, facilities.

The Aircraft Service Division removed the aerial refueling equipment from each airplane and installed air conditioning units, clamshell doors in the rear fuselage, and a jump platform in the rear cabin for deploying pararescue personnel and equipment. Up-to-date radio and electronic search equipment was installed, as were additional fuselage fuel tanks and emergency fuel dump plumbing which increased the HC-97G's range to 5,000 miles.

The first modified HC-97G, 52-916, was delivered to the Air Rescue Service in August 1964 as the largest, fastest and longest-ranged aircraft to be used in the search and rescue role up to that time. The ARS used these Strato-Rescuers in support of the Gemini and Apollo manned space flights from Cape Kennedy, Florida. By 1965, the aircraft were operated by the 55th ARS, at Kindley AB, Bermuda; the 58th ARS, at Wheelus AB, Libya; and the 76th ARS, from Hickam AFB, Hawaii.

9.9 Douglas C-117 Skytrain

Unlike its similar-looking cousin the VC-47, the Douglas C-117A was a factory-built military VIP transport based on the commercial DC-3A. Built at Douglas' Tulsa, Oklahoma, factory alongside the C-47B, the C-117A featured an airline-style interior, seating for 21, and the DC-3A's small cabin door with integral stairs, although it adopted the C-47's improved wing flaps, landing gear and cabin heating system. The Army Air Forces ordered 131 C-117As in 1945, but only 17 had been completed when VJ-Day caused the cancellation of the remainder of the order.

After these 17 C-117As had entered service, ten were modified as C-117Bs with the superchargers removed from their P&W R-1830 engines. The last C-117s were eleven VC-47s which previously had been leased to Pioneer Airlines and, in 1953, were rebuilt and redesignated as C-117Cs.

It probably was this latter model, the C-117C, which was acquired by the Military Air Transport Service in 1953 when nine C-117s appeared on MATS' inventory. These nine C-117Cs were flown by MATS through 1954, but after this date only one C-117C is known to have flown with MATS, C-117C 42-100769. This aircraft eventually was retired from MATS service in 1962.

Above: **Douglas C-117C, 42-100769, shown at Scott AFB, Illinois, in December 1958, was the only C-117 in MATS at this time.** Dave Ostrowski courtesy of Douglas D Olson

9.10 Douglas C-118 Liftmaster

Over 140 Douglas C-118s were operated by MATS from 1948 to 1966 (and beyond by MAC), for roles as diverse as presidential transport to medevac carrier. From the mid-1950s through the early 1960s, the Liftmaster served as MATS' main personnel and logistic transport, participating in many US and NATO global airlift exercises and humanitarian missions.

Left: **Douglas C-118A, 53-3245, of the Atlantic Division of MATS cruising over Southern California.** Douglas, courtesy of Harry Gann

Center, upper left: **53-3245 later in its career, believed on a visit to the UK and apparently sporting a different color on upper fuselage.** via Chris Salter

Center, lower left: **VC-118A, 53-3240, served as John F Kennedy's presidential aircraft with the 1254th ATG(SM) until a new VC-137C could be delivered.** Courtesy of Clyde Gerdes Collection

Left: **VC-118, 46-505, shown in February 1952, served as the presidential aircraft from 1947 to 1953 as Harry S Truman's 'The Independence', flown by the 1254th ATG(SM), MATS.** Air Force

Center, top right: **After being relieved of its 'Air Force One' status in 1953, VC-118, 46-505 was flown in standard MATS markings by the 1254th ATG (SM).** MAP

Center, lower right: **The same aircraft later served with that unit's fleet of VIP transports and is shown at Washington National Airport in June 1961.** Air Force, courtesy of Clyde Gerdes Collection

VC-118

The progenitor of the C-118 was the Douglas XC-112A, the military prototype of the commercial DC-6 series, a design considered by many to be the finest piston-engined airliner ever built. The XC-112A, a pressurized development of the C-54, made its first flight in February 1946. As the DC-6 production line began winding up, the 29th airplane, originally intended for American Airlines, was chosen as the first C-118. Reconfigured as a presidential aircraft, VC-118, 46-505, was delivered on 1st July 1947, and was officially commissioned on the 4th of July as the 'Independence', in honor of President Harry Truman's Missouri hometown. The Independence featured a presidential stateroom at the rear of the cabin, seating for 24 and sleeping berths for 12, weather radar in the nose, and a spectacular blue, white and yellow eagle design painted on its fuselage.

The VC-118 'Independence' joined the Special Air Missions squadron at Washington National Airport and served as the presidential aircraft throughout the Truman administration. Following its retirement from presidential service in 1953, the airplane was repainted in standard MATS colors and flown as part of the SAM fleet at Washington National/Andrews AFB for the following ten years. In 1963, VC-118, 46-505, was transferred from the SAM fleet to the Tactical Air Command. This historic airplane was retired from service in 1965 and now rests in the Air Force Museum.

C-118A

By 1951, the success of the DC-6, DC-6A, and the newest version, the DC-6B, prompted the Air Force to order 101 militarized versions of the DC-6A for the Military Air Transport Service as the C-118A Liftmaster. The first C-118A, 51-3818, was delivered to MATS in July 1952, and by the mid-1950s the Liftmaster equipped the following squadrons:

33rd ATS, 1705th ATG (HVY), McChord AFB, Washington;
48th ATS, 1502nd ATW, Hickam AFB, Hawaii; and the
18th/29th/30th/38th ATS, 1611th ATW, McGuire AFB, NJ.

The 1741st ATS at Palm Beach International Airport, Florida, also had a small fleet of five C-118As for transition training.

Naval use of the Liftmaster as a MATS transport actually had predated the Air Force's, as first deliveries of the R6D-1, the Navy's version of the DC-6A, began in September 1951. The Navy eventually operated 65 R6D-1s on its MATS routes and for its own logistic and tactical support squadrons. Three Navy squadrons flew the Liftmaster for MATS beginning late in 1951:

VR-3, Naval Air Transport Squadron Three, located at NAS Moffett Field, California, began transitioning from the R5D to the R6D-1 in the fall of 1951. The squadron's new Liftmasters were used on MATS Continental Division routes to Alaska and Japan, where they brought back wounded personnel from the Korean War, and eastward as far as Germany. In mid-July 1957, VR-3 was transferred to the 1611th ATW, Naval Air Transport Wing, Atlantic, MATS, at McGuire AFB, New Jersey. At McGuire AFB, VR-3 R6D-1s flew MATS transport routes to Germany, France, England, Spain, Iceland and Greenland, supported the Middle East airlift following the Marine Corps landings in Lebanon in August 1958, the Pacific airlift following the Formosa tensions, various Deep Freeze operations to New Zealand, and numerous classified and unclassified MATS exercises and operations. In August 1963, VR-3 began transition training from the C-118A to the C-130E. The first squadron Hercules arrived in December 1963, and by late 1964 VR-3 had relinquished its R6D-1/C-118Bs for the C-130E.

Air Transport Squadron Six, VR-6, at Westover AFB, Massachusetts, had been flying R5D Skymasters since the late 1940s as part of the Naval Air Transport Wing, Atlantic, MATS. In addition to operating regular Atlantic Division routes, VR-6 specialized in transporting men and supplies on the 'Arctic Airlift' to Bluie West 8, Sondrestom AB, on the southern coast of Greenland, and to Thule, 900 miles from the North Pole.

The squadron received its first R6D-1 in November 1952, eventually acquiring 13 Liftmasters. In July 1955, VR-6 moved its operations to McGuire AFB, New Jersey. VR-6 was a rather large squadron, at various times having 75 pilots and nearly 1,000 personnel. At some time during the late 1960s, the squadron not only operated its own aircraft on Atlantic Division routes, but it also served as an R6D-1 training squadron and a maintenance squadron for VR-3 Liftmasters, and so had custody of 26 aircraft. In June 1958, all of VR-6's R6D-1s were stricken from the Navy inventory (as were VR-3's aircraft) and transferred to the Air Force as C-118As with Air Force serial numbers. VR-6 continued to operate as before, but now flew its Liftmasters with Air Force markings except for the squadron insignia, which was displayed on both sides of the forward fuselage, with 'VR-6' often painted on the nosewheel doors.

NAS Norfolk, Virginia's Fleet Tactical Support Squadron Twenty-Two, VR-22, had assumed a fleet transport and carrier on-board-delivery (COD) mission upon its establishment in December 1950, flying R4D and R5D transports and Grumman TBM COD aircraft. The unit received its first R6D-1 in June 1955, and used its Liftmasters on logistic support missions for the Atlantic Fleet as well as support for both Arctic and Antarctic scientific missions. VR-22 underwent a name and mission change on 1st July 1958, when it became Air Transport Squadron Twenty-Two and was transferred to the Naval Air Transport Wing, Atlantic, MATS, although the squadron still operated out of NAS Norfolk. Over the next 5½ years, VR-22 flew its redesignated and Air Force-owned C-118As on transatlantic MATS routes to Italy, Morocco, Cuba and Puerto Rico, to New Zealand in support of the Antarctic's 'Operation Deep Freeze', and on special missions to Saigon, Indonesia and Liberia.

VR-22 began its transition to the C-130E Hercules in the spring of 1964. The last operational mission flown by a squadron C-118A occurred on 31st January 1965.

Once in service with Air Force and Navy MATS squadrons, the C-118s earned a reputation for reliability and efficiency. The first MATS C-118A non-stop transatlantic flight was made early in 1954, but in June 1959 a MATS VR-3 Liftmaster made the longest recorded non-stop Liftmaster flight of over 17½ hours from Frankfurt, Germany, to McGuire AFB. During 'Operation Safe Haven' late in 1956 and early 1957, MATS C-118As played a key role in airlifting 14,000 Hungarian refugees to the United States. In a ten-day period in November 1962, eight MATS C-118As (and one MATS C-133) transported nearly 1,300 Irish NATO troops and 60 tons of cargo over a 4,900 mile route between Ireland and the Congo.

Remarkably, despite millions of passenger-miles flown by these MATS Liftmasters in over 13 years of service, the C-118s suffered very few major accidents. The first occurred in March 1955 to a VR-3 R6D-1 when it crashed into Pali Kea Peak, northwest of Honolulu, killing all 57 passengers and crew.

Top left: **C-118A, 51-3832, of the 30th ATS, 1611th ATW, McGuire AFB, New Jersey, at Washington, DC, in June 1954.** Courtesy of Lionel N Paul

Left, second from top: **Douglas R6D-1, 128425, of VR-3 at NAS Moffett Field, over the San Francisco Bay.** Navy

Top right: **MC-118A, 53-3279, of the 1405th AMTW, Scott AFB, Illinois.** APN courtesy of Clyde Gerdes Collection

Above right: **C-118A, 53-3261, at Prestwick. The '0-' serial prefix denotes an aircraft over 10 years old.** Chris Salter collection

Left: **Modifications made to a few Liftmasters flown by the 1370th PMW, Air Photographic and Charting Service, included camera ports installed in the forward cargo door, as shown on RC-118A, 53-3224.** Courtesy of Clyde Gerdes Collection

Bottom: **This immaculate VC-118A, 51-3829 of the 1254th ATG, carries the flags of 45 nations visited. The 'Special Air Missions' Liftmaster was photographed at Las Vegas' McCarran Field in September 1962 during the Annual Meeting of the Air Force Association.** Douglas D Olson

The second took place in October 1956 when a VR-6 R6D-1 disappeared over the Atlantic on a flight from RAF Lakenheath to Lincoln, Nebraska, via Lajes AB, Azores, with the loss of 50 passengers and nine crewmen.

VC-118A

In 1955, four standard MATS C-118As (51-3829, 53-3223, 53-3229 and 53-3240) were reconfigured as VC-118As by installing sleeping or conference compartments, a stateroom, lounge, coatrooms and a folding electric ladder. Both cargo doors were sealed shut and an extra window was installed in the rear cargo door. Passenger accommodations ranged from 18 on VC-118A, 53-3229, to 29 on VC-118A, 53-3240.

All of these Liftmasters were assigned to the 1254th ATG at Washington National Airport/Andrews AFB as Special Missions aircraft. When President John F Kennedy took office, VC-118A, 53-3240, was selected to serve as the presidential aircraft until a new Boeing VC-137C could be delivered.

The VC-118A's interior accommodations were updated, a new communications center was installed, and the Liftmaster was given newer electronics. Outwardly, this VC-118A remained in its MATS Special Air Missions paint scheme, although the presidential seal was placed beside the main cabin door. At a later date, the VC-118A was repainted in the standard 'Air Force One' blue and white scheme with 'United States of America' replacing 'Military Air Transport Service' on the upper fuselage.

MC-118A

A small number of C-118As were operated as medevac aircraft by the 1405th Aeromedical Transport Wing at Scott AFB, with the 11th AMTS flying out of Scott AFB and the 12th AMTS from McGuire AFB, New Jersey. These Liftmasters, sometimes designated as MC-118As, flew patients from overseas bases into the USA for treatment, carrying up to 60 litters with seven attendants.

RC-118A

In the early 1960s, a small number of C-118As were converted to RC-118As by installing circular camera ports in the forward cargo door. These aircraft were operated by the 1371st Mapping and Charting Squadron, 1370th Photo Mapping Wing, at Turner AFB, Georgia.

Fairchild C-119C, 50-133, with the Fairchild Hagerstown factory in the background. Fairchild Aircraft, courtesy of Kent A Mitchell

9.11 Fairchild C-119 Flying Boxcar

The C-119 'Flying Boxcar' design began as a development of Fairchild's successful C-82 Packet. The C-82's 2,100 hp R-2800 engines were replaced on the C-119 by 2,650 hp R-4360s, a redesigned flight deck was lowered and moved forward on the more streamlined nose, and the Packet's ventral tail fins were removed. Originally designated as the XC-82B, the prototype eventually became the C-119A. The C-119B replaced the Packet on the production line, featuring a widened fuselage, a slight increase in wingspan, and a 20,000 lb increase in gross weight to 74,000 lbs. Fifty-five C-119Bs were delivered to the Air Force beginning in December 1949, followed by 347 C-119Cs featuring 3,500 hp R-4360s and a large dorsal fin and built at two production lines run by Fairchild and Kaiser Manufacturing Co. The two companies teamed to build 210 C-119Fs, re-engined with Wright R-3350s and with the gross weight increasing to 85,000 lbs. The C-119G was the final version of the 'Flying Boxcar', with nearly 400 of this variant delivered to the Air Force.

While C-119s served mainly with the Troop Carrier Command and Combat Cargo Command in Korea, a small number of 'Flying Boxcars' served with MATS units beginning in 1951. The first of these were attached to the Air Resupply and Communications Service after it had been formed in February 1951. The ARCS used the C-119s to support its various clandestine operations during the Korean War. A number of ARCS C-119s were used to supply the French forces at Danang, Haiphong and Hanoi in 1953, flown by crews of the 581st ARCW at Clark AB, Philippines.

The 1739th Ferrying Squadron, 1708th Ferrying Wing, Continental Division, MATS, at Amarillo AFB, Texas, operated at least two C-119s from October 1953 through 1957. A C-119C and C-119G were flown by the squadron for pilot checkout and proficiency as the 1739th FYS was actively ferrying these models from the factory to operating units.

The Airways and Air Communications Service flew a number of C-119Cs between 1955 and 1959. These aircraft were used to support the installation, maintenance and flight checking of AACS-operated navigational aids and communications facilities by the following units:

3rd AACS Mobile Communications Squadron, Tinker AFB, Oklahoma
1881st Electronics Installation Squadron
1884th Electronics Installation Squadron
1855th Facility Checking Flight, Elmendorf AFB, Alaska

9.12 Lockheed C-121 Constellation

The Military Air Transport Service operated a total of 78 of the elegant C-121 Constellation in six models. The prototype of 22 C-69 Constellations made its initial flight on 9th January 1943, most of these aircraft being used by the Air Transport Command from mid-1944 to the end of the war, when they were sold for airline use.

C-121A

An $11.4 million contract was signed with Lockheed in February 1948 for ten Model 749 Constellations, designated as C-121As (48-608/617). This model's relatively high cruising speed and 44-seat capacity made it more suited as a passenger carrier. Between December 1948 and March 1949, eight of these C-121As were delivered to Westover AFB, Masachusetts, and assigned to the Atlantic Division of MATS. At Westover AFB, the Constellations began transatlantic support missions for the Berlin Airlift, making 15 flights a month to Rhein-Main, Germany, via the Azores, carrying replacement aircrews and high-priority cargo. Return flights were made with one stop at Keflavik, Iceland.

Following the Berlin Airlift, six C-121As were converted to VC-121As to replace the ageing VC-54s in use by the 1254th ATS 'Special Air Missions' unit at Washington National Airport. Each airplane was given a customized VIP interior, with executive compartments, carpeting, galleys, and seating. Beginning in July 1950, the VC-121As were used by the 1254th ATS(SM) to fly governmental and military VIPs worldwide. One VC-121A, 48-610, was given a specific assignment as President Dwight D Eisenhower's presidential aircraft, the 'Columbine II'. In August 1956, in order to simplify maintenance standards, all VC-121As (as well as the VC-121B) were redesignated as C-121As.

As these C-121As eventually were replaced by more modern aircraft, they were operated by the 1254th ATW(SM) mainly on domestic VIP flights. Also, their rather flamboyant MATS markings gave way to a more subdued scheme with 'United States of America' painted on their fuselages. Those aircraft that remained with the Special Air Missions wing were retired between January 1967 and mid-1968.

VC-121B

During its construction, 48-608, the first C-121, was given a VIP interior, including a stateroom, seating for 24, ten sleeping berths, and a smaller passenger door, and redesignated as a VC-121B. The aircraft was delivered to the 1254th ATS(SM) in November 1948 where it was assigned to the Secretary of the Air Force and later to the Secretary of Defense. The VC-121B remained with the Special Air Missions fleet at Washington National Airport/Andrews AFB until its transfer in April 1966.

C-121C

In order to increase MATS' long-range transport capabilities, the Air Force signed a contract for 33 Lockheed Model 1049 Super Constellations, designated as C-121Cs, 54-151/183. Over 20 feet longer than the C-121A, the C-121C grossed 135,000 pounds and its R-3350 engines produced 3,500 hp as compared to the C-121A's 2,500 hp. Between June 1955 and May 1956, these aircraft were delivered to the 1608th ATW at Charleston AFB, South Carolina, divided between the 41st ATS and the 76th ATS. The Super Constellations were flown on Atlantic Division/EASTAF transatlantic routes to Europe, the Mediterranean, the Middle East, and as far east as India. MATS C-121Cs airlifted refugees during the Hungarian Crisis of 1956-1957, and troops to the Lebanon Crisis in 1958, the Berlin Crisis in 1961, and briefly during the Cuban Crisis of 1962. However, by October 1962 nearly all of these C-121Cs had been replaced by the new Lockheed C-130E Hercules.

Four Air Force C-121Cs, 54-159/168/174/181, were operated by Navy Air Transport Squadron Seven, VR-7 Detachment A, at Tachikawa AB, Japan, from 1962 until 1966. These aircraft

C-121A, 48-612, one of eight C-121A Constellations assigned to the Atlantic Division of MATS in 1948-1949. Air Force courtesy of Robert Archer

retained their Air Force serial numbers while flying as Detachment A, 1503rd ATW, MATS.

VC-121E

One Navy R7V-1 Super Constellation, 131650, was transferred to the Air Force while still on the production line. The airplane was converted to VIP configuration and redesignated as a VC-121E, 53-7885. The Super Constellation was assigned in August 1954 to the 1254th ATG(SM) at Washington National Airport and christened as the 'Columbine III' on November 24, 1954. The 1254th ATG(SM) operated this airplane as 'Air Force One', flying President Eisenhower as well as other American and foreign dignitaries until January 1961, when it was replaced by a VC-137A. The VC-121E remained with the Special Air Missions wing as a VIP aircraft until its retirement in April 1966.

C-121G

Along with the Air Force's procurement of 33 C-121Cs, the Navy received 50 R7V-1s, with most of these serving as its contribution to MATS. These Super Constellations were flown by VR-8, beginning in June 1953, and VR-7, which received its first R7V-1 in January 1954, both squadrons based at Hickam AFB, Hawaii, as part of the Pacific Division of MATS. The Navy R7V-1s were flown mainly on the MATS 'Embassy Runs' from Hickam AFB to Manila, Tokyo, Australia, and as far west as India.

VR-7 and VR-8 moved their headquarters to NAS Moffett Field, California, beginning in August 1957. Both squadrons were reassigned to the Naval Air Transport Wing, Pacific, and 32 of their R7V-1s were transferred to the Air Force in May and June 1958 as C-121Gs, 54-4048/4079. These Super Constellations continued making passenger and cargo flights from NAS Moffett Field over MATS Pacific routes to Hawaii, the Far East, Australia and New Zealand, including 'Operation Deep Freeze' support flights in 1959 and 1961, until being replaced by the C-130E during the fall of 1963.

YC-121F

Two Lockheed Model 1049s which had been originally ordered by the Navy as R7V-1s, 131660-131661, were modified as Model 1249A turboprop test beds by substituting their R-3350 engines with 6,000 hp Pratt & Whitney T34s. YC-121Fs, 53-8157 and 53-8158 joined two similarly-powered YC-97Js in a 4,000 flight hour test program to establish the reliability of the T34 engine and propeller combination slated for the new Douglas C-133 Cargomaster.

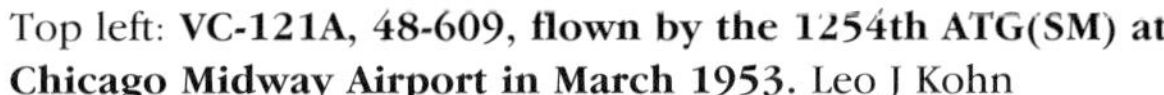

Top left: **VC-121A, 48-609, flown by the 1254th ATG(SM) at Chicago Midway Airport in March 1953.** Leo J Kohn

Above left: **C-121C, 54-180, of the 1611th ATW, McGuire AFB, New Jersey, shown at McEntire ANGB, South Carolina, in October 1961.** Courtesy of Norman Taylor Collection

Below: **Lockheed R7V-1, 128438, operated by VR-8 at Hickam AFB, Hawaii in 1953.** Navy, courtesy of Peter B Mersky

Top right: **VC-121A, 48-610, President Dwight D Eisenhower's 'Columbine II' after it had been relieved of presidential service and placed in the 1254th ATG(SM) VIP pool.** Courtesy of Clyde Gerdes Collection

Above right: **'Columbine III', VC-121E, 53-7885, while being flown by the 1254th ATW 'Special Air Missions' wing as a VIP aircraft in the early 1960s.** Courtesy of Clyde Gerdes Collection

Above: **While this C-121G, 54-4052, shown over San Francisco in 1958, displays Air Force markings, the Constellation's round windows identify it as formerly a Navy R7V-1, 128438, operated by VR-7.** Navy, courtesy of Robert L Lawson

Below: **YC-121F, 53-8157, one of two Constellations powered by the P&W T34 and flown in a service test program by the 1700th Test Squadron (Turbo-Prop), 1700th ATG, at Kelly AFB. Note the airplane's two-foot-wide propellers.** Howard Levy, courtesy of Douglas D Olson

However, the YC-121Fs were delivered late to the 1700th Test Squadron (Turbo-Prop), 1700th ATG, Continental Division, MATS, at Kelly AFB, Texas, and, despite achieving record-setting performance, problems occurred throughout their testing program.

In January 1956, aircrews from the 1700th Test Squadron (Turbo-Prop) were sent to Edwards AFB for indoctrination in flight procedures on the YC-121Fs. The first airplane was ferried to Kelly AFB 11th February 1956, making the 1,200 mile flight from Edwards AFB in 2 hours 45 minutes, averaging 450 mph. The second airplane was received at Kelly AFB on 17th April and the two YC-121Fs began crew familiarization and check-out flights as well as a demonstration flight to Andrews AFB.

The YC-121Fs began overseas operations on 8th May, when 53-8157 flew from Kelly AFB to Rhein-Main, Germany. However, following this flight the aircraft began experiencing cracked propeller pump housings and subsequent loss of oil to the point where, on 29th May, the Air Research and Development Command grounded the two YC-121Fs. Over the following five months the Constellations gained minimal flight time due to continued problems with the YC-121F fuel systems, propellers (causing another grounding in August), and the need to reskin the inboard trailing edge of the upper wing surface of one of the airplanes. The leaking propellers caused a secondary problem to develop, as 'fairly large amounts' of oil were collected from cabin air during tests. To add insult to injury, noise level studies made in the two YC-121Fs during flight revealed pressure levels as high as 120db, with an average of 108db. As a result, the wearing of 'ear defenders' was made mandatory for all personnel flying in the aircraft.

The various problems with the YC-121Fs eventually were overcome so that, in October 1956, a new speed record was set by 53-8157 between Los Angeles and San Antonio, Texas, when the 1,260 mile flight was made in just under three hours. The same airplane made a four-day trip to England in November, covering 9,757 miles in 35¼ flight hours. During 'Operation Safe Haven' in December, four transatlantic trips were flown by a YC-121F to Germany and France, returning to the United States with Hungarian refugees. And, in January 1957, a YC-121F flew from Long Beach, California, to Andrews AFB at an average speed of over 490 mph. By mid-1957, the two YC-121Fs had achieved their test goals, and both the airplanes and the 1700th Test Squadron quickly disappeared from the scene.

9.13 Fairchild C-123 Provider

The C-123 Provider was a development of the Chase XCG-20 all-metal assault glider, capable of carrying 60 troops. The design became a powered assault transport in 1949 when the prototype XC-123 made its first flight on October 14 powered by two P&W R-2800 engines.

Following the delivery of five service test C-123Bs, a production order for 300 of this model was placed in 1953, to be built by the Kaiser-Frazer Corp, which recently had acquired Chase. However, this order soon was cancelled due to a contract disagreement between the Air Force and Kaiser-Frazer. Fairchild was awarded the new contract in 1953, and by mid-1958 had produced a total of 302 C-123Bs.

The Military Air Transport Service operated one C-123B between 1959 and 1963. C-123B, 57-6289, the sixth from last Provider delivered to the Air Force, was flown by the 1254th ATW(SM), at Washington National Airport. While details of this Provider's use by the Special Air Missions wing have been elusive, it seems likely that the airplane was used to transport the presidential limousine to public engagements across the country and to haul aircraft engines and spare parts for SAM fleet aircraft wherever needed.

Below: **Fairchild C-123, 57-6289, operated by the 1254th ATG (SM), at Washington National Airport in April 1961.** Air Force

Above: **C-124A, 50-083, of the Continental Division of MATS displays Arctic red outer wings and empennage.** Air Force/MAP

9.14 Douglas C-124 Globemaster II

The Douglas C-124 Globemaster II was the Military Air Transport Service's main heavy lift transport for over 15 years, operational from 1950 to well into the 1970s (with reserve squadrons). At its peak use with MATS in 1963, 377 C-124s equipped over 20 air transport and troop carrier squadrons in seven wings.

The C-124 was a development of the Douglas C-74 Globemaster, its design coinciding with and reinforcing the lessons being learned from the use of large transports by the Air Force during the Berlin Airlift. The fifth C-74, 42-65406, was retired from MATS service in June 1948 and was flown to the Douglas Long Beach factory for conversion to the YC-124. The airplane's wings, engines, main landing gear and empennage were mated to an enlarged, rectangular fuselage which featured nose-mounted clamshell doors and built-in loading ramps. Also retained on the C-124 were the C-74's integral twin loading cranes, which ran on overhead rails the entire cabin's length, and which could function as a freight elevator through a detachable section of the cabin floor.

The new C-124 could accommodate 95 percent of the Army Field Force's equipment without disassembly, as well as carry 200 passengers, or 127 litter patients, or 68,500 pounds of cargo. Due to its large internal volume, the Globemaster II was one of the few (if not the only) MATS transport that could be loaded to its maximum weight before running out of cargo storage area.

The initial flight of the YC-124 was on 27th November 1949, and the first production C-124A was completed and delivered in May 1950. MATS received the first of its C-124As the following month and began transition training on the new 175,000 lb transport almost immediately. The North Koreans also chose to begin the Korean War in June 1950, and MATS' C-124s played an increasingly important part in supplying allied forces in Korea, although not directly. Following Air Proving Ground tests in Korea with a single C-124A, which had proven successful in October 1951, the Combat Cargo Command began its first operational flights from Japan to Korea with the C-124A in July 1952.

As more MATS C-124 Squadrons became operational from 1951 onward, they took up an increasing part of the Pacific shuttle flights, carrying personnel and supplies westward into Japan, where Combat Cargo aircraft would take over the actual delivery into the Korean war zone, and returning eastward with war casualties. Initial MATS units included the 3rd ATS, 1608th ATW, at Brookley AFB, Alabama; the 32nd and 34th ATS at McChord AFB, Washington; and the 85th ATS, 1501st ATW, at Travis AFB, California. Providing transition training on the C-124 was the 1740th ATS at Palm Beach International Airport, Florida, which had a fleet of seven to nine C-124s throughout the 1950s to perform its mission as part of MATS' Continental Division.

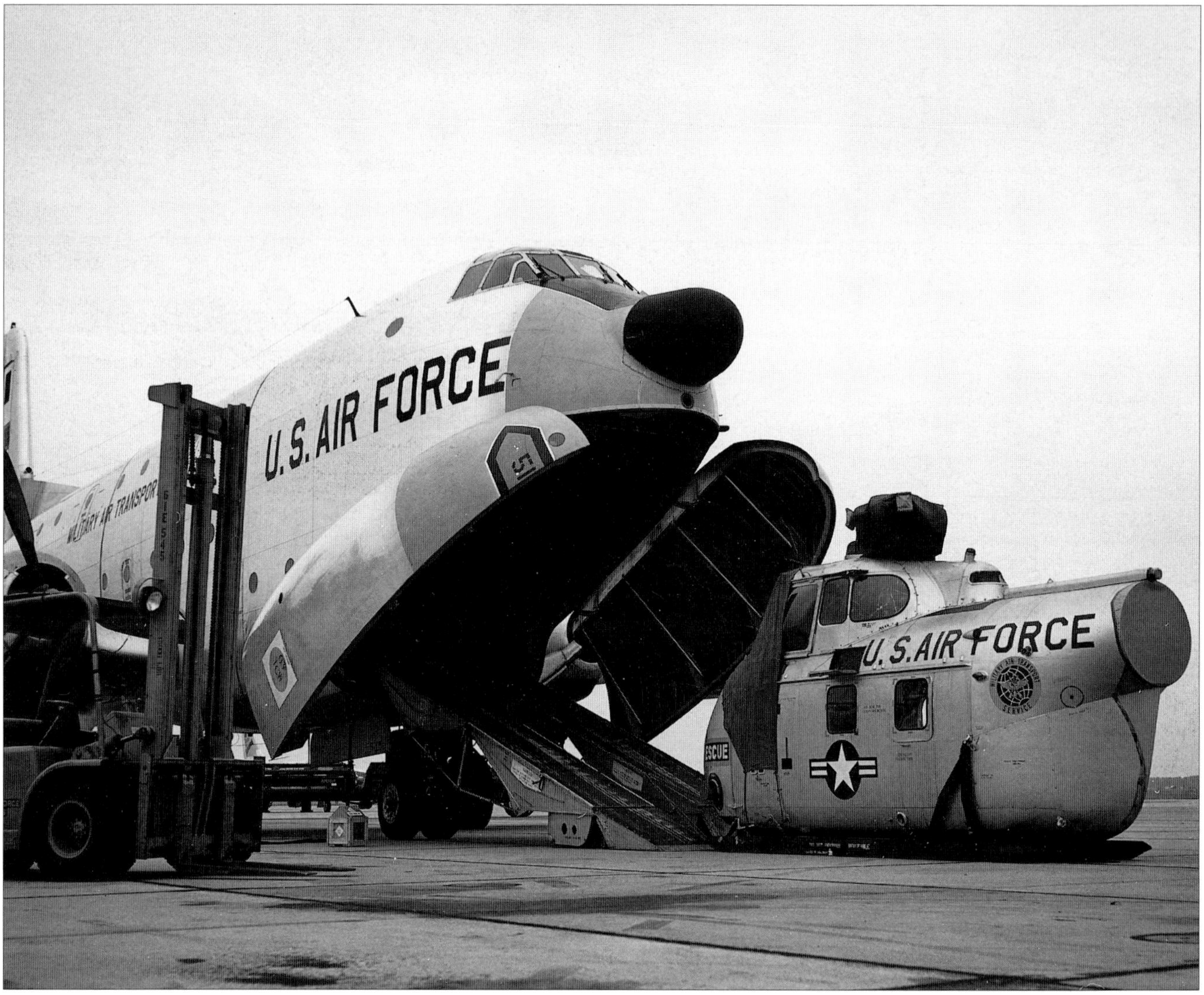
U.S. AIR FORCE
U.S. AIR FORCE

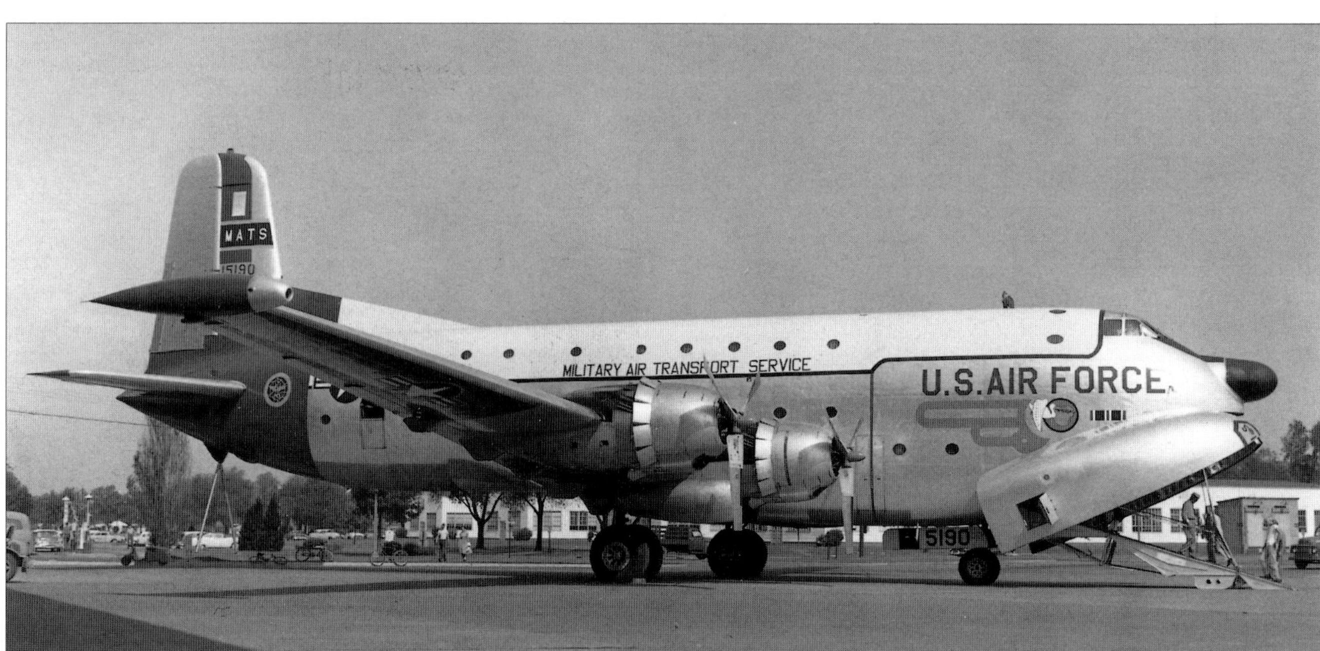

MATS
15190
MILITARY AIR TRANSPORT SERVICE
U.S. AIR FORCE
5190

Photographs on the opposite page:

Top: **A 63rd Troop Carrier Wing C-124C shows off its clamshell doors and integral loading ramps before swallowing a MATS ARS H-19.** Air Force, courtesy of Norman Taylor

Bottom: **Douglas C-124C Globemaster II, 51-5190, of the 9th Troop Carrier Squadron at Scott AFB, Illinois, in May 1958.** Dave Ostrowski, courtesy of Douglas D Olson

Photographs on this page:

Above left: **Douglas C-124C, 52-1035. The Globemaster II was capable of carrying 200 passengers or nearly 70,000 pounds of cargo.** Air Force, courtesy of 1Lt M J Kasiuba

Above right: **63rd Troop Carrier Wing C-124C, 52-950.** Courtesy of Clyde Gerdes Collection

Despite the crashes of two non-MATS C-124As in December 1950 and June 1951, in which over 200 were killed (attributed to faulty engine generators), and the expected teething problems all new aircraft suffer, the C-124 developed into a dependable transport aircraft. In 1952, C-124A production ended with 204 aircraft completed, to be succeeded by the C-124C which featured an increased fuel capacity, a higher gross weight (194,500 lbs) and payload, combustion de-icing heaters housed in wingtip pods, and a nose-mounted APS-42 weather search radar. Most of the earlier C-124As were retro-fitted with these wingtip combustion heaters and search radars. Production of the 243rd and last C-124C was in May 1955, for a total of 446 Globemaster IIs built.

As new C-124s came off the production line during the early 1950s, MATS' share of the Globemaster IIs increased steadily, from 10 in 1951 to 119 in 1954 and 170 in 1956. However, almost overnight, MATS was the recipient of over 150 C-124s as the Tactical Air Command lost two wings of troop carrier Globemaster IIs in a 1957 Air Force realignment, and through the mid-1960s MATS maintained a fleet of over 300 of the aircraft, reaching a high of 377 in 1963. By the end of 1964, the C-124 Globemaster II equipped the following MATS squadrons:

- 4th/7th/8th/19th ATS, 62nd ATW, McChord AFB, Washington
- 28th ATS, 1501st ATW, Hill AFB, Utah
- 75th/85th ATS, 1501st ATW, Travis AFB, California
- 50th ATS/6th TCS, 1502nd ATW, Hickam AFB, Hawaii
- 22nd TCS, 1503rd ATG, Tachikawa AB, Japan
- 9th TCS/20th TCS/31st ATS, 1607th ATW, Dover AFB, Delaware
- 3rd ATS/17th ATS, 1608th ATW, Charleston AFB, South Carolina
- 1740th ATS, 1707th ATW, Tinker AFB, Oklahoma
- 14th/15th/52nd/53rd/54th TCS, 63rd TCW, Hunter AFB, GA
- 7th ATS, 63rd TCW, Robins AFB, Georgia

During its service with MATS, the C-124 participated in nearly every major airlift, including the Army's RotoPlan, the rotation of its combat troops in Europe; 'Long Thrust' airlifts in support of NATO; 'Long Sabre' operations in the Pacific; SAC overseas deployments; troop movements in support of the United Nations' worldwide peace-keeping missions; joint airborne training programs with the US Army; airlift support for Joint Task Force Eight, the US nuclear test program in the Pacific; support for 'Operation Deep Freeze', the US Navy's scientific expedition in Antarctica; and the preparations for airlift and paratroop operations during the Cuban Crisis in October and November 1962. In addition, MATS Globemaster IIs provided humanitarian aid following many of the earthquakes, floods, famines, droughts, fires, and other previously-mentioned disasters and crises that occurred every year. MATS' C-124s, for instance, carried over 500 casualties following the French defeat at Dien Bien Phu in 1954, picking up the survivors at Saigon and transporting them to Tokyo.

9.15 Northrop YC-125B Raider

If the inclusion of the YC-125B in this book sends the more knowledgeable reader into near apoplexy, it should be stated at the outset that this airplane never served with the Air Rescue Service nor with any other MATS organization. The Air Rescue Service markings applied to several of the YC-125Bs appear to have been more a Northrop marketing ploy than actually service-connected.

However, the design of the airplane that became the YC-125B was strongly influenced by Air Rescue Service planners, and one or two Raiders were involved in Air Rescue Service tests during the early 1950s.

Northrop originally intended its N-32 design to be a civil development of the N-23 Pioneer, replacing Ford Trimotors at Central and South American mines, plantations and other locations where short, unimproved airstrips were common. This scheme evaporated almost overnight when, in the spring of 1948, the prototype N-23 crashed, killing its pilot, and after a major partner in the venture, the Central American airline TACA, was forced to cancel its order for 40 N-32s. Fortunately, Northrop had been courting the Air Force with the N-32 and, in March 1948, only days after the Pioneer's crash, a $5½ million contract was signed for 23 YC-125s: 13 YC-125A assault transports and ten YC-125B Arctic rescue aircraft. The YC-125A made its maiden flight on 1st August 1949, and subsequent Raiders underwent flight testing at Edwards AFB and Eglin AFB and static testing at Wright-Patterson AFB.

Unfortunately, what originally was an excellent airplane became a prime example of the worst that can happen when a design is influenced by committee – in the C-125's case, by three committees. The original intent of the Air Force's glider contingent was to use the C-125 as a simple, short-range, powered assault glider, being towed or flown to the landing site, discharging its load, and then using its short-field capabilities to take off for another load.

When the Air Force's Arctic Rescue Group became interested in the airplane, their requirements included provisions for a navigator and a radioman and their extra equipment, six large combustion heaters with their associated ducting, and an autopilot and its control couplings. The Arctic rescue mission profile also increased the C-125's fuel capacity to 1,800 gallons, substantially more than required by an assault transport. Finally, the Army required a reinforced floor to accommodate its artillery pieces, a paratroop door built within the floor ramp, and an oxygen system for 32 paratroopers, all of which increased the C-125's empty weight considerably with no corresponding increase in horsepower.

The airplane that resulted was underpowered, overweight, and dangerously unstable under gusty wind or turbulent flight conditions. This characteristic was borne out in 1949 during maximum performance flight tests at Eglin AFB, Florida, when YC-125A, 48-628, stalled and crashed just before touchdown while landing in gusty crosswinds. In their final flight test report on the YC-125, Edwards AFB test pilots stated that the airplane was 'the worst aircraft stability wise' they had ever flown, and that the Raider had 'no application for Air Force use'.

Most of the 23 YC-125 service test aircraft delivered by 1950 were flown to Sheppard AFB, Texas, where they were used as non-flying engine maintenance training aircraft. But the Air Rescue Service was still hoping the YC-125B would make a suitable Arctic rescue ship, and one YC-125B, 48-622, was fitted with skis and flown in 1950 during the Air Force's SOIAS (Sliding On Ice And Snow) Project. The airplane was found to be superior to the ski-equipped C-82 Packet and, in its report on the tests, the Air Force considered the YC-125B to be 'superior to any large aircraft previously tested on skis in the respect of take-off performance.'

Another YC-125B was flown in 1951 by the Air Rescue Service during cold weather tests at Bemidji, Minnesota. The Air Rescue Service concluded that the airplane had exceptionally good short-field performance, but its payload on skis was so small that the YC-125B was considered operationally unsuitable.

Left: **Northrop YC-125B 48-620 on a test flight over the Pacific Ocean off the Southern California coast.** Northrop courtesy of Gerald Balzer

Lower left: **YC-125B, 48-620, on the Northrop ramp, displaying its factory-applied Air Rescue Service markings.** Northrop, courtesy of 1Lt M J Kasiuba

Below right: **YC-125B, 48-622, is painted in Arctic red markings with 'SOIAS' painted on the fuselage ahead of the national insignia.** Courtesy of Clyde Gerdes Collection

9.16 Cessna LC-126A

In 1949, the Air Force was searching for a relatively fast, rugged, light airplane for Arctic search and rescue missions. It chose the Cessna Model 195 powered by a 300 hp Jacobs radial engine, a throwback to an earlier era which helped earn the civil 195 the nickname, 'The Cadillac of the Air'. Fifteen aircraft were procured as LC-126As, 49-1947/1960 and 49-2757, with 'LC' indicating their status as 'cold weather transports'. These LC-126As were nearly identical to the Model 195, with the exception of a small pilot's emergency escape hatch built into the left side of the cabin, a more austere interior, military radio equipment, and interchangeable sets of Edo floats and Federal skis for the landing gear.

Of the 15 LC-126As purchased by the Air Force, only six were operated by the Air Rescue Service between 1949 and 1953. These aircraft were flown by Alaska's 10th Air Rescue Squadron, which began operating its LC-126As in March 1949 while the unit was attached to the Alaska Air Command. By the time the 10th ARS had been reassigned to the Air Rescue Service on 1st July 1950, the LC-126As were being flown almost exclusively by the Lake Hood Detachment, a seaplane base operated by the 10th ARS' Flight B. The detachment maintained as many as three LC-126As at Lake Hood on a year-round basis, using floats in the summer months and skis in the winter as lakes and rivers provided the only landing facilities in the outlying areas of the Alaskan Territory. The LC-126A was well-suited to the rugged conditions which existed at Lake Hood: the airplane had a large cargo-hauling capacity for its size, was an excellent instrument flyer, and maintenance was simplified by the design's 'swing-out' engine mounts.

The LC-126As operated with the Air Rescue Service in Alaska until approximately August 1953, when the airplanes were transferred to the US Army. Their missions eventually were assumed by the Piasecki SH-21.

Top: **LC-126A, 49-1953, of the 10th ARS, Flight B, Lake Hood Detachment, in 1951.** Air Force, courtesy of Clyde Wilkes

Below: **Cessna LC-126A, 49-1949, of the 10th Rescue Squadron photographed in 1949, less than a year before the squadron was absorbed by the Air Rescue Service.** Colonel H B Allen, courtesy of David Menard

9.17 Lockheed C-130 Hercules

An Air Force decision in 1951 to develop turboprop-powered transports resulted in the design and purchase of the Douglas C-133 Cargomaster and the Lockheed C-130 Hercules. In September 1952, the Air Force signed a contract with Lockheed for two prototype YC-130s, the first of these flying on 23rd August 1954. The production C-130A made its first flight on 7th April 1955, and 219 of this model were built to replace the C-119s in use by the Tactical Air Command and the Troop Carrier Command. The C-130B, with uprated T56 engines and a greater fuel capacity, made its first flight on 12th June 1959, 85 operating with TAC and as satellite recovery aircraft. The C-130E, featuring underwing fuel tanks and an increased gross weight, first flew on 25th August 1961. Future models of the Hercules would confirm the design's remarkable versatility, in a lengthy production run that rivals any other aircraft.

RC-130A

The first version of the Hercules to enter service with MATS was the RC-130A, a variant used for aerial survey and mapping, developed jointly by Lockheed Marietta and the Air Photographic and Charting Service. Following conversion of a prototype RC-130A, 54-1632, 15 RC-130As (57-510/524), were built in 1959. Outwardly, these aircraft featured camera windows along the underside of the fuselage. An Airborne Profile Recorder (APR), for obtaining precise terrain height, was installed with a television viewfinder blister protruding below the nose radome. Additional crew stations were provided for the APR operator, two HIRAN (High Precision Ranging and Navigation) operators, a photo-navigator, and a photographer, as well as spaces for a darkroom, mapping equipment, dropsondes (used to determine wind speed and direction) and a galley.

The first RC-130A was delivered to the 1375th Mapping and Charting Squadron, 1370th Photo Mapping Group, Turner AFB, Georgia, in March 1959, and field operations were begun almost immediately in New York and Iceland. The remaining 15 RC-130As were delivered to the 1375th MCS throughout 1959. By combining the HIRAN and photographic functions, these RC-130As each replaced two RB-50s which previously were required to accomplish the same mission. The RC-130A was capable of cruising for four hours at 34,000 feet, enabling its eight-man crew to map a considerably greater area than had been possible with the earlier aircraft. These RC-130As continued to be flown through 1965 by the 1375th MCS at Turner AFB on widespread mapping and charting missions.

C-130E

By 1960, it was apparent to Air Force planners that MATS' strategic airlift capability was woefully outdated. Aside from the Douglas C-133 and a few Special Air Missions VC-137s, MATS' entire airlift inventory was made up of piston-engined transports.

A design competition held in 1961 resulted in a production contract for the all-jet Lockheed C-141 Starlifter. But as the C-141A would not be available for several years, the Air Force procured new versions of the two already-existing designs to serve as stopgap transports in the interim: the Boeing C-135A and the Lockheed C-130E Hercules.

The C-130E basically was a C-130B structurally strengthened to carry a 45,000 lb payload at a gross weight of 155,000 lbs, 20,000 lbs over the earlier model. Two 1,360-gallon external fuel tanks were mounted beneath the wings, enabling the C-130E to carry a 20,000 lb payload nearly 4,000 miles on its transatlantic or transpacific routes.

Initial deliveries of these MATS C-130Es began in April 1962 to the 41st ATS and 76th ATS, 1608th ATW, at Charleston AFB, South Carolina, and to the 29th ATS and 30th ATS, 1611th ATW, McGuire AFB, New Jersey. Out of over 360 C-130Es eventually produced for the Air Force in three fiscal year blocks (61-2358 /2373; 62-1784/1866; and 63-7764/7899), MATS squadrons at first were authorized to receive only 99 aircraft, but this was increased eventually to over 130 (post-1966) as the Vietnam War intensified. By 1965, nearly 120 C-130Es equipped various MATS units including the 41st ATS and 76th ATS as well as the 86th ATS, 1501st ATW, Travis AFB, California, although these aircraft were transferred to Tactical Air Command by 1967.

The Navy component of MATS also operated C-130Es over their world-wide routes. VR-3, based at McGuire AFB, New Jersey, and assigned to the Naval Air Transport Wing, Atlantic, Eastern Transport Air Force, began transition training from the squadron's C-118As to the C-130E in August 1963. VR-3 received their first C-130E in December. Over the next two years, VR-3 trained with their Hercules in formation and CARP (Computed Air Release Point) missions. Airdrops of heavy equipment and personnel were conducted at Charleston AFB, Pope AFB, North Carolina, Fort Lee, Virginia, and locally at NAS Lakehurst, New Jersey, while MATS scheduled transport missions also were flown worldwide by the squadron's 16 assigned C-130Es.

VR-22, also based at McGuire AFB, had been a Navy MATS squadron since the early 1950s flying the C-54 and, starting in June 1955, the C-118A on MATS transatlantic routes and also to Cuba and Puerto Rico as part of the Naval Air Transport Wing, Atlantic. The squadron's first two C-130Es arrived in February 1964, and by March VR-22 was operating ten C-130Es along with a dozen C-118As.

In the fall of 1965, VR-22 moved to NAS Moffett Field, California, joining the Naval Air Transport Wing, Pacific, in November. The squadron, as part of MATS' Western Transport Air Force, flew its C-130Es over transpacific routes until being disestablished in April 1967.

VR-7, at NAS Moffett Field, had been operating its Lockheed R7V-1 Constellations as part of the Naval Air Transport Wing, Pacific, until 1958, when the squadron was transferred to the Air Force and placed under MATS control. Its R7V-1s were redesignated as C-121Gs, and the squadron continued to fly scheduled routes throughout the Pacific, the Far East, Australia, and New Zealand. VR-7 began the transition to the C-130E in August 1963, and continued to fly the Hercules for MATS on transpacific routes through 1965.

WC-130B

In October 1962, the first of five WC-130Bs, (62-3492/3496), was delivered to the 55th Weather Reconnaissance Squadron, 9th Weather Reconnaissance Group, Air Weather Service, at McClellan AFB, California. The squadron used these WC-130Bs to replace their ageing WB-50Ds for weather reconnaissance missions over the Eastern Pacific.

Top: **Lockheed RC-130A, 57-518, of the 1375th Mapping and Charting Squadron, 1370th PMG, Turner AFB, Georgia.** Air Force, courtesy of 1Lt M J Kasiuba

Above left: **C-130E, 63-7874, flown by the 1611th ATW, McGuire AFB, New Jersey, in 1964.** Massachusetts ANG Museum, courtesy of Tom Hildreth

Above right: **Air Weather Service WC-130B, 62-3496, the last of five operated by the 55th WRS, 9th WRG, McClellan AFB, California.** Air Force, courtesy of 1Lt M J Kasiuba

Below: **This Air Force C-130E, 64-570, photographed in 1965, was flown by one of three Navy Air Transport Squadrons. Note 'NATWP' on the airplane's nose, standing for 'Naval Air Transport Wing, Pacific'.** MAP

In May 1964, three of the WC-130Bs were transferred to the 54th WRS, the 'Typhoon Chasers', at Anderson AFB, Guam, while a year later the 53rd WRS at Hunter AFB, Georgia, received all five aircraft as the 54th WRS and the 55th WRS converted to more modern equipment. The 'Hurricane Hunters' of the 53rd WRS retained their WC-130Bs at least until the late 1960s for weather recon over the Western Atlantic and the Gulf of Mexico.

WC-130E

The first WC-130E to serve with the Air Weather Service was delivered from the factory as a standard C-130E to the 53rd WRS at Hunter AFB, Georgia, in April 1965. The Air Force Logistics Command subsequently modified the airplane to the WC-130E configuration, and by May 1965, five additional WC-130Es (61-2365/2366 and 64-552/554) had been modified for duty with the 53rd WRS at Ramey AB, Puerto Rico, and the 54th WRS at Anderson AFB, Guam. These WC-130Es were used to penetrate hurricanes at 10,000 feet to obtain low-level data, then climb to 30,000 feet for high-level probes. All aircraft served with the Air Weather Service at least through the early 1970s.

HC-130H

The Air Rescue Service first made plans for modifying a C-130 to fit the air search, rescue and recovery role in 1963. The airplane would not only rescue downed airmen, but also would be capable of retrieving data cassettes and film packs ejected from satellites as well as support NASA's manned space flight program.

The HC-130H featured uprated T56-A-15 engines, the C-130E's external fuel tanks as well as up to two additional 1,800 gallon fuel tanks carried within the cargo hold, a radome on the upper fuselage which housed a satellite re-entry tracking system, and the Fulton Recovery System mounted on the airplane's nose. This system provided an air retrieval capability of satellite packs as well as personnel from either water or ground locations.

First flight of the HC-130H occurred in December 1964. Deliveries began in July 1965, and by the end of the year 16 aircraft in the first two contract batches (64-14852/14866 and 65-962/987) had been delivered and were operational with the Air Rescue Service.

Left: **HC-130H, 64-14852, flown by the 57th ARS. The Fulton Recovery System forks are extended on the Hercules' nose.** Air Force, courtesy of John Lameck

Below: **Lockheed C-130E, 62-1785, is painted in Arctic red for operations in polar territories.** MAP

Top left: **The first Convair C-131A, 52-5781, on a pre-delivery flight over Southern California in 1954.**
Convair, courtesy of Robert L Lawson

Lower left: **MC-131A, 52-5804, operated as a medevac transport by the 1st Aeromedical Transport Group (Light). The red cross on the Samaritan's tail was authorized by MATS HQ in 1955.**
A R Krieger, courtesy of Steve Ginter

Top right: **This AT-29C, 52-1096, was one of ten flown by the AACS which were redesignated as AC-131As for a short time in the late 1950s. The brightly-painted aircraft is shown at Oakland Airport, California, in April 1960.** Douglas D Olson

Lower right: **VC-131D, 55-294, flown by the 1254th ATG(SM) at Washington National Airport and Andrews AFB as a VIP transport. The 1254th ATG(SM) insignia is on the Samaritan's tail.** Courtesy of Norman Taylor

9.18 Convair C-131 Samaritan

While nearly four dozen of these Convair twin-engined transports eventually were flown by MATS, the C-131's use by the Air Force was predated by some four years by its similar-looking cousin, the T-29, which was first delivered in February 1950. From 1954 to 1966, MATS operated four variants of the C-131: the C-131A, similar to the civil Convair 240; the YC-131C, two Convair 340s re-engined with the Allison YT-56 turboprop; the C/VC-131D, military versions of the Convair 340; and the C-131E, Model 440s modified to perform the medical evacuation, or medevac, mission.

C-131A

The C-131 Samaritan was procured by MATS in 1954 as a medical evacuation transport, acting as a short-haul 'feeder' to carry the sick and injured to hospitals within the continental United States. Sometimes referred to as the MC-131A, these aircraft were capable of carrying 37 ambulatory patients in rearward-facing, airline-type seats, 27 litters, or a combination of both. The Samaritan boasted an integral, forward air-stair door, a large cargo door at the rear to facilitate loading stretchers, and a pressurized cabin that enabled the airplane to cruise above 20,000 feet at over 230 mph, considerably bettering the performance of the C-47s it replaced in the domestic, trunk-line, medevac role.

The first of 26 MC-131As, (52-5781/5806), was delivered to the 1734th ATS, 1st Aeromedical Transport Group (Light), at Brooks AFB, Texas, on 1st April 1954. By the end of the year, the 26 Samaritans had replaced most of the C-47s and C-54s being flown by the five squadrons of the 1st AMTG(L): the 1734th ATS at Brooks AFB; the 1731st ATS at Scott AFB, Illinois; the 1732nd ATS at Westover AFB, Massachusetts; the 1733rd ATS at Travis AFB, California; and the 1735th ATS at Brookley AFB, Alabama. By mid-1957, these squadrons had been redesignated as follows: the 11th AMS(L) at Scott AFB flew five C-131As; the 12th AMS(L) at McGuire AFB, New Jersey had four C-131As; the 13th AMS(L) at Travis AFB had four C-131As; the 14th AMS(L) at Brooks AFB with four C-131As; and the 15th AMS(L) at Brookley AFB flew five C-131As.

In 1964, the 1st AMTG(L) moved to Scott AFB and was redesignated as the 1405th ATW. Its C-131As were consolidated into the 10th Aeromedical Transport Squadron at Kelly AFB, the 11th AMTS at Scott AFB, the 12th AMTS at McGuire AFB, and the 13th AMTS at Travis AFB.

AC-131A

Between 1957 and early 1959, ten T-29Cs were converted to AT-29Cs for use as electronic flight checking aircraft by the Airways and Air Communications Service, MATS. In an apparent standardization move, the AACS redesignated these aircraft as AC-131As. However, on 3rd May 1960, these aircraft were redesignated back to AT-29Cs, although the Convairs carried the C-131A designation on their stencilled data blocks for some time thereafter.

Above: **Convair YC-131C, 53-7886, flown by the 1700th Test Squadron (Turbo-Prop), 1700th ATG, Kelly AFB, Texas.** Air Force, courtesy of Robert F Dorr

C-131E
By early 1957, the C-131As being flown in the medevac role by the Continental Division of MATS were unable to keep pace with expanded mission requirements. To remedy the situation, eight C-131Es were transferred from the Strategic Air Command to MATS, who reconfigured the aircraft with litter stanchions, litters, seats and other miscellaneous medevac equipment. All C-131Es were assigned, beginning in April 1957, to the 14th AMS at Brooks AFB, while this squadron reassigned its C-131As to the 11th and 13th AMS and to USAF-Europe, and all group medevac C-54s were transferred elsewhere. The 14th AMS used its C-131Es exclusively for runs from Brooks AFB to McGuire AFB and Travis AFB, although their service lives with MATS beyond this initial assignment is not known.

C-131D/VC-131D
Beginning in September 1954, 33 C-131Ds and VC-131Ds, 54-2805/2825 and 55-290/301, were operated by MATS as staff transports, with fifteen VC-131Ds being flown by the 1254th ATG(SM) at Washington National Airport and later at Andrews AFB, Maryland. While all of the aircraft purchased in the 1954 series block were built to the Model 340 standard, six aircraft in the 1955 series were constructed to the commercial Model 440 standard, with passenger accommodations for 44, improved soundproofing, and revised rectangular exhaust outlets. By mid-1961, 13 VC-131Ds were being flown at Andrews AFB by the 1299th ATS(SM), 1254th ATW(SM).

YC-131C
In order to establish the reliability of the Allison T56 turboprop engine and propeller, which was slated to power the production Lockheed C-130 Hercules, two Convair-Liner 340s were converted, in the summer of 1954, to YC-131Cs by replacing their P&W R-2800 piston engines with the new Allison powerplants. The two YC-131Cs, 53-7886/7887, were delivered in January 1955 to the newly-activated 1700th Test Squadron (Turbo-Prop), of the 1700th Air Transport Group, Kelly AFB, Texas, which was assigned to the Continental Division of MATS. This squadron was formed solely to service test new turboprop-powered aircraft: the two YC-131Cs, two Boeing YC-97Js and two Lockheed YC-121Fs, the latter two aircraft types re-engined with P&W T34 turboprops intended for the new Douglas C-133.

The 1700th Test Squadron's goal was to accumulate 3,000 flight hours on the YC-131Cs by 31st January 1956. This was accomplished by flying the aircraft in an 'airline-type' operation beginning on 1st May, flying scheduled and non-scheduled routes from Kelly AFB to Travis AFB, California, and Andrews AFB, Maryland.

Squadron spirit was high to prove these engines for Air Force use. The 1700th ATG Commander, Colonel Claude W Smith, even founded a society 'dedicated to the advancement of turbine-powered transport aircraft, whose range of power, versatility and economy of operation are as limitless as the winds of Aeolus'. The Order of Heron of Alexandria, as the society was called, was named after the Greek mathematician and scholar credited with developing the first known turbine, the Aeolipile. A certificate of membership in the society was presented to each passenger who flew in one of the YC-131Cs.

Despite an early shortage of YT56 engines, the two YC-131Cs set a series of records for twin-engined aircraft, culminating in a claimed world's record performance on 20th/21st August 1955. For this record, both YC-131Cs flew for 23 hours 10 minutes in a 24-hour period, involving four flights and three refuelings apiece.

The 1700th Test Squadron completed its test program with the YC-131Cs in December 1955, six weeks ahead of schedule . The two aircraft continued to fly standard MATS transport missions in the Continental Division for the following year and a half, but eventually they were relinquished by MATS to undergo further conversions: one to test the civil version of the T56, and the other new radar installations.

3.19 Douglas C-133 Cargomaster

The Douglas C-133 was the second production Air Force transport to be designed specifically around the turboprop engine, the result of a major Air Force policy decision, made in January 1951, to utilize turboprops for future transports. Designed to accommodate outsized cargo, the C-133 could carry nearly all Army Field Forces equipment as well as all American IRBMs and ICBMs without disassembly.

In 1952, an operational requirement was established as the Air Force's Logistic Carrier Supporting System SS402L. Douglas Long Beach, busily producing the C-124 and B-66 for the Air Force, submitted their Model DTS-1333, winning the design competition. Detail design was begun in February 1953 and a production contract was signed in 1954 for twelve C-133As, 54-135/146. The first C-133A was completed in February 1956, and made its first flight on 23rd April to Edwards AFB to begin flight testing. As no prototype Cargomasters were built, the initial production aircraft began a flight test program in mid-1956 which resulted in several changes to later production airframes: a larger dorsal fin and a new 'beaver tail' tail cone on the eighth and subsequent C-133As. Beginning on 17th January 1957, five C-133As of this initial batch, plus 56-1998 in the second production contract, were redesignated as JC-133As to reflect their temporary special test status.

First delivery of the 255,000 lb gross weight Cargomaster was made on 29th August 1957, when C-133A, 54-143, was flown to the 1607th ATW, Dover AFB, Delaware. The 1501st ATW at Travis AFB, California, received its first C-133A in October, and by mid-1958 nine Cargomasters equipped these two wings as exclusive operators of the airplanes.

Production of the C-133A progressed through late 1959 at about one airplane per month. Following completion of the 35th C-133A, the C-133B took its place on the production line, the first flight of this model occurring on 31st October 1959.

Below: **Douglas C-133A, 56-2000, flown by the 1607th ATW(H), Atlantic Division, MATS, at Dover AFB, Delaware.**
Douglas, courtesy of Norman Taylor

Bottom: **'The State of Delaware', a C-133A, 54-142, of the 1607th ATW(H), Dover AFB, Delaware.**
Courtesy of Lionel N Paul

The last of 15 C-133Bs was completed in April 1961, bringing C-133 production to an end at 50 aircraft. The C-133B featured uprated T34 engines and incorporated new clamshell rear loading doors, which had been installed on the 33rd and subsequent C-133As. These doors added three feet to the total length of the cargo hold, enabling the Cargomaster to carry the Titan ICBM without the missile having to be disassembled.

Once in service, the C-133 proved to be a valuable, if not completely trouble-free, transport for MATS. A cargo record was set by a C-133A in December 1958, when 118,000 pounds was carried to 10,000 feet, exceeding the old record by 40,000 pounds. On 3rd November 1959, a C-133 made the first airlift of an Atlas ICBM from NAS Miramar, California, to Warren AFB, Wyoming.

As mentioned, the Cargomaster equipped the 1st ATS and 39th ATS, 1607th ATW, at Dover AFB, Delaware, and the 84th ATS, 1501st ATW, Travis AFB, California. At least two Cargomasters were given personalized names by these squadrons: C-133A, 54-142, having 'The State of Delaware' painted on its nose while with the 1607th ATW, and C-133A, 54-140, the 'Spirit of Santa Monica Schools' as one of the 1501st ATW's fleet of 'Suisun Sausages', as the aircraft were known in the San Francisco Bay area.

By mid-1961, MATS possessed a high of 47 C-133s, but accidents to at least ten Cargomasters and persistent maintenance problems with the type's T34 engines kept the number of aircraft in service down to the low 40s during the early 1960s. The Cargomaster's eventual early retirement (in 1971) probably is related to its 13,000 cu ft pressurized cargo hold and to its most notable characteristic, familiar to anyone who has been in the vicinity of the flight path of one of these monsters and has heard the deep throb of 30,000 combined horsepower from the C-133's engines, undoubtedly producing metal fatigue. But despite its shortcomings, the C-133 Cargomaster served MATS well in being the only very large airlifter available in the years before the introduction of the C-141 or C-5.

Below: **An Atlas ICBM is loaded aboard C-133A, 57-1614, at NAS Miramar, California, in November 1959.**
General Dynamics courtesy of Robert L Lawson

Above: **Boeing KC-135A, 60-356, was one of three tankers converted to a partial C-135A standard and flown by the 1611th ATW, McGuire AFB, New Jersey.** Boeing, courtesy of Alwyn T Lloyd

3.20 Boeing C-135 Stratolifter

By 1960, it was painfully obvious to the Air Force that the MATS transport fleet had rapidly become inferior to the civil airlines. The first flight of the Boeing 367-80, prototype of the KC-135 aerial refueling tanker and its commercial derivative, the Boeing 707, took place in July 1954. The KC-135 first flew in August 1956 and became operational with SAC in January 1957, while the Boeing 707 first flew in December 1957 and began passenger flights in December 1958 with National Airlines.

But while three civil all-jet airliners, the Boeing 707, Douglas DC-8, and Convair 880, were becoming operational, MATS was still saddled with nearly-obsolete piston and turboprop-engined transports. Campaigning for the presidency in 1959, Senator John F Kennedy stated, 'Our ability to meet our commitments to more than fifty countries around the globe as been critically impared by our failure to develop a jet airlift capacity.' Even the Air Force Association, a 55,000-strong organization of former Air Corps and Air Force members acting as the unofficial voice of the Air Force, adopted a resolution during their 1960 national convention in San Francisco, asking Congress to modernize the MATS fleet with jet aircraft.

C-135A/B

Eventually, the Air Force issued a requirement in 1960 for an all-jet transport that resulted in the design of the Lockheed C-141 Starlifter. As the Starlifter would take several years to become operational, however, MATS began searching for a jet transport to serve in the interim. In February 1961, the Air Force finally signed a contract with Boeing for 45 C-135As, transport versions of the KC-135A. The tanker's refueling boom and associated plumbing was deleted, although the boom operator's station in the lower rear belly was retained for easy conversion if needed. The 272,000 lb gross weight C-135A's floor was strengthened, cargo tie-down fittings were provided, and two additional toilets, an additional air conditioning system, an insulated cabin liner with lights, and rearward-facing seats for 126 troops were installed. The KC-135A's Pratt & Whitney J57-P-59W 'water burning' turbojet engines were retained on the C-135A. However, after the 15th C-135A had been completed, the remaining 30 aircraft in the contract were delivered as C-135Bs by re-engining them with TF33-P-5 turbofans with thrust reversers. With these engines, the 275,000 lb gross weight C-135B's range increased to 8,000 miles, compared to the C-135A's 5,000 miles.

To speed the delivery of these much-needed jet transports to MATS units, Boeing converted three KC-135As already on the production line (60-356/357/360) to a partial C-135A standard. These three C-135As, known as 'Falsies', were delivered in June and July 1961 to the 1611th ATW at McGuire AFB, New Jersey. The first of the production C-135As was delivered to McGuire AFB on 21st August with the 1611th ATW at McGuire AFB eventually receiving 13 aircraft and the 1501st ATW at Travis AFB, California, one C-135A.

The turbofan-equipped C-135B made its first flight on 15th February 1962, and deliveries to MATS units began on February 28th. Between February and August 1962, these 30 C-135Bs were delivered to the two squadrons of the 1611th ATW at McGuire AFB (the 18th ATS and 41st ATS), and the 44th ATS, 1501st ATW, Travis AFB, each wing receiving fifteen aircraft.

Less than two months after being introduced, the C-135B set a new payload-to-height record when, in April 1962, a Stratolifter carried over 66,000 lbs to 47,000 feet, while another C-135B set a payload-speed record by carrying 30,000 kg around a 2,000 km closed course at 616 mph.

Above: **The MATS Stratolifters could carry 126 fully-equipped troops, as shown by C-135B, 62-4132.** Air Force, courtesy of Clyde Gerdes Collection.

Below: **RC-135A 63-8058, was one of four delivered to the 1370th Photo Mapping Wing, APCS, at Turner AFB, Georgia.** Boeing, courtesy of Alwyn T Lloyd

Once operational, these Stratolifters were used on Eastern Transport Air Force (EASTAF) and Western Transport Air Force (WESTAF) overseas routes, hauling cargo and personnel between the United States and Europe and Japan. For a time, the C-135s became the only MATS transports used for overseas aeromedical evacuation of patients to the US. From 10th-16th October1962, an airlift of four Stratolifters transported over 1,200 Swedish troops and nearly 17 tons of cargo for a United Nations peace-keeping effort in the Congo. The 4,900 mile route from Stockholm to the Congo normally took ten hours, but during the return home, a C-135B established an unofficial MATS record by flying 6,000 miles non-stop from Leopoldville to McGuire AFB in 13 hours. In November 1962, 12 C-135s participated in the Indian Airlift, delivering nearly 1,000 tons of equipment, small arms, and ammunition in 45 missions to Calcutta from bases in the US and Europe, thwarting an invasion of the Assam Valley by Communist Chinese forces.

While these C-135 Stratolifters added a new level of speed and comfort to MATS' capabilities, it was not without a price. During the 1962 Cuban Missile Crisis, a C-135 loaded with ammunition crashed during its approach to Guantanamo, killing all seven crew members. A May 1964 crash of a MATS C-135B at Clark AB, Philippines, killed 75, and 85 persons were killed when a C-135A crashed at Los Angeles International Airport in June 1965. Despite these tragic losses, the C-135 Stratolifters provided a much-needed capability to MATS at a time when few other aircraft were immediately available.

WC-135B

By 1965, the Air Weather Service's fleet of WB-47Es were nearing the end of their service lives. As the AWS Stratojets began to be retired, a replacement aircraft was needed for high altitude storm penetration, weather sampling and reconnaissance. The MATS fleet of C-135Bs, on the other hand, still had plenty of life in their airframes even as they were being replaced by new C-141s coming off the production line. The C-135B converted to the weather recon role offered larger, more comfortable crew accommodations for long missions, more space for equipment, increased performance, and lower operating costs.

On 22nd April 1965, the first two of ten C-135Bs (61-2665/2674) to be modified to WC-135Bs were transferred from MATS to the Air Weather Service, the last being received in January 1966. The aircraft were assigned to the 53rd WRS at Hunter AFB, Georgia, and the 55th WRS at McClellan AFB, California, both squadrons part of the 9th WRG at McClellan AFB.

RC-135A

The final Stratolifters accepted by the Air Force were four RC-135As, 63-8058/8061, delivered to the 1370th Photo Mapping Wing, Air Photographic and Charting Service, at Turner AFB, Georgia. Despite having fiscal 1963 serial numbers, the first two of these aircraft were not delivered until September 1965 due to delays in developing the mapping and surveying equipment they would be carrying.

The RC-135As were designed for aerial photo-mapping and geodetic surveying. Cameras were mounted in a belly compartment located behind the nose wheel, where previously a fuel tank had been placed. Two 30-inch diameter, 2½ inch thick camera windows were placed at the bottom of this camera compartment. The RC-135As also carried the ASQ-28 photomapping and geodetic surveying system. Replacing the APCS's obsolete RB-50s, the RC-135As possessed a range of nearly 5,000 miles at 35,000 feet, quadrupling the area which could be covered by the older aircraft. While these RC-135As served with MATS for only a few months, they soldiered on with the MAC's 1370th PMW until being converted to other uses in the early 1970s.

From the top: **C-135A, 60-374, was one of 15 Stratolifters powered by J57 'water burning' turbojet engines.** (MAP)

While JC-135A, 60-376, was modified for Airborne Astrographic Camera Testing by the Air Force Systems Command, the airplane is shown at Kirtland AFB in 1964 still in MATS markings. Paul Stephenson

Air Weather Service WC-135B, 61-2666, with its sampling pod on fuselage side. The AWS insignia is displayed on the forward fuselage. Air Force, courtesy of HQ AF Weather Agency

JC-135A

C-135A, 60-376, was withdrawn from MATS transport duties in the early 1960s and modified as a JC-135A camera test platform by the addition of numerous camera ports installed along the upper fuselage, reportedly for Airborne Astrographic Camera Testing by the Air Force Systems Command. However, the airplane was photographed at Kirtland AFB, New Mexico, in 1964 with its full MATS paint scheme applied after the modifications had been completed. Whether this airplane was attached to MATS' Air Photographic and Charting Service at this time is unknown.

3.21 Boeing VC-137

By 1958, the Air Force was in the midst of modernizing its aerial tanker fleet with the introduction of the KC-135A. There was pressure to do the same for the MATS Special Missions squadrons carrying governmental VIPs, and so plans were made in 1958 to procure an 'off the shelf' version of the Boeing 707 for the 1254th ATG, MATS' 'Special Air Missions' group at Andrews AFB, Maryland.

VC-137A

In May 1958, three Boeing 707-153s were ordered as VC-137As, 58-6970/6972. These aircraft were designated as C-137s and not C-135s as the commercial 707, on which they were based, was almost an entirely different airplane with a slightly larger diameter fuselage having a double-lobe cross section.

The VC-137As were powered by four 13,750 lb thrust Pratt & Whitney JT3C (J57) water-injected engines with commercial noise-suppression nozzles. The cabins were reconfigured with a communications station at the front, an eight-seat passenger compartment behind this, then a conference room with convertible divans, and an aft passenger compartment with 14 reclining seats. The airplanes also provided two dressing rooms and three galleys for up to 40 passengers and a crew of 18. The first VC-137A made its initial flight on 4th April 1959.

The three VC-137As were assigned to Detachment 1, 1298th ATS, which was organized at Andrews AFB, Maryland, on 1st March 1959, as the runways at Washington National Airport, where the parent 1254th ATG was headquartered, were considered too short to safely operate these large jet transports. The first VC-137A arrived at Andrews AFB on 12th May, and by June all three aircraft had been delivered and were transporting congressional and military VIPs on official business.

While these VC-137As were not specifically assigned as presidential aircraft, President Dwight D Eisenhower did make several trips aboard the aircraft at the end of his administration, as did newly-elected President John F Kennedy at the start of his term, even before he flew aboard his official presidential VC-118A.

In March 1961, President Kennedy directed that all Special Air Missions four-engine VIP aircraft have their MATS markings replaced by the words 'United States of America', and the three VC-137As were so painted.

Left: **'Air Force One', VC-137C, 62-6000, served Presidents Kennedy and Johnson while flown by the 1254th ATW, the 'Special Air Missions' wing of MATS.** Air Force, courtesy of Clyde Gerdes Collection

Bottom left: **VC-137A, 58-6972, flown by the 1298th ATS, 1254th ATG(SM), Andrews AFB, Maryland. The airplane is shown at Hickam AFB, Hawaii, in the spring of 1960 while carrying President Eisenhower.** Chuck Hansen, courtesy of Robert L Lawson

Bottom right: **VC-137A, 58-6972, after receiving the ventral fin modification, but prior to being re-engined with TF33 turbofans.** Courtesy of Clyde Gerdes Collection

VC-137B

In 1963, the three VC-137As were re-engined with 18,000 lb thrust JT3D/TF33 turbofan engines, which, along with other modifications such as the addition of a large ventral fin under the tail, made them equivalent to the commercial 707-120B.

VC-137C

In 1961, Project High Mark was initiated to provide one Intercontinental Series Boeing 707-320B to serve specifically as a presidential aircraft. The airplane was ordered late in the year and designated as VC-137C, 62-6000. Powered by TF33 turbofans, the new 'Air Force One' could seat up to 50 and had a 7,000 mile range. The airplane was painted in a scalloped powder blue scheme reportedly influenced by the First Lady, Jacqueline Kennedy. This attractive design eventually was applied to other VIP aircraft in the MATS Special Air Missions fleet.

VC-137C, 62-6000, was delivered to the 1254th ATW (the 1254th ATG having been upgraded to wing status on 1st December 1960) at Andrews AFB on 10th October 1962. President Kennedy made his first flight aboard the VC-137C on November 10th, and while he had the airplane at his disposal for only a year before his assassination, he and the First Lady travelled aboard the VC-137C extensively. When President Lyndon Johnson took office in November 1963, he had the airplane's interior rearranged with new rearward-facing seating and a redesigned presidential headquarters suite.

9.22 Lockheed C-140 JetStar

The Lockheed C-140 JetStar was developed for a 1956 Air Force requirement for a new jet-powered utility transport, the UCX program. Lockheed's Model 1329, powered by two Bristol Siddeley Orpheus engines, first flew in September 1957. But, while the airplane showed promise, cuts in the Air Force's budget precluded any purchases. With new funding, the Air Force announced in October 1959 that it would purchase a number of JetStars re-engined with four Pratt & Whitney J60 turbojets. In June 1960, five C-140As were ordered as high-altitude navigation aid check aircraft to be flown by MATS' Airways and Air Communications Service. However, before these aircraft were delivered, the AACS was redesignated as the Air Force Communications Service on 1st July 1961, and it separated from MATS as a major Air Force command in its own right.

Eleven JetStars subsequently were ordered as VIP transports by the Air Force in two batches: six VC-140Bs, 61-2488/2493, and five C-140Bs, (62-4197/4201). The C-140Bs were almost immediately reconfigured as ten passenger VC-140Bs and were the first JetStars to become operational in April 1961. By 1963, all eleven VC-140Bs were in MATS' Special Air Missions service with the 1299th ATS, 1254th ATW, at Andrews AFB, Maryland. The JetStars transported the Vice-President, cabinet members and governmental and Pentagon VIPs on short to medium-range trips.

Right: **VC-140B, 61-2488, of the 1299th ATS, 1254th ATW(SM), Andrews AFB, Maryland.** Air Force, courtesy of Norman Taylor

Bottom left: **VC-140B, 61-2489, is shown at Andrews AFB with a small 1254th ATW(SM) decal on its forward fuselage.** Air Force, courtesy of Norman Taylor

Bottom right: **VC-140B, 61-2489, after the 1254th ATW(SM) had its fleet repainted in 'United States of America' markings.** Air Force, courtesy of Clyde Gerdes Collection

9.23 Lockheed C-141A Starlifter

The C-141 Starlifter represented the 'Holy Grail' of transports to the Military Air Transport Service, an airplane embodying all the features MATS had sought for years: large size, high speed, long range, and a great load-carrying ability. Although the Starlifter was with the Military Air Transport Service for only a little over six months, the airplane eventually became the Military Airlift Command's primary airlift asset replacing, to one degree or another, the C-118, C-121, C-124, C-130, C-133, and C-135.

As mentioned elsewhere, by 1960 the civil airlines were converting their fleets to the new Boeing 707s, Douglas DC-8s and Convair 880s coming off the production lines, while virtually all MATS aircraft were still propeller-driven. In an emergency, MATS would be hard-pressed to fulfill its strategic airlift mission. Following the presidential election of 1960, Lockheed C-130s and Boeing C-135s were ordered as interim transports until a new all-jet transport could be placed into service.

The Air Force issued a Specific Operational Requirement, SOR 182, on 4th May 1960, calling for a transport capable of carrying a maximum load of over 60,000 lbs over 3,500 nautical miles. The requirement specified an initial need for 132 aircraft, to be designed for civil certification as well as military use to keep the unit cost as low as possible. The SOR was followed by a Request For Proposals in December 1960 for the Logistics Transport System 476-L. Proposals from four manufacturers were received in January 1961, with Lockheed-Georgia's Model 300 being selected as the winner on 13th March 1961. A contract for five service test C-141A Starlifters (61-2775/2779) was placed on 16th August 1961, and the C-141A's first flight was made on 17th December 1963, the 60th anniversary of the Wright Brothers' first powered flight. Lockheed signed contracts in 1964 for 127 additional C-141As using Fiscal Year 1963/1964/1965 funds (63-8075/8090; 64-609/653; 65-216/281), and later contracts brought total C-141A production to 285 aircraft.

As delivered to MATS, the C-141A was a truly impressive airplane, with a gross weight of 316,000 lbs. Its four 21,000 lb thrust P&W TF33 turbofan engines gave the Starlifter a cruising speed of 550 mph and an operating ceiling of 50,000 feet. Its 9 ft by 10 ft by 70 ft cargo hold could accommodate over 90 percent of all military equipment as well as 138 troops in rearward-facing seats, 80 litters and 23 attendants, or over 70,000 lb of cargo. The C-141 was designed to use the 463L loading system, its main cargo compartment having roller tracks built into the floor for this purpose.

The first operational C-141A was delivered in October 1964 to MATS' Heavy Transport Training Unit, the 1741st ATS, Tinker AFB, Oklahoma. MATS implemented an accelerated service test program with the C-141A that was borrowed from the Strategic Air Command. Called 'Lead The Force', the program used four of the early production aircraft to accumulate flight hours well in advance of the rest of the C-141 fleet. These aircraft were programmed to fly eight hours a day until mid-1968, while two additional Starlifters based at Tinker AFB with the Heavy Transport Training Unit were expected to accumulate twice the number of landings as the operational fleet, testing landing gear, flaps and spoilers and their systems.

The first transport squadron to receive the C-141A was the 44th ATS, 1501st ATW, Travis AFB, California. The Commander of MATS, General Howell M Estes, personally delivered the Starlifter, named 'The Golden Bear' in honor of the state of California, on 23rd April 1965. As C-141As gradually replaced the C-135s flown by the 44th ATS, they were almost immediately placed into service on a growing Pacific airlift between Travis AFB and various airfields in Southeast Asia. By the end of 1965, MATS was operating about 20 C-141As as the build-up of men and supplies for the Vietnam War began.

Opposite page: **MATS Special Air Missions VC-140Bs were repainted in 'Air Force One' blue and white scheme.**
Air Force, courtesy of Clyde Gerdes Collection

Right: **C-141A, 63-8077, at NAF El Centro in March 1965 with the Air Force Flight Test Center insignia on its nose.**
Douglas D Olson

Below: **C-141A, 63-8077, in February 1965 over NAF El Centro while being flown by Navy Lt S R Davis.**
Navy by PHC J M Mitchell, courtesy of Robert L Lawson

Chapter 10

Fighters

10.1 North American F-51 Mustang

The P-51 Mustang was one of the most successful aircraft designs of any era. Over 13,000 were built, beginning in 1940 with the NA-73/XP-51 and ending with the final production version, the lightweight and fastest production Mustang, the P-51H. In 1948 the 'P' (for 'Pursuit') designation was changed to 'F' (for Fighter). Mustangs fought valiantly during the Second World War and Korea, but by the early 1950s most were serving with Air Force Reserve and Air National Guard units.

TF-51H

A small number of TF-51H Mustangs were assigned to the Military Air Transport Service at Andrews AFB, Maryland, presumably serving as proficiency trainers and high-speed transports for MATS Headquarters pilots. The aircraft were attached to the 1403rd Maintenance Squadron beginning in 1951, followed by the 1401st Air Base Wing in November 1953. These MATS TF-51Hs carried 600-series fleet numbers on their tails, with '625' being the highest number noted.

F-51D

An agreement was signed in May 1951 with the Government of Iceland allowing the United States to share facilities at Keflavik International Airport as a stop along the North Atlantic MATS route to Europe. However, as the US also had promised to supply fighter aircraft for Iceland's defense, this placed MATS, as the only Air Force command on the island, in the strange position of having control responsibility for the fighter squadrons that would be based at Keflavik. Icelandic officials also made it clear that they expected these fighters to be in place by 1st September 1952.

With the Korean War raging, the only fighters immediately available were Air National Guard F-51Ds at George AFB, California. Gathering 35 Mustangs from eight squadrons at George AFB, Major Ervin C Ethell formed the 192nd Fighter-Bomber Squadron and, on 26th August, led his unit toward Iceland as a component of the 52nd Air Division, MATS. On 1st September Major Ethell arrived at Keflavik with 24 Mustangs and immediately placed eight aircraft on strip alert with loaded guns.

These Iceland-based F-51Ds provided a token defense force at best as there was no intercept control system set up, nor an air defense radar on the island. There also was the feeling, expressed by many at the time and over subsequent years, especially during MATS' Operational Readiness Inspections (ORI), that MATS personnel had little knowledge or experience with the finer points of running a fighter unit.

The 192nd FBS was redesignated as the 435th FBS on 1st December 1952, as the former squadron was inactivated and returned to state control after having served 21 months on active duty. These MATS 435th FBS F-51Ds remained at Keflavik until 27th March 1953, when they were replaced by F-94Bs flown by the 82nd FIS.

Finally, a single two-place TF-51D was flown briefly in 1952-1953 as a proficiency trainer by the 1739th Ferrying Squadron, 1708th Ferrying Group, Amarillo AFB, Texas. Another F-51D was used for a short time by the Airways and Air Communications Service early in 1954 as a possible high-altitude, high-speed electronic check aircraft for penetration checks of GCA, RAPCON and air traffic control facilities. As the F-51 had no spare room for additional checking equipment, and was not fitted with a UHF radio, the airplane was relinquished for the T-33A as an operational check aircraft.

Opposite page: **North American TF-51H, 44-64688, assigned to the 1403rd Maintenance Squadron, MATS, at Andrews AAFB in 1953.** Courtesy of Clyde Gerdes Collection

This page, top right: **TF-51H, 44-64673, photographed at Boston, Massachusetts, in 1953.** Robert T O'Dell, courtesy of David R McLaren

Above: **North American F-51Ds of the 192nd/435th Fighter-Bomber Squadron, MATS, at Keflavik, Iceland, in 1952.** Air Force, courtesy of Baldur Sveinsson

Right: **Pilots of these 192nd/435th FBS F-51Ds scramble as part of the Iceland Air Defense Force, MATS.** Air Force, courtesy of Baldur Sveinsson

An F-80C, 47-171, similar to a small number of Shooting Stars operated briefly by several MATS units in the early 1950s.
Roger Besecker

10.2 Lockheed F-80 Shooting Star

Hoping to keep pace with jet aircraft development in England and Germany, the Army Air Forces requested, in June 1943, that Lockheed Aircraft Corporation design a fighter aircraft using the new British de Havilland H-1 turbojet. The Lockheed design group, led by Clarence L 'Kelly' Johnson, produced the P-80, which was immediately accepted. The first flight of the XP-80 was made on 8th January 1944, only 20 weeks after construction had begun. Following the brief introduction of two YP-80As into the European Theater during the Second World War, the first of 914 production P-80As was delivered to the Army Air Forces in December 1945 powered by the Allison J33. The P-80B, powered by a 5,200 lb static thrust J33, was delivered beginning in 1946, and 798 P-80Cs, the final production version, were delivered in 1948 and 1949.

A small number of F-80s were flown by the Military Air Transport Service and its sub-commands during the early 1950s. The first assignment apparently was to the 1401st Air Base Wing at Andrews AFB in late 1953 or early 1954, when a small number of F-80Cs were flown as jet transition trainers for MATS pilots. Two F-80s also were briefly flown in 1954 by the 1737th Ferrying Squadron at Dover AFB, Delaware, for transition and familiarization training by the squadron's ferry pilots. Lastly, the Airways and Air Communications Service gained one F-80B and one F-80C early in 1954 as possible high-altitude, high-speed electronic penetration check aircraft for the AACS' GCA, RAPCON and air traffic control facilities. However, as these aircraft had limited space for test gear, and neither had a UHF radio, they were relinquished in favor of the T-33A for this operational checking mission.

10.3 Republic F-84/RF-84 Thunderjet/Thunderflash

Republic Aviation designed the P-84 in 1944 as a jet-powered successor to the company's famous P-47 Thunderbolt. The prototype XP-84 made its first flight on 28th February 1946, powered by a 3,750 lb static thrust General Electric J35. Following service trials with 15 YP-84As, 224 production P-84Bs went into service beginning in mid-1947, followed by 191 P-84Cs and 154 F-84Ds (the Air Force redesignating pursuits as fighters in 1948). The Air Force accepted 743 improved F-84Es and, beginning in 1951, nearly 1,100 F-84Gs with nuclear delivery capability, a total of over 2,400 straight-winged F-84s flown mainly by the Tactical Air Command and the Strategic Air Command.

By late 1949, a swept-winged version of the F-84 was on Republic's drawing boards, with the prototype YF-96A making its first flight on 3rd June 1950. On September 8th, a second prototype made its first flight, re-engined with a Wright YJ65 and redesignated as a YF-84F. Over 1,400 of the swept-wing F-84Fs were operated by TAC and SAC beginning in 1954. Meanwhile, in February 1952 the prototype photo reconnaissance RF-84F made its first flight, with over 300 of this model being delivered to TAC and SAC recon squadrons beginning in March 1954.

The Republic F-84F Thunderflash was flown by the 1738th Ferrying Squadron, 1708th FYG, MATS, at Dover AFB, Delaware.
Courtesy of Clyde Gerdes Collection

With over 4,000 examples of this one aircraft model produced by Republic Aviation, one may well wonder just how these airplanes got to their operating units from the manufacturer's factory. Many were shipped by Military Sea Transport Service (MSTS) vessels, but many also needed to be flown to these units. The Military Air Transport Service's 1737th Ferrying Squadron, 1708th Ferrying Group, at Dover AFB, Delaware, was located only 150 miles south of Republic's Farmingdale, Long Island, New York, factory, and as such was the aerial 'prime mover' of Republic's products for the Air Force. A small number of various models of the F-84 were assigned to the squadron to provide its ferry pilots with aircraft for checkout and proficiency training on the type. The Continental Division of MATS first requested the assignment of F-84s to the 1737th FYS in September 1953, and by January 1954 four F-84s had been received by the squadron. Between 1954 and March 1958, when the 1737th FYS was disbanded, the squadron operated small numbers of the F-84E, F-84F, F-84G and RF-84F as checkout and proficiency trainers.

During these years, there were several mishaps with F-84s assigned to the 1737th FYS. On 28th August 1956, a 1737th FYS RF-84F received major damage when a tire blew out during take-off from Dover AFB, and a squadron F-84F was involved in an accident after taking off from Dover AFB on 4th September 1956, when the airplane's engine suffered internal failure while cruising at 40,000 feet. Lastly, on 10th April 1957, a 1737th FYS F-84F was damaged when its engine exploded during the take-off roll, with the pilot quickly stop-cocking the throttle and evacuating the aircraft.

MATS records indicate that as many as ten F-84s were flown by the 1737th FYS in 1956. By March 1958, however, with the folding of the squadron many of its pilots and personnel moved across the field at Dover AFB to join the 'real MATS' transport wing which was operating C-124s, and the squadron F-84s were assigned elsewhere.

Top: **F-84G, 51-747, flown by the 1737th Ferrying Squadron, 1708th FYG, MATS, for pilot checkout and proficiency training in 1957.** Thomas E Hatch

Above: **2/Lt Thomas E Hatch stands by a MATS 1737th Ferrying Squadron F-84F, 53-7159, at Dover AFB in 1957.** Thomas E Hatch

Below: **Tail markings on 1708th Ferrying Group Sabres included the group insignia as shown on F-86A, 49-1290.** Air Force

10.4 North American F-86 Sabre

While its Navy XFJ-1 was still in the design stage, North American Aviation proposed a version of the Fury to the Army Air Forces in 1944, with the airplane featuring similar straight wings and J35 turbojet. The AAF ordered three prototypes, designated as XP-86s, but the airplane was redesigned shortly after the end of the Second World War when it was decided to adopt swept-back wings. The revised XP-86 made its first flight on 1st October 1947, and a contract was signed in December 1947 for 221 P-86As powered by the 4,850 lb static thrust General Electric J47. The first P-86A made its initial flight on 18th May 1948, and the type was redesignated as the F-86A in June. Over 740 F-86As were delivered, with the later aircraft powered by a 5,200 lb.s.t. J47. In December 1950, the F-86E went into production, with nearly 400 being delivered to the Air Force in 1951 and 1952. The F-86D, an all-weather interceptor featuring an afterburning J47 and a redesigned nose with a large radome, went into production in 1951 with over 2,500 of this model being delivered. The F-86F was built at the new North American plant in Columbus, Ohio, with 700 being delivered between March 1952 and December 1956. The last production version of the Sabre was the F-86H, which boasted a 9,300 lb.s.t. J73 engine, increased wingspan and a lengthened fuselage, among other improvements. Nearly 500 F-86Hs were delivered from the Columbus factory between January 1954 and August 1955.

As with the Republic F-84s produced in New York and ferried to operating units by Dover AFB's 1737th FYS, the North American Sabres built on the south side of Los Angeles International Airport were delivered by the 1738th FYS located at Long Beach Airport, some 18 miles to the southeast. When this squadron was organized at Long Beach Airport late in 1952, the 1738th FYS was charged with the responsibility for ferrying single-engined jet aircraft, in particular the North American F-86s. In December 1952, 'Project High Flight' was established to ferry F-84, F-86 and T-33A aircraft across the North Atlantic. The first ferry flights in this program began in March 1953, with air deliveries made to USAF-Europe squadrons and MDAP recipients when Military Sea Transport Service carriers could not accommodate the increased demand for these aircraft.

While the 1708th FYG Det.12, at Kelly AFB Headquarters, had several F-86s for pilot checkout and proficiency training from April 1954, and the 1737th FYS at Dover AFB, Delaware, flew one assigned F-86 beginning in late

Above: **Three units of the 1708th Ferrying Group, MATS, flew several models of the F-86 similar to this F-86A, 49-1251, photographed in 1953.** Courtesy of Clyde Gerdes Collection

1954, it appears that the 1738th FYS at Long Beach Airport possessed only one T-6 trainer and several C-45s and C-47s at this time. This may have been due to safety considerations at the Long Beach Airport, surrounded as it was by residential neighborhoods, and the unfortunate crash of a squadron F-86F on 12th January 1954, when the Sabre was approaching Long Beach Airport for a landing and crashed on nearby Signal Hill, killing the pilot and several civilians on the ground. By May 1955, the 1708th FYG Det.12 at Kelly AFB had eight F-86s, and the 1737th FYS at Dover AFB one Sabre.

On 1st July 1956, the 1738th FYS at Long Beach Airport was discontinued and re-established at Kelly AFB with one F-84F, nine T-33As, ten F-100A/F-100Ds, and four F-86Fs, while a smaller 1708th FYW Detachment 17 was organized at Long Beach International Airport. On 8th November 1956, the 1708th FYW Det.17 was discontinued once-and-for-all at Long Beach, and the four F-86Fs with the 1738th FYS at Kelly AFB were flown until early 1958.

10.5 Northrop F-89 Scorpion

As mentioned elsewhere, for many years the Military Air Transport Service had been using Iceland as a staging base for its North Atlantic transport route to and from Europe. With this experience in mind, MATS signed an agreement with the government of Iceland in May 1951 allowing it to share the facilities at Keflavik International Airport. However, the Icelandic authorities also had been promised American aircraft to provide for their defense and MATS, as the only US command presence on Iceland, was given control of the fighter squadrons which subsequently were deployed to the island. F-51Ds from the 192nd FBS/435th FBS provided the initial commitment at Keflavik beginning in September 1952. These aircraft were replaced in April 1953 by F-94Bs flown by the 82nd Fighter Interceptor Squadron.

Plans were announced early in 1954 that the 82nd FIS on Iceland would be replaced by F-89Cs flown by the 57th FIS at Presque Isle AFB, Maine. The 57th FIS had been activated on 20th March 1953, and was assigned to the 528th Air Defense Group. The initial flight of 57th FIS Scorpions departed Presque Isle AFB on 20th October 1954, and by January 1955 the squadron had relieved the 82nd FIS with 15 F-89Cs, two T-33As, and one TB-25K. Despite the North Atlantic's severe weather, which delayed the arrival of the squadron's full complement of 25 Scorpions and caused numerous problems with airframe corrosion, the 57th FIS accumulated the highest number of flying hours in June of all Air Force F-89 units.

Below: **F-89Cs of the 57th FIS, Iceland Air Defense Force, MATS, at Keflavik, Iceland, in 1955.** Air Force, courtesy of Larry Davis

Above: **F-89D, 54-241, of the 57th FIS, slid off an ice-coated runway during take-off at Keflavik, Iceland, in March 1957, after losing its nosewheel.** Air Force, courtesy of Baldur Sveinsson

Right: **57th FIS F-89D, 54-226, with MATS insignia on the Scorpion's nose and F-89J wing tanks for the ferry flight to Keflavik, Iceland.** M Balogh Sr, courtesy of David Menard

Poor weather also delayed the 57th FIS' conversion to the F-89D during 1955, but the switch-over was completed by August 1956, making the 57th FIS the last squadron to operate the F-89C. The F-89D featured new wingtip rocket pods, each containing 52 2.75-inch folding-fin air-to-air rockets, extra fuel carried in the nose and in wing pylon tanks, and uprated engines. With this conversion, the 57th FIS continued to apply the squadron's emblem to their Scorpions' fins: a black knight's helmet and lightning bolt superimposed over clouds.

The 57th FIS operated its F-89Ds at Keflavik as part of the Iceland Air Defense Force through the 1950s. The often severe winter weather limited flying, airframe corrosion was a constant problem, and icy runways and foreign object damage to the Scorpions' low-slung engines from Keflavik's gravel-strewn runways all claimed their share of accidents. By 1960, attrition had reduced the squadron's strength to twelve aircraft from a high of 25 in 1957. MATS' involvement with the Iceland Air Defense Force came to an abrupt end on 1st July 1961, when the US Navy assumed command of Keflavik IAP as well as Iceland's defense.

F-94B

The 82nd Fighter Interceptor Squadron at Larson AFB, Washington, was notified early in 1953 that they would be relieving 435th FBS F-51Ds as part of the newly-activated 65th Air Division, MATS, at Iceland's Keflavik International Airport. As the only Air Force presence on the island, the Military Air Transport Service had control of Iceland's air defense as a result of a May 1951 agreement with the Icelandic Government.

The 82nd FIS deployed its F-94B Starfires to Keflavik in March 1953, and officially replaced the 435th FBS on April 1st, attached to the new Iceland Air Defense Force, MATS. These 82nd FIS F-94Bs provided Iceland's defense as part of the Northeast Air Command until they in turn were replaced in November 1954 by F-89Cs from the 57th FIS.

MATS' 1708th Ferrying Group Detachment 12 at Kelly AFB, Texas, operated a single F-94 beginning in May 1954. The Starfire was used briefly as a check and proficiency trainer for the detachment's ferry pilots who would be flying new production aircraft from the factory to operating units.

10.6 Lockheed F-94 Starfire

Lockheed Aircraft Company created the Starfire in 1949 as an early two-seat, jet-powered, all-weather fighter/interceptor by adding a nose-mounted radar, a radar operator's station in the rear seat, and an afterburning J33 or J48 engine to the basic T-33A airframe. The first of 110 F-94As went into service in June 1950, followed by 357 improved F-94Bs in 1951, and 387 redesigned and re-engined F-94Cs the following year.

10.7 North American F-100 Super Sabre

North American Aviation began the Super Sabre's design early in 1949 as a development of the F-86 Sabre. In November 1951, the Air Force ordered two prototype YF-100As and the first block of production F-100As. The YF-100A, powered by the XJ57-P-7, made its first flight from Edwards AFB on 25th May 1953. The first production F-100A first flew on 29th October 1953, and between November 1953 and March 1954, a total of

203 F-100As were delivered with most going to the Tactical Air Command. The F-100C was equipped with five underwing hard points and aerial refueling for use as a fighter-bomber. A total of 476 F-100Cs were delivered from North American's plants at Inglewood, California, and Columbus, Ohio. The F-100D, featuring a larger tail, inboard wing landing flaps, and a supersonic autopilot, was delivered beginning in January 1956 with nearly 1,300 built at Inglewood and Columbus. The final production version of the Super Sabre was the F-100F, a two-seat operational trainer which made its first flight in March 1957 as the TF-100C. A total of 339 F-100Fs were delivered to the Air Force by October 1959.

Early in July 1956, the 1738th Ferrying Squadron, 1708th Ferrying Wing, was moved from Long Beach International Airport to Kelly AFB, Texas, due to safety considerations at Long Beach. By July 1956, the 1738th FYS, designated specifically to ferry single-engine jet aircraft, was operating six F-100As and four F-100Ds, as well as four F-86Fs, one F-84F, and nine T-33As for pilot checkout and proficiency training, and one administrative VC-47A.

However, the training and checkout of prospective squadron F-100 pilots at Kelly AFB was restricted until a new, longer runway could be opened, as the existing runways left little margin for error. The squadron discovered that a misjudgement on the landing point or a collapsed drag chute on these F-100s usually resulted in an accident.

Throughout 1956 and 1957, new F-100Cs and F-100Ds were coming off the North American production lines at a high rate. These aircraft were ferried to USAF-Europe squadrons by using the 'Project High Flight' route over the North Atlantic at a dozen aircraft a week in April 1956. By December 1956, the 1738th FYS was flying 13 F-100Ds at Kelly AFB. The squadron retained its F-100s into 1958 for checkout and proficiency training of the squadron ferry pilots.

Left: **'Jan IV', a Lockheed F-94B, 50-816, of the 82nd FIS, MATS, at Keflavik, Iceland, in 1953.** Heraldur Guomundsson, courtesy of Baldur Sveinsson

Below: **F-100A, 53-1640, flown by the 1708th Ferrying Wing at Kelly AFB, Texas. The 1708th FYW emblem is painted on the Super Sabre's tail fin.** Courtesy of David Menard

Chapter 11

Gliders

11.1 Waco G-15A Hadrian

In 1944, the Waco Aircraft Company of Troy, Ohio, designed the CG-15, an improved model of their CG-4 troop and cargo glider, of which over 12,000 were built during the Second World War by various manufacturers. The CG-15's wingspan was some 21 feet shorter than the CG-4's, and the model had improved landing gear and aerodynamics and could carry up to 16 troops. Waco delivered 427 CG-15As before production was stopped at the end of the war. In June 1948, the Air Force redesignated its remaining gliders as G-15As.

One G-15A was used occasionally for rescue missions on the polar ice cap during 1950-1952 by Alaska's 10th Air Rescue Squadron. The glider could carry a respectable load of rescue personnel and supplies and, with its large skis, still land on thinner ice than most other aircraft. The G-15A also was towed by a 10th ARS C-47 to airlift supplies for various Arctic tests of equipment and personnel gear.

Below: **Waco G-15A, 45-5399, and SC-47B, 43-49565, of the 10th ARS, Elmendorf AFB, Alaska.** Air Force, courtesy of David Menard

Chapter 12

Helicopters

12.1 Sikorsky H-5

The Sikorsky R-5 was a development of the R-4 training helicopter, switching the R-4's side-by-side seating to a tandem arrangement. Five prototypes of the XR-5 two-man observation helicopter were ordered in 1943, the first flying in August. Later in the same year, the Army Air Forces purchased 26 YR-5As for service tests and 34 R-5As for the search and rescue role. These aircraft were powered by a 450 hp P&W R-985 engine and had provisions for a litter carrier to be mounted on each side of the fuselage. Subsequent models included 25 R-5Ds (R-5As modified to carry two passengers and featuring a rescue hoist and nosewheel), 38 H-5Gs (helicopters being redesignated 'H', rather than 'R' for rotary-winged, in 1948), and 17 H-5Hs with dual wheel/pontoon landing gear.

When MATS was formed in June 1948, the Air Rescue Service had only 18 H-5s of all models, but by the end of 1949 40 were in operation. With the start of the Korean War on 25th June 1950, the 3rd ARS possessed nine H-5s dispersed between its headquarters at Johnson AB and three detachments at Ashyia, Misawa and Yokota, Japan. The squadron deployed the first H-5s to Taegu, Korea, on July 22nd, the aircraft beginning medevac missions almost immediately. By mid-August, six of the 3rd ARS' nine H-5s were operating within Korea, while an additional 14 H-5s were brought in by the fall of 1950. One 3rd ARS H-5 pilot evacuated 16 wounded soldiers in one day, and in the first six months of the war personally accounted for 81 litter patients being evacuated from the front lines. During two days of operations, from 22nd-23rd October 1950, two 3rd ARS H-5s and three L-5s combined forces to evacuate 47 paratroopers who had become surrounded at drop zones near Pyongyang, and on 24-25th March 1951, ARS H-5s teamed with a single YH-19 to evacuate 148 paratroopers stranded at the drop zone at Munsan-ni. Two 3rd ARS H-5s are known to have been lost, one crashing after running out of fuel and the other which was blown into a hillside after its rotor downwash had detonated a Communist anti-tank mine 300 feet below the helicopter as it cruised above a road.

By war's end, while the H-5s flying with the 3rd ARS had accounted for 53 percent of the squadron's total sorties and 20 percent of their total flight hours, the Sikorskys were credited with performing 91 percent of the rescues made by the Air Rescue Service in Korea. Despite these figures, the Sikorsky H-19 began replacing its smaller brother in February 1952, and by 1955 the H-5s all had been retired from the Air Rescue Service.

Photographs on the opposite page:

Top: **SH-5G, 48-555, of the 3rd Air Rescue Squadron, taking off with a wounded Korean Marine from a Korean airfield in July 1951.** Air Force, courtesy of NASM

Bottom left: **YH-5A, 43-46623, flown by the 10th ARS at Ladd AFB in the summer of 1951.** Air Force, courtesy of George Horn

Bottom right: **Air Rescue Service H-5G, 48-549, equipped with pontoons and capsules for carrying patients.** MAP

12.2 Sikorsky H-6A

The Sikorsky R-6 was developed in 1942 alongside the R-5 as a refinement of the Navy's Sikorsky R-4. The prototype XR-6 made its first flight on 15th October 1943, but due to several problems the helicopter barely left the ground. Through constant refinement the R-6 was developed into a successful helicopter, the XR-6 setting records in March 1944 for speed, altitude, distance and endurance. Eventually, 26 YR-6A and 193 production R-6As using a 245 hp Franklin engine were built for the Army Air Forces, the US Navy as the HOS-1, and England as the Hoverfly. A few R-6As were used at the end of the Second World War for field trials in China, accomplishing several rescues, but the design's impact on the war was negligible.

Two H-6As were operated briefly by the Air Rescue Service by the 2nd Rescue Squadron at Kadena Field, Okinawa. These H-6As had been flying with the 2nd RS at least since 1948, and were taken into the MATS inventory when it absorbed all Air Rescue Squadrons operating in the Far East in May 1949. These 2nd ARS H-6As were used to support the tactical reconnaissance wing based on Okinawa at the time, as well as a squadron of F-51s stationed at Naha AB. The two H-6As flew with the 2nd ARS at least into early 1950 before being retired.

12.3 Bell H-13 Sioux

One of the most versatile helicopter designs of all time, the H-13 was the military version of the civil Bell Model 47. The first YR-13s were delivered to the Air Force in 1947, and in time over 1,500 H-13s were operated by all services for field ambulance, reconnaissance, observation, training and utility missions.

The 1707th Field Maintenance Squadron of the 1707th ATW, Palm Beach AFB, Florida, was assigned two H-13s in December 1954. The squadron apparently acted as a Transition Training Unit (TTU) on the H-13, but it also flew one C-45, one C-47 and two VC-47s for familiarization and administrative purposes. At least one of these 1707th FDM H-13s were equipped with pontoons, as it was involved in a major accident on 2nd July 1955, when the helicopter pitched to the right while attempting a water landing and the rotors were destroyed with no serious injuries to the pilot.

The 1707th Field Maintenance Squadron existed at least through 1957, but it is not known how long the unit operated the H-13.

VH-13J

In 1957, the Air Force took delivery of two Bell Model 47Js, to be operated by the 1254th Air Transport Group (Special Mission), at Bolling AFB. These aircraft, (57-2728/2729),designated as VH-13Js, were used specifically to transport President Eisenhower and his staff around the Washington, DC, area, providing 'doorstep-to-doorstep' service from the White House lawn.

The VH-13Js were powered by a 240 hp Lycoming O-435 engine, giving them a range of about 250 miles. Equipped with a fully-enclosed cabin and VIP interiors, the VH-13Js carried four, with the pilot sitting in front and three passengers on a bench seat at the rear. In 1962, the Bells were redesignated as UH-13Js.

RESCUE

12.4 Sikorsky H-19 Chickasaw

Sikorsky designed the S-55 in 1948 to meet an Air Force requirement for an Arctic search and rescue helicopter. An order for five service test YH-19s was placed in 1949, with the Chickasaw's first flight being made in November. In designing the H-19, Sikorsky engineers chose a unique arrangement for the 550 hp Pratt & Whitney R-1340 powerplant, locating it in the nose with an angled, extended drive shaft passing between the pilots to connect to the main rotor transmission. This placed the large, unobstructed main cabin directly under the rotor center-of-gravity, negating balance concerns, and enabled the pilots to sit high enough for excellent visibility. Engine maintenance also was simplified through the use of two large clamshell doors on the Chickasaw's nose.

YH-19

In March 1951, nine months after the start of the Korean War, two new YH-19s were deployed to Korea by an Air Proving Ground team. Operating with Sikorsky H-5s flown by the 3rd Air Rescue Squadron's Detachment F, the YH-19s assisted in the evacuation of wounded and injured paratroopers from the drop zone at Munsan-ni, transporting 148 men in 77 sorties flown over two days. The two YH-19s, 49-2014 and 49-2016, seem to have been flown later in the war by the 3rd ARS itself. These aircraft were painted black with yellow markings, and reportedly were used by the squadron to pick up agents along North Korea's western coastline.

SH-19A/B

When the 3rd ARS began to receive its own H-19As in February 1952, the unit used the aircraft mainly for overwater search and rescue missions, taking advantage of their 120-mile range. The 3rd ARS subsequently deployed two H-19As to Cho-do Island off the west coast of North Korea. These aircraft orbited over the Yellow Sea in areas designated as bail-out sites for damaged or mechanically disabled aircraft. On 12th April1953, two 3rd ARS H-19As were dispatched from Cho-do to a designated bail-out site where Air Force ace Joseph McConnell ejected from his damaged F-86. McConnell was one of four American aces of the Korean War rescued by the Air Rescue Service. A total of 102 Air Force airmen were rescued behind enemy lines by ARS helicopters during the war, not counting dozens of additional airmen from other services, allied flyers, or air crew rescued within friendly territory.

Opposite page, top: **The two Bell VH-13Js flown by MATS' 'Special Air Missions' wing provided 'doorstep-to-doorstep' service for the White House.** Bell Helicopter, courtesy of Wayne Mutza

Bottom left: **Sikorsky H-6A, 43-45398, of the 2nd Rescue Squadron, Kadena Field, Okinawa, in August 1948, nine months before all Far East Air Rescue Squadrons were absorbed by the ARS.** Air Force, courtesy of NASM

Bottom right: **1st Lt Robert Wardner in the cockpit of 2nd RS H-6A, 43-45398, at Kadena AB, Okinawa. The helicopter's door and side panel have been removed during the summer's heat.** Air Force, courtesy of Robert Wardner

Early in October 1952, the 581st Wing of the Air Resupply and Communications Service, MATS, deployed a detachment of four H-19As, six pilots and 13 enlisted men to Cho-do Island to conduct clandestine operations in North Korea. These aircraft, painted silver with all 'rescue' markings absent, operated under the Fifth Air Force for inserting and retrieving agents along the coastal mud flats north of the DMZ, as well as occasionally assisting the 2157th ARS and 3rd ARS in rescuing downed flyers in the Yellow Sea. Flown by the 581st ARCW 'Helicopter Flight' headquarters at Seoul City Air Base ('K-16'), Korea, these H-19As flew single-ship, low-level night missions across the Yellow Sea.

While the Korean War was raging in the Pacific, a project was formulated by Air Rescue Service Headquarters to ferry two H-19As across the Atlantic. The flight was intended to explore several areas of concern: the practicality of ferrying helicopters over the Northern Atlantic route; techniques to extend the helicopter's range; and pilot fatigue while flying helicopters. Two new H-19As, 51-3893 and 51-3894, were picked up at the factory and flown to Westover AFB, Massachusetts. The Chickasaws were lightened by removing their pontoons, rescue hoists, cabin heaters and sound-proofing blankets, and the aircraft were fitted with three 100-gallon auxiliary fuel tanks in the cabin. The H-19As, with the names 'Hop-A-Long' and 'Whirl-O-Way' painted across their noses in red, began their trek on 15th July 1952, flying from Westover AFB to Presque Isle, Maine. Despite numerous delays due to bad weather, the two H-19As reached Wiesbaden, Germany (via Labrador, Greenland, Iceland, Scotland and the Netherlands), where they were delivered to the 9th ARS to begin search and rescue duties. While it took 20 days and nearly 52 hours of flying time to cover the 3,984 mile route, the mission proved that ferrying the H-19 over the North Atlantic was feasible, if not impractical.

By 1955, the new SH-19B had entered service featuring a more powerful Wright R-1300 engine as well as several airframe improvements, and a high of 97 SH-19s were being flown by the Air Rescue Service worldwide. Of the countless rescue situations in which the SH-19s participated over the 13-plus years they flew with the ARS, a few are notable. From 2nd-6th April 1954, SH-19As of the 59th ARS dropped 30,000 pounds of food in 66 sorties to some 4,000 victims of floods that had hit the Tigris River Valley in Iraq.

When a Portuguese ship ran aground in the Azores on 19th September 1958, 30 passengers died trying to reach shore. A single SH-19B from the 57th ARS was dispatched to rescue the remaining survivors. The crew managed to save 48 people by hovering above the stricken ship, hoisting them up into the helicopter and flying them to a hilltop 1½ miles away. The mission took 4½ hours and one refueling to accomplish.

On 7th June 1959, a 58th ARS SH-19 out of Wheelus AB, Libya, rescued seven men from an Air Force C-47 which had crashed into the Mediterranean. Despite 40-knot winds, the crew managed to hoist the survivors aboard and, even in this overloaded condition, flew the 60 miles to the nearest land while skimming the wavetops.

In December 1960, the Air Force Chief of Staff directed that all 70 independent Local Base Rescue (LBR) units be consolidated under a single command and transferred to the Air Rescue Service. On 1st October 1961, the ARS assumed command of these LBR units, including 58 SH-19Bs. But as the turbine-powered Kaman HH-43B was deemed the helicopter of choice for these

Above: **Bell VH-13J, 57-2729, operated by the 1254th ATG (SM) to transport Presidents Eisenhower and Kennedy. Note the 1254th ATG(SM) insignia on the cabin.** Bell, courtesy of Wayne Mutza

Left: **A Sikorsky SH-19A of the 3rd ARG hoists an aircrewman from Far East waters.** Air Force, courtesy of NASM

Opposite page, from the top:

H-19A, 51-3886, one of four flown by the 581st Air Resupply Squadron in Korea with 'Air Resupply' painted on its side. These markings were removed after only a few days. Joe Barrett, courtesy of Carl H Bernhardt

LBR units, the SH-19Bs were quickly disposed of. The last ARS Chickasaws were phased out in 1964 with the 57th ARS at Lajes Field, Azores.

VH-19/UH-19

At least two VH-19Bs, (51-3942 and 53-4436), and one UH-19D, (55-3228), were operated by the 1299th ATS, 1254th ATG(SM), at Andrews AFB, Maryland, from approximately 1957 to 1961. The Chickasaws were part of the Special Air Missions fleet of aircraft, used to transport Washington, DC-based VIPs on short-range trips throughout the East Coast. The aircraft were painted in an attractive medium blue and white scheme with red trim, and carried the 1254th ATG(SM) emblem as well as the MATS insignia on their fuselages.

YH-19, 49-2016, flown by the 3rd Air Rescue Squadron in Korea, shown at K-13 in 1951. Air Force, courtesy of Larry Davis

Air Rescue Service SH-19A, 51-3862, at the Dayton Airport in September 1953. Art Krieger, courtesy of Douglas D Olson

SH-19B, 52-7539, at Hamilton AFB in March 1959. The Chickasaw carries a ribbon painted on its nose and the inscription: 'USAF Outstanding Unit Award 1955 – Northern California Floods 23-28 December'. William T Larkins

VH-19B, 51-3942, flown by the 1254th ATG(SM), at NAS Anacostia in May 1957. The 'Special Air Missions' group insignia is on the aircraft's nose, with a large MATS emblem on the rear fuselage. Warren Shipp courtesy of Douglas D Olson

12.5 Piasecki/Vertol H-21 Workhorse

The Piasecki H-21 is one of several examples of a Navy aircraft being adopted by the Air Force. Piasecki's HRP series had seen service with the US Navy since 1945. In 1949, the Air Force ordered 18 YH-21s, based on the HRP-2, and embarked on a lengthy service trial program with these aircraft.

SH-21A

The Air Force ordered 38 H-21As in 1951, with most of these earmarked as Arctic search and rescue aircraft with the Air Rescue Service. The SH-21A was powered by a Wright R-1820 radial engine, de-rated to 1,250 hp as it was felt this was sufficient power to accomplish the SAR mission. The Workhorse's 14-passenger cabin was insulated and heated, and the pilot had a full panel of blind-flying instruments at his disposal. A 400 pound capacity hydraulic hoist was positioned above a sliding door on the helicopter's right side aft of the cockpit, and a large sliding door was located at the rear of the main cabin on the left side. When operating from water, the SH-21A could be fitted with inflatable ring floats which attached to each wheel, although these seldom were used in service.

SH-21B

Although the SH-21A was procured specifically as a SAR aircraft, the SH-21B saw wider service in slightly greater numbers than its predecessor. Between November 1955 and January 1958, the Air Force accepted 163 H-21Bs into its inventory, but the Air Rescue Service appears to have operated only 16 of both models in 1957, with the number of Workhorses in its inventory declining after that year. The SH-21B was powered by the same engine as the SH-21A, but it was fully-rated at 1,425 hp. The B-model had a larger rear door, two additional windows in the 20-passenger cabin, an autopilot, and provisions for jettisonable, external auxiliary fuel tanks, which frequently were used in service. However, even with these auxiliary tanks, the SH-21B's range was considered insufficient and this, along with a low cruising speed, forced the Air Rescue Service to retire all but four SH-21Bs by 1961. From 1961 through 1965, these four ARS SH-21Bs (HH-21B after 1962) were flown by Local Base Rescue units in the United States.

(V)H-21B

In the late 1950s, at least two H-21Bs, 52-8682 and 52-8701, were operated by the 1254th ATG at Andrews AFB for VIP 'Special Missions' flights on the East Coast. The Workhorses were painted in an attractive medium blue, white and red scheme similar to Special Missions VH-19s used by the 1254th ATG(SM) at the time.

CH-21B

A small number of CH-21Bs were flown by the Air Photographic and Charting Service in the early 1960s, used for support of its many photomapping detachments. The 1375th MCS, 1370th PMW, at Turner AFB, Georgia, began to phase out these CH-21Bs in 1964, replacing them with the CH-3C.

On 1st April 1962, the Air Weather Service was designated as the 'single manager' for aerial sampling missions for the Department of Defense. One of the sampling programs gained in this

Above: **Piasecki H-21B, 53-4341, of Detachment 15, Central Aerospace Rescue and Recovery Center, Goodfellow AFB, Texas, in January 1965.** Norman Taylor

Left: **Air Rescue Service SH-21B, 53-4366, in the red Arctic markings adopted for cold weather operations. Note the aircraft's external auxiliary fuel tanks.** Courtesy of Robert Esposito

Below: **Special Air Missions H-21B, 52-8682, of MATS 1254th ATG(SM), at Anacostia, Maryland.** Howard Levy, courtesy Douglas D Olson

expansion involved ground-launched balloons which were recovered by helicopter. The AWS gained six CH-21Bs from this program. These were assigned to the 59th WRS, 9th WRG, organized on 8th July 1963, at Goodfellow AFB, Texas. The squadron was short-lived, however, as the Air Weather Service consolidated all of its balloon support activities on 8th May 1964. The 59th WRS was inactivated, and its mission was assumed by the 6th Weather Squadron (Mobile), 4th Weather Group, at Tinker AFB, Oklahoma. The six CH-21Bs subsequently were transferred to the Air Rescue Service.

12.6 Kaman H-43 Huskie

H-43A

The Kaman H-43 was the first helicopter to be purchased by the Air Force specifically as an airborne crash rescue and fire suppression aircraft. Following an Air Force evaluation of current designs, the Navy's Kaman HOK-1 was chosen for this role and 18 were ordered as the H-43A. Powered by a 600 hp P&W R-1340 piston engine, the H-43As were delivered between November 1958 and July 1959 to the Tactical Air Command where they served in the Local Base Rescue role.

H-43B

Meanwhile, in a joint Air Force/Army development program, an HOK-1 was chosen to test the new Lycoming XT53 gas-turbine engine, with the first flight occurring on 27th September 1956. The Air Force ordered 116 H-43Bs in 1958 and another 59 late in 1961. Deliveries of the H-43B began in June 1959, with the aircraft being operated at virtually all Air Force bases worldwide as part of each base's local crash rescue unit.

Like the piston-powered H-43A, the H-43B featured Kaman's two counter-rotating, intermeshing main rotors which produced no torque and so required no tail rotor. The light, powerful T53 turbine produced 860 shp, and was compact enough to enable the H-43B to feature large clam-shell doors at the rear of the cabin. The H-43B was capable of carrying either its pilot, two firefighters and a fire fighting kit and a crash entry kit; two pilots and ten passengers; or two pilots, a medical attendant and four stretcher patients. The Huskie's four landing gear were fitted with 'bear paws', small skids which enabled the helicopter to land on all types of terrain.

As part of its new global SAR concept, the Air Force directed that all air rescue operations be consolidated under one command. Consequently, in December 1960 the Air Force Chief of Staff transferred all 70 Local Base Rescue units to the Air Rescue Service.

This transfer became effective on 1st October 1961, and, almost overnight, the Air Rescue Service gained 17 H-43As and 69 H-43Bs as well as a number of SH-19s and SH-21s. By the end of the year, the ARS operated an LBR unit at every major Air Force base around the world.

The typical ARS LBR unit consisted of two Huskies, four pilots and seven airmen. One H-43 and its crew were always on 24-hour alert. The H-43B's turbine required no warm-up, and the Huskie could be airborne in 30 seconds, with only another 30 seconds needed to attach the 1,000 pound Fire Supression Kit (FSK), popularly known as 'The Sputnik' due to its resemblance to the Russian satellite.

The FSK hung below the Huskie on a sling, and held 80 gallons of water, a container of foaming agent, a nitrogen pressure bottle, and a fire hose. Eight hundred gallons of fire supression foam could be generated, theoretically giving 54 seconds of protection to crash victims and the fully-suited firefighters. The Huskie pilot would unload the FSK and firefighters as near as possible to the crash scene, then hover above the burning wreck, using the helicopter's down-wash to direct the smoke and flames away from victims and their rescuers. A rescue hoist was available on the Huskie, as were rescue flood lights for nighttime missions.

Just 2½ weeks after the ARS assumed the Local Base Rescue mission with the Huskie, a world class altitude record was set by an H-43B on 18th October 1961, when it flew to 32,000 feet. An earlier altitude record had been set by an H-43B on 25th May 1961, when the Huskie reached 26,369 feet while carrying a 1,000 kg payload. A third record was established on 5th July 1962, when an HH-43B (as the Huskie was redesignated in mid-1962) flew 888.4 miles non-stop, a remarkable record for a helicopter utilized in the Local Base Rescue mission with a 75 mile radius of action.

HH-43F

The HH-43F was basically an HH-43B powered by a 1,100 shp T53L-11A turbine engine. The first flight of the HH-43F was in August 1964, and although a number of production HH-43Fs were purchased by the Air Force, most of the HH-43Bs eventually were converted to the later model.

By 1965, over 150 HH-43Bs were being flown by two standard Air Rescue Service squadrons, the 41st ARS, Hamilton AFB, California, and the 48th ARS, Eglin AFB, Florida, as well as 61 ARS Local Base Rescue units at Air Force bases worldwide.

Kaman HH-43B Huskies were flown by Air Rescue Service aircrews in at least two aerial mapping projects for MATS' 1370th Photo Mapping Wing, Air Photographic and Charting Service. In the first, beginning in March 1962, approximately 160 personnel, three photo or electronic survey RB-50s, one supply C-54, and two HH-43Bs operated as Aerial Survey Team 7, flying out of Jackson's Airdrome, Port Moresby, Australia. Their mission was to measure and map the area between Northern Australia and Eniwetok Island, including 88,000 square miles of aerial mapping photography and 72,000 linear miles of measurements. The Huskies functioned as supply helicopters, selected on the basis of their excellent high altitude performance.

During one 27-day period, one HH-43B flew 122 passengers and over 40 tons of supplies from two small Military Sea Transport Service cargo ships to six mountaintop HIRAN (High Precision Ranging and Navigation) sites.

The second project, known as 'Project King's Ransom', involved the aerial photographing and mapping of the entire country of Ethiopia during 1964-1965. Aerial Survey Team 4, 1370th PMW, at Turner AFB, Georgia, had to establish 14 HIRAN sites throughout the country, all on almost inaccessible mountaintops from 4,000 to 12,000 feet high. Again, the Huskies were chosen to do the job due to their excellent high altitude performance. The HH-43B detachment in Ethiopia rotated personnel from 11 Air Rescue Service detachments in Europe, Turkey, and the 55th ARS from Kindley AB, Bermuda.

The HH-43Bs first assisted in establishing the mountain top HIRAN sites by using cabin space and external sling loads to transport generators, electronic equipment and supplies. Once the station had been established, the Huskies kept each station supplied with personnel, food, water, fuel and mail. A typical flight might begin near sea level in almost desert conditions, flying over rough terrain with gusty winds and rapidly moving clouds, finally landing on a mountain knoll in an area barely large enough for the HH-43B's wheels to fit. The first 1½ months of operations saw the detachment fly 120 hours while hauling 87,000 pounds of supplies and carrying over 100 passengers to these remote stations.

Above: **Kaman HH-43B, 59-1583, hovers above the Fire Suppression Kit at an airfield in Vietnam.** Air Force, courtesy of Clyde Gerdes Collection

Opposite page:
Air Rescue Service Sikorsky CH-3C, 63-9688, displaying its retractable landing gear. Air Force, courtesy of Wayne Mutza

Below: **H-43A, 58-1829, in Korea before all Local Base Rescue units were transferred to the Air Rescue Service in 1961.** Courtesy of Wayne Mutza

Below: **HH-43B, 62-4512. This model's compact T53 turbine engine provided space for clam-shell doors at the rear of the cabin.** Tom Hansen, courtesy of Wayne Mutza

12.7 Sikorsky CH-3 Sea King

CH-3B

The Sikorsky S-61 first flew on 11th March 1959, as the Navy's HSS-2 Sea King, designed as an all-weather, anti-submarine helicopter. In April 1962, the Air Force received three HSS-2s on loan from the Navy. The stripped-down aircraft were used as 27-seat transports by the 551st Base Flight at Otis AFB, Massachusetts, flying personnel, high-priority cargo and mail to the radar sites at Texas Towers 2 and 3 in the Atlantic. Along with three additional transport Sea Kings received by the Air Force, the aircraft were designated as CH-3Bs.

In 1964, CH-3Bs began replacing HH-21Bs flown by the 1375th Mapping and Charting Squadron, 1370th Photo Mapping Wing, MATS, headquartered at Turner AFB, Georgia. These CH-3Bs were used to support photo-survey missions at various deployed sites around the world.

CH-3C

On February 8, 1963, the Air Force signed a contract for 22 S-61Rs, designated as the CH-3C. This version's first flight took place on 17th June 1963, and the first delivery was in December to Tyndall AFB, Florida, the aircraft being used for the recovery of drone aircraft and satellite capsules and nose cones. By 1965, CH-3Cs were flown by Detachment 15, Eastern Air Rescue Center, Patrick AFB, Florida, where they were used to support the Gemini manned space program. The CH-3C was powered by two 1,250 shp T58 engines. Unlike Navy versions of the S-61, the CH-3C had a built-in ramp at the rear for loading passengers or cargo. The CH-3C also had a full all-weather capability. By 1964, the search and rescue version, designated as the HH-3C, was in use by the 48th ARS at Eglin AFB, Florida, and by November 1965 the type was flown by the 38th ARS at Udorn RTAB, Thailand, where it would soon earn the official nickname, 'The Jolly Green Giant', for heroic service during the Vietnam War.

CH/HH-3E

In 1965, the HH-3Cs were succeeded on the production line by the CH-3E, fitted with uprated engines. The already-delivered CH-3Cs subsequently were modified to CH-3Es. The HH-3E was similar to the CH-3E, but was equipped with drop tanks, a refueling probe, and armor plate for use as a combat SAR aircraft in Vietnam. The first of these was delivered to the Air Rescue Service on 5th November 1965, and by the end of the year the ARS possessed eleven CH-3C/HH-3C and HH-3Es.

Chapter 13

Liaison

13.1 Piper L-4 Grasshopper

The Army Air Corps received four Piper J3C-65 Cubs in 1941 for service trials, designated as YO-59s. Twenty O-59s were ordered and delivered soon afterward, powered by a 65 hp Continental O-170 engine. A total of 299 O-59s and 649 O-59As were flown by the Army Air Forces as liaison and courier aircraft. These Cubs were redesignated as L-4As, and in mid-1942 a further 980 L-4Bs were ordered. Additional procurements of 1,801 L-4Hs, 1,680 L-4Js, and the impressment of over one hundred civil Cubs used for primary flight instruction brought the total to nearly 5,500 L-4s built between 1941 and 1945.

At war's end, most of the L-4s were declared surplus to the Army Air Forces' needs and were sold by the War Assets Administration to civilians. The Army Air Forces retained many aircraft, however, and a number of L-4s were in the US Air Force inventory when it was created in September 1947. When the Military Air Transport Service was formed in June 1948, it inherited three L-4 Cubs. Three L-4s were being flown at Bolling AFB during this time period: 42-15214 until July 1949; 42-15285 until July 1949; and 43-29345 until April 1950. A fourth L-4 was based at Andrews AFB from September 1948 until May 1949, when it was assigned to Bolling AFB until August 1950.

The Air Rescue Service also operated one L-4 in 1948. The most likely candidate is 43-1037, flown at West Palm Beach Airport, Florida, until 1st July 1948, when it was transferred to Orlando AFB, Florida, headquarters for the Air Rescue Service. Additionally, one L-4, 43-1234, was operated at Harmon AB, Newfoundland, from 1st June 1948, to 26th April 1949; and 43-1198, flew at Goose Bay, Labrador, from January 1948 to November 1949.

13.2 Stinson L-5 Sentinel

The Army Air Corps signed a contract in 1942 with the Stinson Aircraft Division of the Consolidated-Vultee Aircraft Corp for a revised version of the Stinson Voyager. The O-62 was slightly larger than the Voyager, and was powered by a 185 hp Lycoming O-435, 2006 being manufactured. Reflecting the airplane's liaison role, its designation was soon changed to L-5. A proposal to convert 688 L-5s to a 24-volt electrical system under the designation L-5A is believed not to have been undertaken. Nearly 700 L-5B ambulance versions of the Sentinel followed, while 200 L-5Cs fitted with a K-20 reconnaissance camera were built and 558 L-5Es featuring drooping ailerons. The last production Sentinel was the L-5G, powered by a 190 hp O-435, and with a 24-volt electrical system, of which 115 were constructed.

When MATS was formed in June 1948, six L-5s were carried on its inventory, the aircraft presumably being flown as proficiency trainers. By 1949, this number had increased to 16 Sentinels, but by 1953 all of MATS' L-5s had been retired.

In contrast, when the Air Rescue Service was officially designated in May 1946, it possessed over 30 L-5s for the search and rescue mission. By the time the ARS was absorbed by the Military Air Transport Service in June 1948, only 23 L-5s were being flown. Some interesting modifications were made to the L-5s flown in 1948 by the 4th Rescue Squadron Flight D at Hickam AFB, Hawaii. The squadron's L-5s, painted in typical ARS silver with black-bordered yellow bands on the fuselage and wing tips, were equipped with a small pod attached to the left wing struts which carried a dropable one-man life raft. Mounted on the L-5s' right wing struts were a tidal wave warning siren and a loudspeaker horn.

Piper L-4B, 43-495, similar to several operated by MATS and the ARS. Vince Weckesser, courtesy of Earl Blum and Bill Stratton

Stinson L-5, 42-98633, flown by the Air Rescue Service, MATS. Air Force, courtesy of NASM

Top: **Air Rescue Service L-5, 42-98572, of Air Rescue Unit 8, Flight A, at Hamilton AFB, California, in June 1948.** William T Larkins

Above left: **Camouflaged L-5E, 44-17863, flown by the 3rd ARS in Korea.** US Army, courtesy of Larry Davis

Above right: **The first Convair L-13B, 46-073, with Arctic red outer wing panels and empennage.** Air Force

Bottom right: **L-13B, 47-399, one of 29 L-13As 'winterized' for Arctic search and rescue duties with the Air Rescue Service.** Boardman C Reed

The L-5 was used with limited success by the 3rd Air Rescue Squadron during the Korean War. On 7th July 1950, the 3rd ARS dispatched two L-5s to Korea from their base in Japan. Several rescue pick-ups were attempted, but the mountainous Korean terrain strewn with rice paddies proved unsuitable for the Sentinels. On October 22nd-23rd, three L-5s and two H-5s, based at Pyongyang with the 3rd ARS, Det.F, evacuated 47 injured paratroopers from drop zones at Sukchon and Sunchon. At war's end, of the 170 Air Force aircrewmen rescued by the ARS behind enemy lines, only two were attributed to the L-5s.

13.3 Convair L-13

The L-13 was designed in 1945 by the Stinson Division of Consolidated-Vultee as an all-metal replacement for the versatile Stinson L-5. The L-13 was intended to be an aerial 'Jack-of-all-trades', capable of performing the liaison, observation, aerial ambulance, photographic, wire laying, courier, and light cargo missions while operating on wheels, skis or floats. The L-13's single-strut braced wings and tail surfaces could be folded, and its landing gear was adjustable from 92 inches to 61 inches for towing or hauling by truck.

The Army Air Forces purchased two XL-13s, 45-58708/58709, which were tested by the Army Ground Forces in 1945 but were not accepted. With its 245 hp Franklin O-425 air-cooled engine, the XL-13 was basically a good design, capable of taking off or landing in only 230 feet and of carrying up to six people in its relatively large cabin. But the airplane became caught in an interservice squabble between the newly-formed Air Force and the old Army over their relative roles and missions. The Air Force/Air National Guard eventually took delivery of 300 L-13As, (46-68/213 and 47-267/420), beginning in 1947.

However, the combination of 'right airplane – wrong mission', and the Franklin O-425's tendency to be unreliable due to overheating, doomed the L-13A to a short service life which ended in 1954 when all aircraft were 'discarded'.

L-13B

Following tests with L-13A, 46-73, 28 L-13As, (46-110/111 and 47-395/420), were 'winterized' as Arctic search and rescue aircraft. All cracks in the cabin were sealed, a 40,000 BTU combustion heater and ducting was installed, heat-retaining blankets for the cabin were provided, and covers for the wings, tail and engine were furnished for open-air parking.

The Air Rescue Service received 14 L-13A/B aircraft in 1948, and by 1949 were operating a total of 38 of both models for search and rescue duties. A small number of L-13Bs are known to have operated in Alaska in 1950 by the 10th ARS, but all Air Rescue Service L-13Bs were declared surplus in 1950 and were retired from service.

Left: **L-20A, 52-6119, one of four Beavers flown by the Air Rescue Service.** Air Force, courtesy of David Menard

Below: **De Havilland U-6A, (L-20A redesignated) 52-6102, assigned to Detachment 15, Central Air Rescue Center, Goodfellow AFB, Texas, photographed in July 1964.** Norman Taylor

13.4 de Havilland L-20A Beaver

De Havilland Aircraft of Canada Ltd began the design of the Beaver in September 1946 as an all-metal replacement for the bush airplanes then in use in Canada and Alaska. Construction of the prototype DHC-2 was begun in January 1947, and the Beaver made its maiden flight in August. While the prototype was powered by a 295 hp supercharged Gypsy Queen 5 engine, for the production models de Havilland chose the sturdy and dependable P&W R-985 Wasp Junior of 450 hp.

Early in 1951, the US Air Force and Army issued a design requirement for a new liaison aircraft. A competition between seven aircraft designs was won by the de Havilland DHC-2. The Air Force subsequently purchased four Beavers (plus two for the Army) for service evaluations, designating them as YL-20s. Before the Air Force could purchase the L-20 in quantity, however, Congressional approval was sought and granted to overcome the then-current 'buy American' policy of not contracting with foreign manufacturers. Between 1952 and 1960, nearly 1,000 L-20s were delivered to the US military, with about 200 operated by the Air Force. While the Army Beavers usually were painted olive drab, the Air Force left their L-20As in natural aluminum, with those used in Arctic climates bearing standard red wing panels and tail surfaces. Air Force Beavers were used mainly for light utility transport, medical evacuation, liaison, and courier missions. The L-20A could carry from five to seven passengers, and, with the passenger seats removed, over 1,000 pounds of cargo in the 1,125 cubic foot cabin.

While medical evacuation was one of the L-20's primary roles with the Army, this was not the case for Air Force Beavers. In mid-November 1953, the 1706th Air Transport Group (AE), MATS, began a 60-day operational test program with the L-20A. The tests, conducted at Travis AFB, California, were to determine the feasibility of using the L-20A as a 'feeder aircraft' in MATS' aeromedical evacuation system. These tests were discontinued on 20th January 1954, with the recommendation that the L-20A not be used as a feeder aircraft due to 'certain professional, flight and economic limitations.'

The Air Rescue Service began using a small number of L-20As beginning in approximately 1954, when at least one Beaver was being flown at Harmon AB, Newfoundland, by the 52nd ARS. By 1958, four L-20As were operated by the ARS, although from 1961 through 1965 only one L-20A (redesignated U-6A in 1962) was in Air Rescue Service use, flown by Detachment 15, Central Air Rescue Center, at Goodfellow AFB, Texas.

13.5 Aero Design L-26 Commander

The L-26 Commanders were the military variants of a series of civil aircraft designed, beginning in 1944, by Ted R Smith and his fellow Douglas Aircraft Company engineers in their spare time. Basing the prototype L3805 on Douglas' successful A-20 attack bomber, the Douglas engineers scaled down the design to produce the forerunner of a new class of light twin executive aircraft. The group left Douglas in 1950 and started Aero Design and Engineering Co at Bethany, Oklahoma, where thousands of Aero Commanders were constructed between 1951 and 1985.

L-26B

The Air Force conducted a study in the fall of 1954 to consider a replacement for its Beech C-45s being used around the world for combat readiness training, air attache duties and for Special Air Missions use by MATS' 1254th ATG(SM) at Washington National Airport. Several designs were studied, but it was decided that none offered a great enough improvement over the C-45 to warrant new procurement.

A change of heart in the Air Force's thinking was forced in the spring of 1955 by none other than the White House. President Dwight D Eisenhower recently had purchased a farm in Gettysburg, Pennsylvania, and Eisenhower had asked his personal pilot, Lt Col William Draper, to look into the possibility of using a light aircraft to fly him into his farm's 2,200-foot grass airstrip. Draper discussed this request with his superiors at the 1254th ATG(SM), and it was discovered that the SAM Group had been receiving numerous requests from government and military VIPs for short trips involving only one or two people. These requests were met by using the 1254th ATG's large, twin-engined Convair C-131Ds, so the economies of operating a light twin for these missions became obvious as well.

Following another study of available light twin aircraft, the Aero Commander Model 560 was selected as both a presidential aircraft and as a short-range VIP transport for use by the Special Air Missions Group and Air Force Headquarters Command. A contract for 15 Aero Commander Model 560As, designated as L-26Bs, 55-4634/4648, was signed in May 1955. These aircraft basically were off-the-shelf Model 560As, with only changes in instruments and the installation of wing and tail de-icing boots being required by the Air Force, although the retention of the type's civilian radios would give the Air Force fits over the following 14 years.

The delivery schedule for these L-26Bs called for the first airplane to be available for service in July 1955. However, the White House insisted that an airplane was needed by May 23rd for orientation, checkout and actual VIP missions. A standard Aero Commander Model 560, N2724B, was subsequently leased from Aero Design and delivered on the 24th to the 1254th ATG(SM), MATS, at Washington National Airport. The first presidential flight aboard this airplane occurred on 3rd June and N2724B was flown until replaced by the first L-26B, 55-3634, which was delivered on 2nd August 1955.

L-26C

During a presidential vacation trip to Denver, Colorado, in August 1955, the recently-delivered L-26B, 55-4634, was flown to Denver to act as a stand-by aircraft. Upon returning to Washington, DC, Lt Col Draper made a request through MATS to HQ Air Material Command to replace two L-26Bs on the current contract with supercharged Model 680 Aero Commanders. Evidently, Lt Col Draper had test flown a new Model 680 while in Denver, and he felt the added performance was needed to meet this 'unanticipated mission requirement'. Approval for the contract change was granted in March 1956, and the final two aircraft were delivered in April 1956 as L-26Cs with supercharged engines.

By the summer of 1956, five Aero Commander L-26Bs, 55-4634 and 55-4636/4639, were being flown by the 1299th ATS(SM), at Bolling AFB, Washington, DC, transporting cabinet-level VIPs, and the two L-26Cs, 55-4647/4648, operating as presidential aircraft with the 1298th ATS(SM) at Washington National Airport. While still a presidential aircraft, L-26B, 55-4634, participated in the 'Greenbrier Air Lift', when President Eisenhower met with American and foreign dignitaries at White Sulphur Springs, West Virginia, on 26th March 1956. The presidential L-26B also took part in the 'Gettysburg Airlift' in the fall of 1955 when President Eisenhower was at his Gettysburg farm recuperating from a heart attack. In July 1956, after the President's operation, one of the L-26Cs was fitted with a bed to carry Eisenhower to his farm.

The Presidential Election of 1960 had an almost immediate effect on the use of the Aero Commanders flown by the 1254th ATG(SM), as they were no longer needed for flights to Gettysburg, Pennsylvania, and were replaced by helicopters for the shorter flights made by President John F Kennedy. Also, by the summer of 1961 Bolling AFB was being phased out as an active flying field, while Andrews AFB, Maryland, began assuming a greater Special Air Missions role. Beginning in July 1961, two L-26Bs, 55-4637 and 55-4639, and the two Presidential Flight L-26Cs were transferred to the 1299th ATS(SM) at Andrews AFB. The aircraft joined a fleet of 13 C-131Ds, one C-123B, and three VC-140Bs providing VIP transportation for the Vice-President, members of the President's Cabinet, members of Congress, and other high-ranking US government officials and visiting foreign dignitaries. These four Aero Commanders continued flying with the Special Air Missions Wing, redesignated as U-4A/U-4Bs in 1962, until transferred to other commands in the late 1960s.

Below left: **Aero Commander U-4A, 55-4639, flown by the 'Special Air Missions' 1254th ATW(SM), at Andrews AFB, Maryland, in 1964.** Air Force

Below right: **Presidential U-4B, 55-4647, at Philadelphia in 1962, painted in the attractive blue, white and day-glo scheme used by the 1254th ATW(SM) for VIP flights.** Robert Esposito

Bottom: **L-26B, 55-4637, at Bolling AFB, Washington, DC, in April 1961 carrying the 1254th ATW(SM) insignia under the pilot's side window.** Air Force

Chapter 14.8

Trainers

14.1 North American T-6 Texan

The T-6 Texan can trace its ancestry to the North American BC-1, which won a 1937 Army Air Corps competition for a basic combat trainer. In 1940, these aircraft were classified as advanced trainers and redesignated as AT-6s. The AT-6 in its several models trained a generation of pilots during the Second World War, and for some time afterward. By war's end, over ten thousand Texans were built by North American Aviation at their plants at Inglewood, California, and Dallas, Texas, for the Army Air Forces, US Navy, and several nations under Lend-Lease agreements. In June 1948, all Texans were redesignated as T-6A/C/D/Fs when the 'AT' category was dropped.

Over 2,000 T-6s were remanufactured beginning in 1949, with both cockpits being modernized, additional fuel capacity, and an F-51 landing gear and steerable tail wheel being adopted among other improvements. These modified Texans were redesignated as T-6Gs and were given new serial numbers.

The Military Air Transport Service operated about a half-dozen T-6s upon its formation in June 1948 and for the following two years, presumably at various locations as proficiency trainers and 'base hacks'. By 1951, only one T-6 was in MATS' inventory, but by August 1953 five T-6s were being operated by the three squadrons of the 1708th Ferrying Group:

Two T-6s by the 1737th FYS, Dover AFB, Delaware;
Two T-6s by the 1738th FYS, Long Beach Airport, California;
One T-6 by the 1739th FYS, Amarillo AFB, Texas.

Both the 1737th FYS and the 1738th FYS still had one T-6 apiece in June 1954, but by the end of the year all Texans were replaced by the T-33A as squadron proficiency trainers.

14.2 Beech T-11 Kansan

The Beech AT-11 bombing and gunnery trainer was developed in 1941 from the AT-7 navigation trainer. The AT-11 featured a bombardier's station and flexible machine gun in the transparent nose, a gun position behind the cockpit, and a small bomb bay within the fuselage. Over 1,500 AT-11s were built between 1941-45. In July 1946, only two months after being designated, the Air Rescue Service was flying nine AT-11s for search and rescue missions. In 1948, all AT-11s were redesignated as T-11s.

When the Military Air Transport Service formed in June 1948, it possessed two T-11s and two SNBs, the Navy version of the airplane. After a Beech remanufacturing program in 1951, as many as 40 T-11s and two SNBs were being operated by MATS as multi-engine proficiency trainers and 'base hacks'. By mid-1953, only ten T-11s were being flown by the following MATS units:

2 by 1726th Support Squadron, McChord AFB, Washington
1 by 1700th Air Transport Group, Kelly AFB, Texas
2 by 1707th Air Base Wing, Palm Beach, Florida
1 by 1708th Ferrying Group Detachment, McClellan AFB, California
2 by 1737th Ferrying Squadron, Dover AFB, Delaware
1 by 1738th Ferrying Squadron, Long Beach, California
1 by 1739th Ferrying Squadron, Amarillo AFB, Texas

The last MATS T-11 apparently was flown by the 1700th ATG at Kelly AFB until February 1954.

14.3 Convair T-29

The T-29, the navigation training version of Convair's civil Model 240, was generally similar to its transport cousin, the C-131, but preceded it in service by some four years. The first flight of the XT-29 was made in September 1949. The production T-29A, 48 of which were built featuring four astrodomes and 14 stations for student navigators in its unpressurized cabin, was delivered between March 1950 and October 1951. The T-29B, 105 of which were delivered between April 1952 and August 1953, had pressurized accommodations for ten student navigators and four student radar operators, as well as three astrodomes and one periscopic sextant on top of the fuselage. The 119 T-29Cs delivered between September 1953 and April 1955 had more powerful R-2800 engines and space for 14 students and their instructors. Finally, between January 1954 and August 1955, 93 T-29Ds were delivered, this variant featuring the 'K' system bombsight with no astrodomes for its six students and two instructors.

AT-29C

The Airways and Air Communications Service received authorization, in December 1953, for 54 two-engine transport aircraft to perform the important flight checking mission, ensuring that the many AACS-operated electronic navigation aids and ground/air communications facilities were functioning within acceptable tolerances. However, by mid-1954 the AACS had only 23 C-47s to service 1,016 facilities, with the number of sites expected to double by mid-1957.

An additional requirement for high-altitude flight checks was partially met by the use of a specially-equipped B-47B in a joint AACS, Strategic Air Command and Air Proving Ground project. AACS Headquarters requested that use of a twin-engine transport capable of cruising at 20,000 feet be authorized, naming the Convair C-131 as its choice for this mission. In July 1954, MATS Headquarters agreed with this request, recommending that 70 modified C-131Ds be procured for the AACS.

Above: **North American T-6 flown by the 1739th Ferrying Squadron, Amarillo AFB, Texas, photographed in 1953.** Walter D House

Above: **Beech T-11, 43-10462, flown by the 1739th Ferrying Squadron, Amarillo AFB, Texas, in 1953.** Walter D House

While Air Force Headquarters agreed that the C-131D would be 'highly desirable' for this high-altitude flight check mission, budget restrictions prevented the airplane's use for the AACS' 'second line' requirements. Reluctantly, the AACS submitted another request in September 1954 for an additional 35 C-47s and temporarily shelved their desire for the C-131.

An opportunity to obtain a higher performance replacement for the AC-47s came two years later, as older models of the T-29 became available. By mid-1957, the first four AT-29Cs became operational with AACS Headquarters and its 1800th AACS Wing at Andrews AFB and the 1850th AACS Flight at Hamilton AFB, California. Curiously, as additional T-29s completed their electronic modifications at the FAA's Will Rogers Modification Center in Oklahoma City, all were redesignated as AC-131As. On 3rd May 1960, all AACS AC-131As were again redesignated back to AT-29Cs. By early 1959, a total of ten AT-29C/AC-131As had completed their modifications and were in service with AACS flight checking squadrons. On 1st July 1961, the Airways and Air Communications Service was detached from MATS and renamed the Air Force Communications Service.

VT-29A/B/D

As the T-29A, T-29B and T-29Ds ended their usefulness as navigation/bombing trainers, a number were converted as staff and VIP transports with MATS. All were given airline-style interiors, while some aircraft retained their astrodomes and others, apparently flown by the 1254th ATG(SM), had their astrodomes removed and faired over. Most of these VT-29s continued to fly through 1965 with MATS as staff transports.

14.4 Lockheed T-33A Shooting Star

The Lockheed T-33 design began in 1947 as a lengthened F-80C, providing room for a second cockpit under an extended canopy. Lockheed had constructed 128 TF-80Cs when the airplane's designation was changed to T-33A in May 1949. When production had ended in August 1959, nearly 5,700 T-33As had been built as the standard Air Force jet-powered trainer.

Photographs on the opposite page:

Second down: **Convair AT-29C, 52-1098, of the Airways and Air Communications Service, at Oakland Airport in May 1961.** Douglas D Olson

Third down, left: **AT-29C, 52-1139, after being redesignated as an AC-131A by the AACS.** William T Larkins, courtesy of Steve Ginter

Third down, right: **T-29A, 49-1942, flown by the 1611th ATW, McGuire AFB, New Jersey, in 1964.** Courtesy of Steve Ginter

Bottom left: **VT-29A, 50-183, flown as a VIP transport by MATS.** D W Ostrowski, courtesy of Steve Ginter

Bottom right: **VT-29B, 51-5122, flown by the 1254th ATG(SM) at Andrews AFB.** Courtesy of Clyde Gerdes Collection

The Military Air Transport Service began operating the T-33A in 1952, with MATS air transport groups and wings using the airplane as a proficiency and transition trainer. By 1957, a high of 75 T-33As were flown at MATS bases worldwide, with a large number being operated at MATS Headquarters at Andrews AFB, Maryland, and at other major MATS-affiliated bases, the Shooting Stars being used as proficiency trainers and high-speed transports for senior officers.

Beginning in 1954, the 1708th Ferrying Group Headquarters at Kelly AFB, Texas, its three squadrons at Dover AFB, Amarillo AFB and Long Beach, California, and several of its detachments, used a number of T-33As for pilot transition training, proficiency training, and as lead aircraft on transatlantic and transpacific group ferry flights where the ferried aircraft lacked the proper navigational gear. The 1708th FYG operated 17 T-33As in 1956, but the group was disbanded within a few years.

(A)T-33A

In December 1953, Headquarters Air Force authorized the Airways and Air Communications Service several aircraft types for flight checking its widely-scattered electronic navigation aids and communications facilities, including one 'single engine fighter type aircraft'. This aircraft was needed to perform high altitude, high speed operational penetration checks of GCA, RAPCON and air traffic control facilities.

The AACS originally had requested a T-33A to perform this mission, as the airplane could carry additional equipment and an observer in the second cockpit. The AACS instead first received an F-51, then an F-80B and F-80C, none of which had been equipped with a UHF radio.

By mid-1956, the AACS finally had received its first three T-33As, which were operated by AACS Headquarters at Andrews AFB, Maryland, and its 1800th AACS Wing. By the end of 1957, the AACS was operating eight T-33A flight check aircraft: one by HQ AACS at Andrews AFB; two by ConAACS Area at Tinker AFB, Oklahoma; and one each by the following facilities checking flights:

1850th AACS Flight, Hamilton AFB, California;
1851st AACS Flight, Mitchel AFB, New York;
1852nd AACS Flight, Robins AFB, Georgia;
1853rd AACS Flight, Chanute AFB, Illinois;
1854th AACS Flight, Randolph AFB, Texas.

In mid-1961, just before the Airways and Air Communications Service was redesignated as the Air Force Communications Service and was separated from MATS, the AACS possessed nine T-33A flight check aircraft.

Lastly, the 57th Fighter Interceptor Squadron, one of the MATS-controlled fighter squadrons responsible for the defense of Iceland, deployed to Keflavik International Airport in January 1955 with a complement of F-89Cs, one TB-25K, and two T-33As. Later in the year, the squadron would receive a third T-33A, using the trio as proficiency trainers and squadron 'hacks'. These 57th FIS T-33As remained under MATS jurisdiction until July 1961, when the US Navy assumed the responsibility for Iceland's air defense.

By 1960, the Military Air Transport Service was operating 58 T-33As. In 1965, MATS' last year of existence, only six Shooting Stars were still on the MATS inventory.

Photographs of Lockheed T-33s appear overleaf.

Above: **Lockheed T-33As of the 1708th Ferrying Wing at Love Field, Dallas, Texas, in January 1956.** Courtesy of Lionel N Paul

Left: **T-33A, 53-5077, one of several flown by the 57th Fighter Interceptor Squadron as part of the MATS-administered Iceland Air Defense Force, Keflavik, Iceland, photographed in June 1957.** Courtesy of Baldur Sveinsson

Left: **MATS T-33A, 57-0723, flown by the 1405th Aeromedical Transport Wing, at Scott AFB, Illinois.** MAP

Bottom: **T-33A, 56-1758, assigned to the 1611th ATW, McGuire AFB, New Jersey, in 1964.** Robert Esposito

14.5 North American T-39A Sabreliner

North American Aviation Co began the design of its Sabreliner in 1956 as a small civil business jet when, in August 1956, the Air Force announced a requirement for the UTX utility transport and combat readiness trainer. The prototype NA246 Sabreliner was completed in May 1958, but the airplane's first flight was delayed until September 16 as its General Electric J85 turbojet engines were unavailable. The Air Force chose the Sabreliner as the UTX winner and signed a contract with North American for the T-39A in January 1959, and this first production version made its initial flight on 30th June 1960.

The T-39A differed from the prototype NA246 mainly by the substitution of 3,000 lb thrust Pratt & Whitney J60 engines. The T-39A's cabin normally had seating for four passengers, although as many as seven could be accommodated. A total of 143 T-39As were delivered to the Air Force between June 1961 and September 1963, with most of these Sabreliners being used as high speed utility transports rather than as trainers.

The Military Air Transport Service received two T-39As in 1962, and by the following year was operating four Sabreliners: 61-634/ 638/ 650 and 681. At least two of these aircraft were flown out of Scott AFB, Illinois: T-39A, 61-650, by the 1405th Air Base Wing, and T-39A, 61-638, by the 1405th Aeromedical Transport Wing.

It is likely that the remaining two Sabreliners were flown by MATS Headquarters at Scott AFB as VIP staff transports.

Above: **North American T-39A, 61-0634, flown as a VIP transport by MATS in the early 1960s.** MAP

Below: **T-39A, 61-0650, assigned to the 1405th Air Base Wing shown at Andrews AFB in May 1963. The 1405th ABW emblem is on the Sabreliner's fuselage.** Robert C Mikesh

Right: **The relatively spacious cabin of the Sabreliner had seating for four plus two pilots.** Air Force

Chapter 15

Utility

15.1 Lockheed U-2

The history of the U-2's Central Intelligence Agency-inspired design, secrecy-shrouded production, and the airplane's subsequent deployment and overflights of Communist territories – all accompanied by official denials or plausible 'cover stories' is well-known, if not well-documented. Not generally appreciated, however, is the fact that there actually was a tenuous connection between MATS' Air Weather Service and early U-2 operations, as well as an apparent closer involvement some seven years after Francis Gary Powers was shot out of the sky over Russia.

In April 1956, a press release issued by the National Advisory Committee for Aeronautics (NACA) announced 'a new type of airplane, the Lockheed U-2' which, with logistical and technical assistance from the Air Weather Service, would be used to study turbulence and 'obtain high-level meteorological data'.

The U-2s were assigned to three Weather Reconnaissance Squadrons, Provisional, units which ostensibly were attached to Air Weather Service Headquarters. The 1st Weather Reconnaissance Squadron, Provisional (WRSP-1), was activated at RAF Lakenheath, England, between 15th April and 14th July 1956, before moving on to Wiesbaden, Germany. WRSP-2 was organized in August at Incirlik, Turkey, while WRSP-3 was based at NAS Atsugi, Japan. WRSP-1 eventually moved to Incirlik and various detachments from all three squadrons were deployed to other 'Operating Locations' worldwide.

The downing of Powers' U-2 over Sverdlovsk on 1st May 1960, brought to light the fact that these actually were CIA aircraft flown by civilian CIA pilots on temporary loan from the Air Force, performing CIA-designed intelligence gathering missions. However, lost in the frenzy following Powers' last flight is the fact that some of the WRSP WU-2As occasionally were involved in AWS/NACA high-altitude weather research flights, carrying among other sensors the AMQ-7 temperature-humidity measuring system.

The markings carried by these CIA/NACA/AWS WU-2As during the late 1950s and early 1960s are uncertain, and may have ranged from bare metal aircraft with standard Air Force markings to the dull, all-black scheme with red serial numbers typically attributed to the CIA. However, as late as 1967 one U-2 was reliably spotted while landing at Anderson AFB, Guam, painted gray overall and bearing the standard Air Weather Service yellow-bordered dark blue tail band containing the word 'WEATHER'. This aircraft may have been operated by the 54th WRS, which was flying WB-57s off the island at the time, or by Detachment 1, 55th WRS, at Eielson AFB, Alaska.

Top: **Lockheed WU-2A, 56-6714, in May 1965. The sampling orifice is located at the tip of the airplane's nose.** Roger Besecker

Below: **WU-2A, 56-6722, with black and white markings.** Courtesy of Clyde Gerdes Collection

15.2 Cessna U-3A Blue Canoe

The US Air Force announced a requirement, late in 1956, for an 'off the shelf' light commercial twin-engined airplane to be used for liaison and light cargo missions. An evaluation was made of several existing designs, and the Cessna Model 310 was declared the winner in 1957. The Model 310 had first flown in January 1953, with production deliveries beginning the following year.

An initial order for 80 L-27As, 57-5846/5925, was delivered between May and December 1957, followed by a second order for 80, 58-2107/2186, accepted between May and November 1958. The L-27A was nearly identical to the commercial Model 310, but auxiliary fuel tanks, a special interior and a revised instrument panel were added at Air Force request. The aircraft were painted in a blue and white scheme, earning them the semi-official nickname of 'Blue Canoe', referring to the peculiar shape of the L-27A's fuselage. In the 1962 tri-service redesignation system, these L-27As were classified as utility aircraft and were redesignated as U-3As.

The U-3A is an airplane that, for whatever reason, the Military Air Transport Service did not acknowledge as having operated. However, at least two aircraft, U-3As 58-2170/2171, have been photographed in MATS markings in 1965 at McGuire AFB, New Jersey.Considering their sequential serial numbers, it may be that these two aircraft were delivered to MATS late in 1958.

Below: **Cessna U-3A, 58-2170, photographed at McGuire AFB, New Jersey, in 1965.** Robert Esposito

Bottom: **U-3A, 58-2171, in 1965.** MAP

The MATS Terminal at RAF Burtonwood, England, photographed in May 1957. P H Butler

Bibliography

Air Force Bases Volume II - Outside the United States: Harry R Fletcher; Center for Air Force History, USAF, Washington, DC, 1993.

Air Force Communications Command 1938-1991 - An Illustrated History: Thomas S Snyder (ed); AFCC Office of History, Scott AFB, IL, 1992.

Air Transport at War: Reginald M Cleveland; Harper & Brothers Publishers, New York and London, 1946.

Air War over Korea - A Pictorial Record: Larry Davis; Squadron/Signal Publications Inc., Carrollton, TX, 1982.

Air Weather Service - Our Heritage, 1937-1987: Rita A Markus et al; Military Airlift Command, Scott AFB, IL, 1987.

Beyond the Wild Blue - A History of the US Air Force 1947-1997: Walter J Boyne; St Martin's Press, New York, 1997.

Bridge Across the Sky - The Berlin Blockade and Airlift, 1948-1949; Richard Collier; McGraw-Hill Book Company, New York, 1978.

The Development of Strategic Airlift for the Armed Forces of the United States, 1941-1965: Roland D Hinds; HQ Military Airlift Command, Scott AFB, IL, 1968.

Eagle in the Egg, The: Oliver LaFarge; Houghton Mifflin Co, The Riverside Press, Boston, MA, 1949.

Eagles of the Pacific - Consairways ... Memories of an Air Transport Service during World War II: Edwin and Jeanne Spight; Historical Aviation Album, Temple City, CA, 1980.

Flight to Everywhere: Ivan Dmitri; McGraw-Hill Book Co, New York & London, 1944.

Flying the Hump - Memories of an Air War: Otha C Spencer; Texas A&M University Press, College Station, TX, 1992.

Flying the Weather - The Story of Air Weather Reconnaissance: Otha C Spencer; The Country Studio, Campbell, TX, 1996.

From a Dark Sky - The Study of US Air Force Special Operations; Orr Kelly, Presidio Press, Novato, CA, 1996.

A History of the United States Air Force 1907-1957 : Alfred Goldberg (ed); D Van Nostrand Company Inc, Princeton, NJ, 1957.

How They Won the War in the Pacific - Nimitz and his Admirals: Edwin D Hoyt; Weybright & Talley, New York, NY, 1970.

The Hump - The Great Military Airlift of World War II: Bliss K Thorne; Lippincott, New York, 1965.

The Hurricane Hunters: Ivan Ray Tannehill; Dodd Mead & Company, New York, 1955.

Lifeline in the Sky - The Story of the US Military Air Transport Service: Clayton Knight; William Morrow & Company, New York, NY, 1957.

MATS - The Story of the Military Air Transport Service: Stanley M Ulanoff; Franklin Watts, New York, 1964.

Mighty MAC - Airlift, Rescue, Special Operations: Rene J Francillon et al; Osprey Publishing Ltd, London, 1988.

The Military Airlift Command - A Brief History: Office of MAC History, Scott AFB, IL, 1977.

Military Airlift Command - Historical Handbook 1941-1984: Dick J Burkard; Military Airlift Command, USAF, Scott AFB, IL, 1984.

Operation Lifeline - History and Development of the Naval Air Transport Service: James Lee; Ziff-Davis Publishing Co, Chicago & New York, 1947.

Over the Hump: William H Tunner; Duell Sloan & Pearce, New York, 1964.

Over the Hump - Airlift to China: William J Koenig; Ballantine Books, New York, 1972.

Rescue !: Elliott Arnold; Duell Sloan & Pearce, New York, NY, 1956.

The Role of the Naval Air Transport Service in the Pacific War: Naval Air Transport Service, 1945.

The Story of MATS: US Air Force, Govt Printing Office, Washington DC, 1951.

Thor's Legions - Weather Support to the US Air Force and Army 1937-1987: John F Fuller; American Meteorological Society, Boston, MA, 1990.

The United States Air Force in Korea 1950-1953: Robert Frank Futrell; Duell Sloan & Pearce, New York, 1961.

US Military Aircraft Designations and Serials 1909 to 1979: John M Andrade; Midland Counties Publications, Leicester, England, 1979.